Educational Transitions in Post-Revolutionary Spaces

Also available from Bloomsbury

Citizenship Education in Conflict-Affected Areas, Bassel Akar
Conflict, Education and Peace in Nepal, Tejendra Pherali
Education in the Arab World, edited by Serra Kirdar

Educational Transitions in Post-Revolutionary Spaces

Islam, Security, and Social Movements in Tunisia

Tavis D. Jules and Teresa Barton

Bloomsbury Academic
An imprint of Bloomsbury Publishing Plc

B L O O M S B U R Y
LONDON · OXFORD · NEW YORK · NEW DELHI · SYDNEY

Bloomsbury Academic

An imprint of Bloomsbury Publishing Plc

50 Bedford Square	1385 Broadway
London	New York
WC1B 3DP	NY 10018
UK	USA

www.bloomsbury.com

BLOOMSBURY and the Diana logo are trademarks of Bloomsbury Publishing Plc

First published 2018

© Tavis D. Jules and Teresa Barton, 2018

Tavis D. Jules and Teresa Barton have asserted their right under the Copyright, Designs and Patents Act, 1988, to be identified as Authors of this work.

British Library Cataloguing-in-Publication Data

A catalogue record for this book is available from the British Library.

ISBN:	HB:	978-1-4742-8213-0
	ePDF:	978-1-4742-8215-4
	ePub:	978-1-4742-8214-7

Library of Congress Cataloging-in-Publication Data

A catalog record for this book is available from the Library of Congress.

Typeset by RefineCatch Limited, Bungay, Suffolk
Printed and bound in Great Britain

To find out more about our authors and books visit www.bloomsbury.com. Here you will find extracts, author interviews, details of forthcoming events and the option to sign up for our newsletters.

Contents

Lists of Tables and Figures

Tables

Figures

Acknowledgments

This five-year research project was made possible with several grants and assistance from several individuals and institutions. Dr. Jules is particularly appreciative to Professor Peter Schraeder, who introduced him to Tunisia in 2011 and is grateful for the initial funding under the Tunisian Research Fellowship. The Office of the Provost at Loyola University Chicago provided the second round of funding for this research under the "Stimulating Multidisciplinary Research at Loyola's Lakeside Campuses."

Dr. Jules is beholden to the Office of Research Services (ORS) at Loyola University Chicago who funded several research and data collection trips to Tunisia. Special thanks to Tracy Foxworth who has worked tirelessly during the past five years in ensuring that my numerous requests were taken care of in a timely manner. Le Centre d'Etudes Maghrébines à Tunis (CEMAT), in particular Laryssa Chomiak, has been instrumental in securing early access to research sites and taking the time to sit with several research assistants and Dr. Jules on several occasions to provide in-depth contextual information that was invaluable in assisting our team in understanding the Tunisian context. Colleagues at Université de la Manouba, Faculty of Letters, particularly Professor Mounir Khelifa, provided invaluable assistance during the early days of this research project and Dr. Jules is appreciative for their collaboration. Dr. Jules is indebted to the various Deans at the School of Education, Loyola University Chicago, who have been instrumental in supporting this research during the last five years.

Several research assistants in Tunisia were instrumental in collecting, transcribing, and translating archival and interview data as well as providing research support; we are particularly beholden to Yosra Chatti, Châari Souhir, and Yosr El Benna. We are grateful to Dina S. Paulson for her editorial support.

We are grateful for the several graduate students at Loyola University Chicago, Landis Fryer, Devin Moss, Briellen Griffin, and Michel Mesterharm, who have contributed time, research support, and editorial assistance to this project.

Finally, Dr. Jules is grateful to his friends who have been supportive, Hakim M. A. Williams, Lara Smetana, Kristin and Jason Davin, Susan and Gary Graham, Said Darwish, Mustapha Boufares, and the Ben Othmen Family. Teresa Barton is grateful for the support from faculty from the School of Education at Loyola University Chicago and to her partner, Anthony Bushik.

List of Abbreviations

AfDB	African Development Bank
AFTURD	The Association of Tunisian Women for Research and Development
AIHR	Arab Institute for Human Rights
AIU	Alliance Israe'lite Universelle
APR	Assembly of the Representatives of the People
ATFD	The Tunisian Association of Democratic Women
CEDAW	Convention on the Elimination of All Forms of Discrimination Against Women
CENAFF	National Center of Training the Trainers in Education
CGTT	General Confederation of Tunisian Workers
CIE	Comparative and International Education
CPS	Le Code du Statut Parsonnel (the Code of Personal Status)
DCFTA	Deep and Comprehensive Free Trade Agreement
DEA	Diplôme d'Études Approfondies
DEUPC	Diploma of University Studies of the First Cycle
DEV	Department of Virtual Education
DOS	Discursive Opportunity Structures
Ennahda	The Islamic Tendency Movement
EQIP	Education Quality Improvement Program
ERSAP	Economic Recovery and Structural Adjustment Programme
FDI	Foreign Direct Investment

FTDES	Tunisian Forum for Social and Economic Rights
GDP	Gross Domestic Product
GNP	Gross National Product
GPC	Compagnie des Phosphates de Gafsa (Gafsa Phosphate Company)
HPA	Historical Policy Analysis
IBRD	International Bank for Reconstruction and Development
ICT	Information Communication Technologies
IDA	International Development Association
IMF	International Monetary Fund
IOM	The International Organization for Migration
ISET	Higher Institutes of Technological Studies
ISIS	Islamic State of Iraq and Syria
JORT	Journal Officiel de la République Tunisienne
le Bac	Baccalaureate
LMD	Licence–Maitrise–Doctorat (Bachelor–Master–PhD)
LTDH	Tunisian Human Rights League
MENA	Middle East and North Africa
MOBHERS	Ministry of Basic and Higher Education and Scientific Research
MOE	Ministry of Education
MOET	Ministry of Education and Training
MOHESR	Ministry of Higher Education and Scientific Research
MOHESRT	Ministry of Higher Education, Scientific Research and Technology
MONE	Ministry of National Education
MSA	Modern Standard Arabic
MSRTCD	Ministry of Scientific Research, Technology and Competency Development

MTI	Islamic Tendency Movement Party
NCA	National Constituent Assembly
NLS	National Literacy Strategy
OECD	Organization for Economic Co-operation and Development
OTA	Tunisian Order of Lawyers
PAQSET	Education System Quality Improvement Project
PHEI	Private Higher Education Institutions
PISA	Program for International Student Assessment
PLO	The Palestine Liberation Organization
PNEA	National Adult Education Program
POS	Political Opportunity Structures
PSD	Socialist Destourian Party
RCD	Democratic Constitutional Rally
SAP	Structural Adjustment Program
SERST	Secretariat of State for Scientific Research and Technology
SESP	Secondary Education Support Project
SMEs	Small and Medium-Sized Enterprises
STERP	Scientific and Technical Education Reinforcement Project
UGTT	General Confederation of Tunisian Workers
UNDP	United Nations Development Programme
UNFT	National Union of Tunisian Women
USAID	United States Agency for International Development
UTICA	Tunisian Confederation of Industry, Trade and Handicrafts
UVT	Virtual University of Tunis (Université Virtuelle de Tunis)
VET	Vocational and Employment Training
WSIS	World Summit on the Information Society

1

The Tunisian Paradox and Authoritarian Bargaining

The poem, *To the Tyrants of the World*, written in the late 1920s by the distinguished Tunisian poet, Abou el Kacem Chebbi, became the rallying cry in 1956 for Tunisia's independence from France. It was invoked again in 2011 during *al-sahwa*—the "Tunisian Uprising" or the "Jasmine Revolution" (later called the Arabic Spring or Arabic Awakening as it swept across North Africa and the Middle East)—as young Tunisians took to the streets to demand the removal of President Zine El Abidine Ben Ali (from 1987 to 2011) and his kleptocratic comrades, including his family and the Trabelsi family, his in-laws. Under his twenty-three years of rule, the Ben Ali and Trabelsi families elevated themselves to the status of Royals with a cult following and Mafia-style way of living based on drug smuggling, rent seeking, private property extortion, and blackmail (Maalej 2012; Schofield 2008). So, when Tunisians took to the streets, they chanted:

- *khobz w ma wben Ali la* (No to Ben Ali even if it takes living on bread and water)
- *Ben Ali ya jaban shaàb tounes la yuhan* (Ben Ali the coward, the people of Tunisia cannot be humiliated)
- *Ben Ali ya jaban, shaàb tounes la yuhan* (Tunisia is free, the Trabelsis must leave)
- *RCD dégagé* (RCD out)
- *twallishi ilkhobza ballushi, la la lil-Ghannouchi* (even if the loaf of bread becomes free, no no to Ghannouchi).

The "revolutionary contagion" that eventually gripped the Middle East as young cyber-activists, artists, human rights activists, feminists, and critical intellectuals took to new media or social media platforms (Facebook, Google, YouTube, and Twitter) and other podiums to claim liberty, solidarity, and equality was unparalleled and unprecedented. Unlike earlier violent demonstrations in

Tunisia—such as the Bread Riots of 1983–1984 and the Gafsa uprising in May 2008 that were brutally suppressed, censored, and curtailed—in 2011, ordinary educated people, utilizing core competencies acquired from schooling, took their demands to the streets and online, drawing more and more people into their center. This form of "open activism," using political communication and participation, meant that the Ben Ali regime could not suppress the people, quell demonstrations, nor hide the ensuing atrocities as it had done after the 2008 Gafsa uprisings—that occurred over hiring practices at the state-run Gafsa Phosphate Company (GPC)—some 360 kilometers from Tunis, the capital.

Social media provided a platform for a counter-narrative against the propaganda machinery (television and radio) of the state. Within this context of a proliferating new and social media we explore the role of education in Tunisia during times of political transition. We study how roles and modes of education have been actors of dissent responding to various conflict and crisis situations in Tunisia across three periods: (i) the pre-colonial and colonial period; (ii) the authoritarian period—1958 to 2011; and (iii) the post-*al-sahwa* period—2011 onwards. Our aim is to analyze the discursive policymaking and policy practices that occur at the national level in Tunisia, and which inform the country's model of education across these three periods. We pay attention to the impact of the external environment (both global and regional) on the formation and development of these educational models and practices, specifically as they relate and respond to the new, socially mediated, street or "ground up" forms of educational resistance and conduct.

Unlike other Arab states, Tunisia is a homogeneous "resource-rich, labor-abundant" (Economist 2016) country that has extractive industries, natural resources, and a population of almost eleven million people. Since independence, Tunisia's two dictators held sway over the people under a tightly woven authoritarian bargaining agreement that was endorsed by the elites in the coastal cities. Authoritarian bargaining or "dictator's dilemma" (Tullock 1987; Wintrobe 1990, 1998, 2007) refers to the principal instruments—repression and loyalty—that dictators use to survive and stay in office. At its core, authoritarian bargaining "reflects the 'contract' between dictators and different constituencies whereby the latter acquiesce to constraints on their political participation and liberties in exchange for economic security" (Desai, Yousef and Olofsgård 2007: 5). Under this implicit agreement between dictatorial regimes, the ruling elites and citizens, dictators are granted legitimacy through sham elections and in return, they provide political stability and moderate social and economic improvements. The scholarship on the dictator's dilemma suggests that dictatorial or authoritarian regimes use the political apparatus and institutions to find a delicate balance between the support garnered for the general population and that of the ruling elites. Under this social pact, citizens relinquish political freedoms in exchange for access to public goods and economic benefits. Authoritarian bargaining, which promises greater social benefits to its citizens, provides a strategic vantage point to examine the role of education under dictatorship.

Since independence in 1956, the two dictatorial regimes in Tunisia—from 1956 to 1987 under Habib Bourgubia, and from 1987 to 2011 under Ben Ali—made schooling the center of their authoritarian bargaining agreement, policies, and priorities and the engine of national development. In the English language, there is an idiomatic expression that says, *"Don't bite the hand that feeds you."* When young Tunisians took to the streets demanding freedom from authoritarian rule in 2010, they were not only *biting the hand that fed* them, they were peaceably rising against a regime with the only instrument they knew, which is *al-ttaelim* (education). Education as both ideological and political capital has been used by Tunisian youth to counter the ideological changes imposed by dictatorial governance and to promote socio-political revolutions that oppose it.

As Facci (2011: 79) notes in citing Paulo Freire, "nobody liberates nobody, nobody liberates themselves alone: human beings liberate themselves in communion." In this way, education not only plays a significant role in national economic development but also raises the "archaeology of consciousness" of the citizen through *conscientization*—the processes of reflection and action (Freire 2000). The educator is, therefore, responsible for fostering dialogue and liberation by enabling students to reach different levels of political understanding: magical consciousness, naive consciousness, critical consciousness, and political consciousness (Freire 2000). In this sense, magical consciousness suggests the individual is unable to do anything about their socio-economic portion. Naive consciousness speaks to the ability of the individual to make a distinction between themselves and the outside world. Critical consciousness is where the individual discovers not only the distinction between themselves and the world, but they also act to change things. Finally, political consciousness, the highest form of discovery, occurs when the individual shares their perception of reality and the individual then mobilizes with others to try to influence the political scenery.

At this point, it is important to recognize there were models of education enacted by the Tunisian state (which, to some extent and under some leadership, had positive effects for its citizenry) (see Chapter 2); but other models of education, based in Freirian principle, were the ones growing explosively with the greater impact on (re)defining what contemporary modes of education and activism look like. This is the difference of referring to the educator as "the state" and the educator as "the people." It is the growth of the people as activists, as educators, and how they become inspiration for others, that is our interest in this book.

Table 1 Tunisia's demographic indicators at a glance

Indicator	Year	Data
Capital		Tunis
Religion		Muslim (official; Sunni), 99.1%; other (includes Christian, Jewish, Shia Muslim and Baha'i) 1%
Population	2014	10.98 million
Language		Arabic (official), French
Child labor (ages 5–14)	2014	3% or 50,364 children
Number of mobile phones per 100 people	2015	128
Life expectancy at birth (years)	2015	75
Number of Internet users per 100 people	2015	46.2
Literacy rate	2015	79%
Net Enrollment Rate in primary education	2014	98.7% (1,063,291)
Primary School Teachers	2013	61,002
Primary completion rate	2014	101.7%
Net Enrollment Rate in secondary education	2014	91.0% (1,071,729)
Gross secondary enrollment	2014	90.6%
Expenditure on education (all levels)	2014	21.6%
Expenditure on tertiary education	2014	28.1%
Gross enrollment in tertiary education	2014	35.2%
Enrollment in vocational schools	2013	99,345
Effective transition rate from primary to lower secondary	2012	92.8%
Youth not in education, employment, or training	2013	25.4%
Unemployment with primary education	2010	22.3%
Unemployment with secondary education	2011	42.5%
Unemployment with tertiary education	2011	30.8%
Fertility rate		1.99

Sources: United States Department of Labor (2014); World Bank World Development Indicators Databank (2016); World Economic Forum (2016)

The strategic utilization of one's education to mobilize became the *only* weapon to denounce, scribble, and vent the anger and frustrations of years of repression, unfulfilled promises of economic development, and an unprecedented level of graft that Ben Ali and his regime had inflicted upon Tunisians. In fact, the regime's post-Franco, colonial, semi-bureaucratic, *Tunisified*, secular, uncontrolled education system had slowly imparted to Tunisians that *"Tunisian rights are human rights and human rights are Tunisian rights."* In other words, the post-independence authoritarian bargaining agreements had stressed that human rights and Tunisian secular rights are conjoined twin pillars of the Tunisian's identity; however, citizens perceived that the Ben Ali regime had gravely infringed upon these rights for years. In short, *al-sahwa*, which took the global landscape by surprise in January 2011, has its historical heredity, incubation, fermentation, expansion, explosion, and contagion in Tunisia's national education developments. It was the school system that equipped students with disobedient objects and tools (digital, oratory, and written) as the student movement for social change grew with passion. The school system reinforced the authoritarian bargaining agreements between the regimes and the citizenry. The school system taught about sustainable democratic institutions and the possibility of freedom from tyrannical rule. The school system ultimately developed and prepared students to become dissenters and to lead the peaceful overthrow of Ben Ali's regime.

The post-Franco colonial education system, with all its bureaucratic trappings, was responsible for radically transforming and reorienting the political clarity of Tunisians who had, before January 2011, begun to discuss in their homes and cafes: *What type of society do we want to produce? How do we produce it?* And, *for what and for whom is it to be produced?* The media and scholars in covering *al-sahwa* have exposed every possible explanation under a macroscopic lens, except the role, if any, the education system played in fostering, cultivating, and incubating disobedience and finally unleashing it at the right time, in a peaceful, respectful, mobilizing, and almost bloodless way. When education is discussed in the Tunisian context, if at all, it is linked to unemployment and underemployment and to the popular company belief that students are not learning the necessary labor market skills (as discussed in Chapter 5).

In the next section, we introduce our study, which was based on five years of fieldwork by Dr. Jules, in Tunisia. We employed an "analysis for policy," where researchers critically examine past and existing educational policies rather than doing an "analysis of policy," which involves providing information to be used for policymaking (Gordon et al. 1977).

Mapping the Methodological Terrain—Narrative Comparisons and Comparative-historical Analysis

Methodologically, this study draws upon the discursive traditions within Comparative and International Education (CIE). We were interested in the role education plays under different regimes during times of transition, be they democratic or dictatorial. We sought to understand the different approaches Tunisia's two dictatorial regimes took to drafting and enacting education policy reforms and the implications of these, if any, in the period following the fall of the Ben Ali regime in 2011. To look at these education policy reforms, we focused primarily on the discursive aspect of policy by collecting and analyzing policy texts and other policy artifacts on educational developments and then exploring their parallels and metamorphoses across different historical periods. Our findings were illuminated through a "causal narrative [that] offers insight into causal processes, process tracing [that] explores causal mechanisms and pattern matching [that] tests theory" (Lange 2013: 14). We took the causal narrative and determined how different dictators used authoritarian bargaining agreements across different periods. In analyzing the discursive patterns found in Tunisia's national education policy documents, we focused on the documents from Tunisia's independence in 1958 through 2011. During this period, Tunisia had three major reforms: (i) the 1958-Education reforms aimed at re-nationalizing, *Tunisifying*, and Arabizing the education system by making basic education accessible, taught in Tunisian Arabic rather than in French, mandatory and, free for all children from six years old; (ii) the 1991-Education reforms that extended the duration of free basic education from six years, established in the 1958-Education reforms, to nine years and split the Ministry of Education and Sciences into the Ministry of Education and the Ministry of Higher Education Scientific Research; and (iii) the 2002–2007 School of Tomorrow (*L'école de Demain*) reforms aimed at providing quality education for all.

We used a vertical case study to analyze the different plans, policies, and papers that were active during the education reforms across these three time periods. The vertical case study draws "'vertical' attention across micro-, meso-, and macro-levels, or scales; a 'horizontal' comparison of how policies unfold in distinct locations; and a 'transversal,' processual analysis of the creative appropriation of educational policies across time" (Bartlett and Vavrus 2014: 131). Emerging from a "comparative-historical approach," "historical-comparative," or "comparative-historical analysis" (Cowen 2000a; Jules and Barton 2014; Lange 2013; Larsen 2010; Mahoney and Rueschemeyer 2003; Schriewer

2002), and grounded in a Historical Policy Analysis (HPA) (Hanberger 2003; Jules 2013a, 2013b; Schram 1993; Torgerson 1996), we kept our methodological focus on the vertical case study within the field of CIE. By applying the vertical case study to an analysis of Tunisia's national policy documents, we show how the policy discourses on education across these three periods of transition in Tunisia affected the educational landscape experienced by the Tunisians and how their experiences impacted the larger Arab region.

To gage how different policy streams allow for education reforms to occur in Tunisia, we focus our analysis of policymaking at the national level and pay attention to the impact of the external environment on national decisions. We define policies as discursive, vital expressions of social power that epitomize the values of authoritative actors and institutions, whose knowledge about the social world are echoed in these texts (Ball 1990; Jules 2016). Michel Foucault reflected this well, writing, "[policies] can be said and thought, but [it is] also about who can speak, when, where and with what authority" (Ball 1990: 2). We seek to understand how "new patterns of power, regulation and inclusion/exclusion [in policy] can lead to new ways of organising public space and distributing common goods and to new opportunities to stabilise or change society" (Simons, Olssen and Peters 2009: 38). By focusing on the new educations formed within and in response to each of the three policy time periods, our vertical case study departs from a more traditional "education politics" framework defined as "the processes whereby [an educational] agenda is translated into problems and issues for schools and schools' responses to those problems and issues" (Dale 1994: 39) toward perceived solutions.

In deconstructing how national education policies and priorities were framed in Tunisia, we do not reinforce old patterns of methodological nationalism by limiting "one's analysis to state policies and politics within the state and assuming a fixed linkage between government and territory in a single nation, [which] actually re-enforce[s] a given state of affairs at the national and international level" (Simons, Olssen and Peters 2009: 38; see also Robertson and Dale 2008). In our analysis of policy discourse, we sought to account for changes in Tunisia by placing them within the broader context of external change. To do this, we moved away from "comparison" and toward "translation" (Dale 2006; Santos 1995; 2004) by not confining ourselves to national, partial problem-solving assumptions, but concentrating on the scalar nature of the governance of education. As discussed above, we focused on studying Tunisia vertically because its "national policies ... have themselves acquired international, transnational and global dimensions, [so] then we need to ask how this has become so and what implications this has for thinking about national policy programs, local policy initiatives and internationalizing policy dialogue" (Rizvi 2006: 203). As Marcus (1995) suggests, our processes involved *mapping, visiting, questioning,* and *following* policy to determine "the 'whos' and 'whats' but also the 'wheres' of policy—the places and events in which the 'past, present and potential futures of education co-exist'" (McCann and Ward 2012: 48). Our work therefore entailed "staying close to practice" by "'following policies' and 'studying through' the sites and situations of policymaking" to explain "... how policy actors circulate policies among cities, how they draw on circulating policy knowledge and how and for whom they put these engagements to use as they assemble their own 'local' policies ..." (McCann and Ward 2012: 42).

Our study focused on discursive, semi-structured interviews conducted between 2011 and 2016 with ministry officials from the Ministry of Education and the Ministry of Higher Education, nongovernmental representatives, university deans and faculty members, teachers, and college students. Essential to our approach was the ability to illuminate "... the inescapably social nature of those continuous processes of translation, intermediation and contextualization/decontextualization/recontextualization, through which various forms of policy mobility are realized" (Peck and Theodore 2012: 24). Our comparative-historical approach focuses on: (i) the pre-colonial and colonial period; (ii) the authoritarian period—1958 to 2011; and (iii) the post-*al-sahwa* period—2011 onwards. Narrative comparisons of educational policies fall into three broad categories that allow us to: (i) consider a broad array of factors that contribute to perceived convergence or divergence of policies and practices to global norms across different periods or process-oriented comparison; (ii) pull out specific mechanisms and explicate these, or make mechanistic comparison; and (iii) focus on both a particular causal relationship and areas of similarities and dissimilarities, or on ideal–typical comparisons (Lange 2013). Thus, following Mahoney and Rueschemeyer (2003) the comparative-historical inquiry we use has three features: (i) we explain causal configurations; (ii) we focus on explaining the unfolding of temporal processes over time; and (iii) we describe sequels within delimited historical contexts.

Since our analysis centered on "... social processes like revolutions, [and] ... involve[d] many people within a complex social environment over an extended period" (Lange 2013: 14), our starting point was asking broad "research questions about concrete real-world phenomena" (Lange 2013: 14), for example: *What role did education play in the Tunisian revolution?* As Lange (2013: 14–15) suggests, "the most common comparative methods employed in the comparative-historical analysis are small-N comparisons. These comparisons usually explore how causal processes are similar and different and, in so doing, pay attention to the impact of context and causal mechanisms ... [using] historical methods to gather, assess and present data." In using narrative comparisons to historicize Tunisia's education system, we can highlight nomothetic and ideographic insights that further show how social, economic, and political factors shaped the educational decisions of different dictatorial regimes.

A comparative-historical approach, combining comparative and within-case methods, complements the vertical case study because this allowed us to compare the educational priorities outlined in different dictatorial authoritarian bargaining agreements. We chose this framework and methodology to understand the "processes [of the policy documents] and [to explore its] causal determinants ... through a detective-style analysis which seeks to highlight the causal impact of particular factors within particular cases" (Lange 2013: 4). In other words, "within-case methods constitute the 'historical' in comparative-historical analysis—that is, they are temporal and analyze processes over time" (Lange 2013: 4). For us, a comparative-historical approach was not about the "juxtaposition of historical patterns across cases," but instead it was used to draw attention to "the processes over time and the use of systematic and contextualized comparison" (Mahoney and Rueschemeyer 2003: 10) of education policy priorities. We seek to highlight space, scale, endogenous, and exogenous influences within transitology literature. As we examine specific histories of Tunisia in the following chapters, we aim our temporal analysis at explaining the evolution of social and political structures during times of transition (Mahoney and Rueschemeyer 2003).

Al-sahwa and the Liberation Caravan: The Uneducated Martyr

Bayat (2010: 4) in discussing social movements suggests that:

> [social movements] combined three elements: an organized and sustained claim making on target authorities; a repertoire of performances, including associations, public meetings, media statements and street marches; and "public representations of the cause's worthiness, unity, numbers and commitment."

The 2010 protests and *al-sahwa* that brought down the Ben Ali regime in January 2011 were part of a gradual internal "revolutionary contagion" that has its heredity in 2008. The interior regions of Tunisia—particularly the four governorates of the North-West, the three governorates of the Central-West, and the six governorates of the South—have historically been neglected, but these regions are expected to produce the exports and feed the country. Tunisia has a relatively small, well-educated population, is geographically close to Europe with economic and political connections to France and the United States and has a slow economic growth, a significant number of trade unions, and a high unemployment rate. All these characteristics made Tunisia a powder keg primed for explosive change. However, a closer reading of slogans chanted by mobs of protestors during the final days of the Ben Ali regime shows that *al-sahwa* was organized by far-reaching networks of actors with years of experience in battling restrictions of political expression.

As Tunisians began to organize in December 2010 after the self-immolation of a fruit vendor, Mohamed Bouazizi (discussed in detail in Chapter 7), they used the "space to revolt" (Le Saout 1988) while keeping in mind the Bread Revolt of January 1984 (eighty-nine killed) and the Gafsa uprising and suppression of 2008. In fact, Tunisians point out that *al-sahwa* began in 2008, not 2010, with the Gafsa Mining Basin protest that ran for six months as the unemployed (predominantly university graduates), high school students, temporary workers contracted on municipal building sites, and families of workers who suffered from an accident in the phosphate mines rioted, blocked roads, used sit-ins, and burned tires. In 2008, the phosphate mining area controlled by GPC was doing well, yet the so-called "economic miracle" the Ben Ali regime boasted about was nowhere to be seen. In the country's interior regions, youth unemployment remained high and the quality of education declined.

The problem with GPC was that in the 1970s, when it shifted to open-pit mining, jobs began to decrease and local economies dependent on the mines were not diversified. Some estimates suggest that when compared with 1980, by 2006, the modernization toward open-pit mining had caused the region a 75 percent reduction in GPC's workers (Gobe 2010). In 2008, the people of Gafsa began protesting the results of the placement examinations for GPC workers that came into force in 1986 between GPC and the Regional Union of the UGTT. Many alleged that GPC's hiring practices were rife with corruption and nepotism and that the company reneged on its promise to ensure 20 percent of its total workforce was composed of young people from the region, which was part of the 1986 agreement with trade unions. For many young people in the Gafsa area, once they completed *le Bac* (the Baccalaureate) their only option was to work in the mines since they could not afford external costs (food, rent, and textbooks) associated with attending higher education, even though it is free and based on merit. Post-Gafsa tensions reached another milestone in 2007 when unemployed graduates of the University of Tunis denounced the corrupt practices of the Ben Ali regime and founded the Union of Unemployed Graduates, which was not recognized by the Ben Ali regime.

The 2010 uprising against Ben Ali's regime began that August in the border town of Ben Guerdane and spread in December to the agricultural regions of Sidi Bou Zid, Kasserine, and Thala in the Central-West region. In the Western media, the 2010 uprising is often misunderstood and misappropriated. For example, the city of Sidi Bou Zid, with an unemployment rate at that time of 30 percent, which was the triggering mechanism for the larger uprising, is often dismissed as a backwater town. However, if one studies the history of Tunisia, one will quickly learn Sidi Bou Zid had suffered greatly from the "pillage-cum-privatization" (Clancy-Smith 2013) of the Trabelsi family as they privatized natural resources, such as water and other agrarian activities, such as food-processing and the growing of fruits across the region. In fact, Mohamed Bouazizi's self-immolation was not the first one in protest of Ben Ali's and the Trabelsis' corrupt practices. The actions of the intelligence-based police (*al-mukhabarat*) of harassment and intimidations resulting in the self-immolation of Bouazizi was *the last straw that broke the backs of Tunisians*: having a good education was serendipitous and played a major role in the contagion that followed.

On December 17, 2010, the twenty-six-year-old street vendor, Mohamed Bouazizi, would have begun his day in Sidi Bou Zid like any other day. However, it was different on that day because of two degrading encounters he had with *al-mukhabarat* (a historically entitled civil servant group under the Ben Ali regime) and other government officials. The first encounter was harassment by a policewoman that prohibited him from selling his fruits and vegetables. The other happenstance occurred when he was sent away from the governor's office after he complained about his encounter with the policewoman. A disgruntled Bouazizi eventually set himself on fire not only to protest his encounters with authority but also to express national frustrations with the corrupt *al-mukhabarat* and a privileged inner circle that seemed to be accumulating vast amounts of wealth and patronage while ordinary citizens, like him, were struggling for basic needs. Bouazizi's self-immolation was an act of martyrdom to draw attention to the plight of unemployment and underemployment, food insecurity and inflation, inadequate living standards, lack of freedoms, and deficiency of government responsiveness (Gelvin 2013). However, most of all, Bouazizi's act was one against the institution of *al-mukhabarat*. Bouazizi's death on January 4, 2011 would eventually set off a cascading series of events leading to the revolutionary contagion as mass mobilization and protests gained fervor and spread to the cities of Sfax and Ben Guerdane before reaching the coastal capital of Tunis and then taking the other interior regions by storm. Unlike previous uprisings in specific areas of Tunisia, the revolutionary contagion gained countrywide momentum not only because of the issues (corruption, nepotism, and pillage-cum-privatization) but also because of the diverse array of people (lawyers, judges, students, and civil society activists) both employed and unemployed, who came out to voice their anger and disgust at the regime. However, more importantly, protestors had the backing of the powerful General Confederation of Tunisian Workers (UGTT), which historically Ben Ali had paid patronage to under the authoritarian bargaining agreement they had stuck by him and the regime in times past.

Bouazizi's sacrifice was not a unique experience among youths; in fact, before his self-immolation, several young Tunisians had killed themselves to draw attention to the plight of poverty and lack of opportunities. The development of a "culture of suicide" (Clancy-Smith 2013; Mabrouk 2013) had become rampant among the country's most marginalized and disenfranchised youth. In discussing the impact of liberalizing the Tunisian economy to foreign investors as part of the pillage-cum-privatization upon vulnerable groups, Mabrouk (2013: 12), in citing the United Nations Development Programme (UNDP), argues the culture of suicide that emerged in Tunisia was "a culture which disdained the value of life, finding death an easier alternative because of a lack of values and a sense of anomie," which was "particularly true of unemployed and marginal youth, so that death was more attractive than life under such conditions . . ." Thus, we suggest it was the opening-up of the economy to benefit a selected few and not others that spawned the discontent, disillusionment, and disenfranchisement that would, in the post-*al-sahwa* period, serve as an incubator for the recruitment of Tunisian youth by *Daesh* (*al-Dawla al-Islamiya fil Iraq wa al-Sham* a.k.a. the Islamic State) who were fleeing in droves to eke out a living and find better paying jobs.

Tunisians, both educated and undereducated, could resonate with Bouazizi's story; that is, the government had failed them in:

[a] country that has for a resource the intelligence of its sons and daughters, over which we have always taken a gamble and we continue to do so, since we prefer to face the challenges and difficulties, strong in that of an educated and cultured people rather than to enjoy an illusory peace with an illiterate people.

We are, as we have already said, proud of their growing number and we will work to meet the challenge it imposes on us, since our educational choices figure among the constants of our political and civilisational project, that the compulsory and free nature of education is one of the inviolable principles, despite the social and economic costs they entail and that the spreading of academic institutions across the country, without exception, is a reality that we use, irreversibly, to consolidate in each phase.

Our education policy, like our policies related to family, women, youth and children, as well as efforts by the state to ensure the care of the poor, preserve purchasing power and to subsidise the prices of commodities which cost the state budget more than 1,700 million dinars a year (I say 1,700 million dinars), make us proud.

Last speech of Ben Ali, delivered on January 10, 2011

As the public later found out, Bouazizi had dropped out of secondary school and became a street vendor to support his family. His lack of education and the profession that he chose, a street vendor selling fruit and vegetables, placed him neither as elite nor as one of the hundreds of thousands that were either unemployed or underemployed. Instead, he fell into a unique category that houses many Tunisians who did not benefit from the free market capitalist promises that never materialized under Ben Ali; he was an invisible person with no rights or recourse since he did not have ties to corrupt feudal clans that controlled the informal economy. Bouazizi's story highlights the power of education in constructing the middle class. If a person was not in the regime's inner circle and was suffering from the plight of under-education, particularly in the interior regions and toiled in the informal or "shadowy" economy, they were neglected by the regime and viewed as worker-bees in the pillage-cum-privatization moneymaking schemes of the regime. Yet, ironically, Bouazizi's family was paid off by the Ben Ali regime before he fled the country and they immediately moved from Sidi Bou Zid to the posh coastal suburb of La Marsa where they bought a Mediterranean villa. Bouazizi's sacrifices—dropping out of high school to support the family and finally standing up to corrupt officials—brought the family into the landed middle class that many Tunisians aspire to attain. The second lesson of Bouazizi's story is that five years after *al-sahwa* much of Tunisian youth retain a pessimistic outlook. Young people are still disillusioned and argue they are no better off today than they were under Ben Ali. In fact, they claim that *al-sahwa* has failed them since it did not provide the jobs, hope, or opportunities promised.

An Overview of the Retrospective: Negotiating the Transition Between the Old and the New

Once the dust of *al-sahwa* settled and the collateral damage was calculated, the Arab Awakening had dismantled autocratic regimes across the region. In fact, all the pundits in predicting democratic changes to the Middle East never once identified Tunisia as a potential regional catalyst, protagonist, and instigator for change. In his 2010 article, *Why Are There No Arab Democracies*, Larry Diamond suggests that "the emergence of a single democratic polity in the region, particularly in a country that might be seen as a model" (Diamond 2010: 102) could hail the beginning of an era of democratization across the Middle East and North African (MENA) region. Prescient as his article is, Diamond overlooked Tunisia and instead predicted Lebanon, Iraq, or Egypt as potential harbingers of democracy in the region. Like Diamond, many leaders and pundits often forget that "Tunisia has its own personality," as Tunisia's first president, Habib Bourguiba (from 1957 to 1987) used to say (Barakat 2015). Moreover, "Tunisian exceptionalism" has existed since the dawn of independence. In fact, Bourguiba was an ardent proponent of promulgating Tunisia's Arab–Islam character that has been forged across ages dating back to *al-Amazigh* (the free people) or Tunisian *Berbers* (see Chapter 2). However, Tunisian exceptionalism, which is steeped in its Arab–Islamic character, often oscillates between the Arab East (*al-tamashruq*) and Westernization (*al-tamaghrub*) since adherents of Tunisification (*al-tawnasa*) or Tunisian identity (*al-dhatiyya al-atunisyya*) emphasize local patriotism (*wataniyya*) (Barakat 2015). While *al-sahwa* created ripples in the fabric of the Middle East, Tunisia has a rich history of revolutionary transition led by the educated middle class. As discussed across this book, if we look at Tunisia's history throughout the last 3,000 years, we can observe that dictators and dictatorial regimes, in whatever form, have been good at educating Tunisians, giving them freedoms and then suppressing those freedoms; ultimately resulting in violent demonstrations, revolts, and the eventual toppling of the regime in power. Demonstrations, revolutions, and dictatorial changes are part and parcel of the social fabric of Tunisia. However, what has remained consistent is that Tunisia's benevolent dictators, from the times of the Carthaginians (in 814 BCE), have always invested heavily in the educative development of Tunisians. Education has historically been and continues to be linked to Tunisian distinctive North African culture. In fact, the Ministry of Education and Training (MOET) (2002: 5) notes, "education aims at . . . strengthening [students'] sense of . . . cultural belonging in its national, Maghreb, Arab, Islamic, African and Mediterranean dimensions, widening their outlook into human civilization." Of course, several scholars have raised the Tunisian puzzle; that is, they have questioned the quality of the education provided by the state and if it is relevant or adequate for the labor market needs of the time. However, that particular puzzle is for a different book. The puzzle of this book is the role that education plays in delivering and sustaining the different dictatorial authoritarian bargaining agreements. The overwhelming answer to this puzzle, at least dating back to the French occupation, was that the type of education offered by the state did not always match the skills needed in the market. After independence in 1956, education focused on filling vacant bureaucratic offices left by the French. Under Ben Ali, educational development was intertwined with the notion of preparing Tunisians for the knowledge society. In the post-*al-sahwa* period, education is touted as a panacea for democratization, economic stabilization, and securitization.

Across the eight chapters of this book, we make the argument that education contributed significantly to both the pre-*al-sahwa* period (*ma kabla al-sahwa*) and post-*al-sahwa* period (*ma baada al-sahwa*) in shaping the young Tunisian revolutionaries that took to the streets in December 2010 and January 2011, eventually peacefully toppling the Ben Ali regime and his comrades. As *al-sahwa al-Tunisia* (the Tunisian uprising) or *Sahwa Movement* (the Awakening Movement) or *al-Sahwa al-Islamiyya* (the Islamic Awakening) swept across the Arab world, changing its shape and metamorphosing into expanded forms of "people power," the common denominator of the movement was that they were educated. It was *not* the foreign educated elites, the landed gentry, the Tunis-based *grand families*, the intelligentsia, or the emerging coastal (or *Sahel*) bourgeoisie who mobilized and led or backed *al-sahwa* as it was during the fight for Tunisian Independence. It was *not* Western-backed, Shiite-backed or Sunni-backed armies, or military generals leading a *coup d'état* that started *al-sahwa*. It was *not* the coronation of an Arabic Royal house with a new sultan, prince, or king that led to *al-sahwa*. It was ordinary educated people (with secondary and tertiary levels of education), with basic technological literacy and a mobile telephone in the hand (for text-messaging, photo-documentation, and video live streaming) that brought a United States-backed regime and its cronies, that had ruled Tunisia for twenty-three years, to its knees. In fact, it was Ben Ali in his third-to-last speech as president, trying to quell tensions, who acknowledged that:

> ... unemployment is the concern of developed and developing countries in the world. We in Tunisia spend all efforts to curb it and treat its effects and its repercussions especially among families without any resources. The State will spend extra efforts in this regard during the next period. We accomplished outstanding results in the area of education both quantitatively and qualitatively. This has attracted the respect and laudability of concerned international agencies and constitutes a fixed central choice in our policy of building an educated population. One of the most prominent results is the development of university graduates in higher education institutions that are found across the regions of

the country without exception, which saw last year, for example, the graduation of over 80,000 students, which is a figure that we are proud of and whose challenges we accept to employ this high rate of graduates among those applying for jobs through various employment mechanisms and programs. In spite of the difficulties posed by this kind of new kind of unemployment, it remains a source of optimism in the future – the optimism of an educated population perseverant in more promotion and advancement.

Speech given on December 28, 2010 [*trans.* Maalej 2012]

In hindsight, Ben Ali and his comrades did not foresee that the tool of education they vehemently advocated for as a necessary *good for the masses*, as a necessary *good for economic prosperity*, as a necessary *human right*, and as necessary for *access to the middle class*, would be responsible for the downfall of him and his regime.

While the world was not looking, the social eruption that catapulted Tunisia into the spotlight in January 2011 was a powder keg that had been simmering since 2008. In this book, we advance three crisis narratives that help to explain the relationship between revolutionary educational thinking and social change in Tunisia. We suggest that:

i.   *Skills shortage: There continues to be a drastic disparity between the* quality of education and training offered and the *skills demanded by the labor market and those acquired by graduates (at all levels of the education system).* For example, since independence, Tunisia's public university system (private universities were not encouraged or supported until 2008, see Chapter 5) has undergone one major reform in 2008 that introduced the *Licence-Maitrise-Doctorat (LMD) system.* As such, in retaining the francophone system of higher education, even after the 2008 reform, the public university system and to a large extent the private suppliers of higher education continue to produce graduates with job skills for acquainted bureaucratic positions that never benefited from reforms. Skills mismatch is a growing problem with graduates. Students who have earned a *Licence* or higher are more likely to be unemployed for eighteen to twenty-four months after graduating.

ii.   *Open and free access to education:* Since independence in 1956, the number of jobs promised under the Bourguiba and Ben Ali regimes, based on reforms in education—that focused on access, equity, and quality over time—and experimentation with diverse economic models touted under the authoritarian bargaining agreements—liberalization, socialist collectivization, mixed economy, and neoliberalism (which are aspects of state-led interventionism)—*did not materialize.* State-led interventionism *was first cloaked in nationalism with socialist tendencies under Bourguiba and these same policies were promoted as free market capitalism under Ben Ali.* This allowed the regimes (and their allies) to intervene in the market process to correct perceived market failures and promote the Tunisian social bargaining. The lack of jobs created a cycle where access to free public basic education eventually produced surplus labor at the secondary level where students were then encouraged to take up bachelor's degrees while looking for a job. If a student was unable to find a job with a bachelor's degree, they were encouraged by the regime to begin studying for a master's degree and eventually a doctoral degree. At the end of the cycle of degree after degree, supply outstripped demand and quality of the education offered diminished. An overeducated youth population conjoined with the socio-economic fallout of neoliberal transformations that coincided with a "youthful age structure" or "youth bulge" (much of the population is young adults), comprising youths aged fifteen to twenty-four, barred young people from entering the job market. For example, the unemployment rate in Tunisia for 1995, 2000, 2010, and 2011 respectively was 15.7, 15.6, 13, and 18.9 percent. However, for 2011, 42.3 percent of youth were unemployed. The side effect of unemployment and underemployment is the emergence of a booming informal economy with high youth participation and an environment ripe for the *recurring radicalization of youth.*

iii. *Tunisian exceptionalism*: Tunisian exceptionalism is embedded in structural and historical advantages that have befallen Tunisia: (i) Tunisia has existed as a political entity for 3,000 years (see Chapter 3); (ii) as noted earlier (see Table 1), Tunisia is almost entirely Sunni and void of the sectarian and tribal differences that beset Iraq, Syria, and Libya; and (iii) Tunisia's post-independence institutions are some of the most liberal in the Arabic world, particularly when it comes to women's rights and marriage (see Chapter 8). Since the early 1960s when Tunisia received the first World Bank loan for an education project, Tunisia has managed to develop the "Tunisian way" of doing business in education. In this sense, the pre-*al-sahwa* regimes were skillful in "cherry-picking" the external "conditions for reform" they bound themselves to with international knowledge banks (such as the World Bank and IMF), and aid agencies (such as USAID and the European Union's Mediterranean Partnership Agreements). Higher education in Tunisia, which remains free of user fees, is an example of the "Tunisian way." This is compounded by the fact that given Tunisian colonial history with France, Tunisia often looks to France for policy solutions to perceived problems since it has maintained its colonial education bureaucratic structures, with minor tweaks every so often, since independence.

These three narratives can be cumulatively summed up as the Tunisian model. Under this model, both dictatorial regimes suppressed dissidents, quelled uprisings, and jailed perceived rebels; they did so in the name of democracy while receiving compliance from the population in return for growing the middle class and keeping the public education system free and open to all. We do not propose these narratives as a panacea for *al-sahwa*, but we use them to facilitate a broader discussion on the role that education plays during times of transitions or "transitologies" (Cowen 2000a). In doing this, we draw upon the literature in educational transitologies (see Chapter 2) to explain the frustrations of young Tunisians that persist in the post-*al-sahwa* period and to discuss Tunisia's post-*al-sahwa* education system. Following Clancy-Smith (2013), we employ a long-term historical perspective or policy histogram recognizing that several contributing factors (such as globalization, social media technologies, and the "youth bulge") facilitate *al-sahwa*, but they are not solely responsible for the mass mobilizations and demonstrations that occurred. The youth bulge existed long before independence and it was exacerbated by statist educational policies under both Habiba Bourguiba and Ben Ali. As such, we study *al-sahwa* as a historical phenomenon whose origins are derived from several causal explanations and its ends are not in sight (Hudson 2014; Wallerstein 2011).

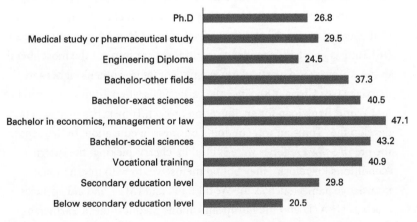

Figure 1 Youth unemployment rate by educational level in Tunisia (2007)

Sources: Jelassi, Bouzguenda and Malzy (2015); Stampini and Verdier-Chouchane (2011)

In fact, one of the key arguments this volume proposes is that across Tunisia's long, colorful history of plunder, conquest, and looting by invaders, several revolutionary movements have mobilized and revolted against the dictators who were supported by the elites, and demanded changes. As such, a historical understanding of the role of education in aiding and abetting *al-sahwa* is warranted because we habitually overlook "that 'national' histories have always been constructed in transnational context and circumstances and that ruptures and continuities exist in continuous, yet contingent, dialogue and tension" (Clancy-Smith 2013: 18).

This book historically explores Tunisia's education system by chronicling the trajectories of the political transformations leading up to January 14, 2011, when former president Ben Ali fled Tunisia after weeks of nonviolent demonstrations. We explore the role of education in training, mobilizing, and transforming the Tunisian landscape in the pre-*al-sahwa* and post-*al-sahwa* periods by explaining the current "Tunisian paradox." On the one hand, Tunisia is hailed as the success model of democratic transitions and human rights in the Arab world (since 2014 it has one of the most advanced constitutions in the Middle East and in 2015 *the National Dialogue Quartet* received the Nobel Peace Prize); notwithstanding the rise of internal jihad militantism and conflict on its border with the failed state of Libya. On the other hand, Tunisia's educated youth is unemployed and disgruntled, often exclaiming that Ben Ali's corrupt regime did more for the country. Such sentiments and other deteriorating social conditions have resulted in Tunisia producing the largest contingent of foreign fighters for *Daesh*.

In sum, our aim is not to examine if *al-sahwa* has created a functioning template for the rest of the Middle East, however flawed, with the potential to establish great Arab democracies. A lot has been written about the long-term transformation of the Arabic region that began with *al-sahwa*. Scholars have sought to analyze the associated economic, political, strategic, ideological, and religious underpinnings of the revolts. However, what is missing from the current wave of analysis is the role that education played in the historical development of *al-sahwa*. As such, we provide a compelling argument grounded in chronological historical account that explains the origins of *al-sahwa* and the fundamental role that education and the educated middle class played in mobilizing, steering, and dictating a "leaderless revolt" against a corrupt, dictatorial, autocratic leader, his regime and military-based police system, and a clan of Ben Ali wife's extended family networks. Our central argument is that, unlike the scores of movements, dating back to the 1970s, that sought to bring down the two dictatorial regimes in Tunisia and were subsequently suppressed by the prevailing security-based political orders, *al-sahwa* was different because the tech-savvy educated youths could marshal the technological resources of globalization to shed light on the atrocities of the autocratic system. Unlike their forefathers who came of age in an agrarian-based economic system in the post-colonial era, today's Tunisian youth are generally viewed as open-minded; they are glued to their cellular telephones, with access to terabytes of information, use social media to their advantage, and are multilingual (French and Arabic). However, most of all, the average young person was and continues to be disillusioned by the fact that *al-sahwa* did not create mass changes in their economic, social, and, to a large extent, political life, something that we return to in the final chapter of this book. It is the potent combination of these characteristics that makes Tunisia an easy recruiter for *Daesh*. In fact, *al-sahwa* was built as a great coming of change and prosperity, driven by a sense of inclusion for all, but its trajectories and expectations were never defined and therefore its success and failure are measured by individual barometers rather than national surveys.

Based on the methodological design, this book's subsequent analysis unfolds across the remaining chapters. Chapter 2 details the theoretical framework that drives this study. In doing this, we draw upon the transitologies literature in education to explain the role of education during different periods of transitions. Chapter 3 discusses the educational developments during the pre-colonial and colonial periods and the role of education in shaping and sustaining different regimes. Chapter 4 provides the idea of using authoritarian educational policies to sustain power in the post-independence period. Chapters 5, 6, and 7 expand upon the idea of using authoritarian educational policies to sustain power under dictatorships by utilizing different topical case studies on: (i) the role of higher education in meeting the needs of the labor market; (ii) the role of women in society; and (iii) the use of information communication technologies in education. In Chapter 8, we conclude the book by discussing the role of education in the post-*al-sahwa* period as the transition toward democratic rule commences in earnest.

2

Theoretical Insights on Educational Transitologies

The rallying cry of "people power" was chanted and scribbled on walls and banners as young Tunisians took to the streets to demand their freedoms and the removal of a corrupt regime, an entrenched ruling family, and their allies. The leaderless avant-garde campaign to break loose of the chains of the Ben Ali regime was unique. Whereas classic revolutions are "violent, utopian, professedly class-based and characterized by a progressive radicalization, culminating in terror," unarmed Tunisian youth used "nonviolent, anti-utopian [techniques], based not on a single class but on broad social coalitions and characterized by the application of mass social pressure—people power—to bring the current powerholders to negotiate" (Garton Ash 2009: 19). In this chapter, we draw upon theoretical insights from the literatures in: (i) Sociology—the ideas around "political opportunity structures" (Eisinger 1973; Koopmans and Olzak 2004; Tilly 1978); and (ii) Comparative and International Education (CIE)— predominantly the concept of "education transition" or "education transitologies" (Cowen 2000b; Jules and Barton 2014; Rappleye 2012) to understand the national educational characteristics that shape mass mobilizing and nonviolent people power in Tunisia. In other words, the focus is on understanding the role education has played in shaping different transitory periods across Tunisia's history. In combining acumens from these two literatures we seek to illustrate the consequences and causes of different policy periods under which Tunisia has undergone distinctive types of education reforms. Kingdon's (1984) notion of "policy window" frames our discussion of three periods: (i) the pre-colonial and colonial period; (ii) the authoritarian period; and (iii) the post-*al-sahwa* period— of educational change and reforms in Tunisia. The concept of a policy window encompasses three streams: (i) the *problem stream* consists of identification and recognition; (ii) the *policy stream* focuses on alternatives; and (iii) the *political stream* incorporates institutional and structural changes. Collectively, changes occur simultaneously in all three of these streams, thus opening a window of opportunity for reforms to happen. In broadly considering the historical trajectories of education reform in Tunisia, we begin by probing: *At what moment does the right policy window of opportunity open and create a space to facilitate and engage in educational import and export?* As such, we are proposing a broad scaffolding (or a collection of research strategies and methods) for studying education reforms during times of political transitions in the aftermath of revolutions.

In bringing concepts together from these two fields, our aim is to study Tunisia's education reforms and their impact from the perspective of a "vertical case study" that seeks "to situate local action and interpretation within a broader cultural, historical and political investigation" (Vavrus and Bartlett 2006: 95). We argue that such a nuanced approach is warranted since the existing scholarship on the study of transitions in education during turbulent times, or educational transitologies in CIE, has primarily been used to explain post-socialist constructions and the transition from socialism or communism to liberal democracies (Cowen 2000; Jules and Barton 2014; Silova 2009; Rappleye 2012). However, little attention has been given to: (i) the types or models of national education systems that post-authoritarian regimes and post-revolutionary regimes seek to (re)construct; (ii) which reform areas are given priorities; (iii) what pre-revolutionary and authoritarian elements of the previous system are retained; and (iv) how new education reforms are justified (Jules and Barton 2014).

Moreover, *al-sahwa* and the ensuing Arab Awakening—that toppled regimes in Egypt, Libya, and Yemen; cultivated uprisings in Bahrain and Syria; encouraged major demonstrations in Algeria, Iraq, Jordan, Kuwait, Morocco, and Oman; and facilitated minor rebellions in Lebanon, Mauritania, Saudi Arabia, Sudan, and Western Sahara—provides us with opportunities to study the role and function of national education systems in the pre- and post- periods of internal disruptions, revolutions, and dictatorial transitions. These events permit us to trace discursive patterns found in national education systems and to suggest a framework that accounts for the processes of globalization at the national level that affect these education systems. Our framework highlights during times of political disruptors: the projectability of "scopic systems" (Sobe and Ortegón 2009), which imply a singular way of viewing the global; and the broader cultural, historical, and political nature of vertical sites that exist within "policyscapes" (Carney 2009), which are spaces constituted by the flow of policies that impact and permeate every level of education.

We use these concepts, and we explain how they help us to (re)frame the various governance mechanisms that manage and regulate national education developments before the opening of new educational spaces. We do not just use these "flashy" terms to make the existent literature in CIE and sociology denser. In drawing insights from the ways in which these concepts are defined and used in CIE, we are hoping that by (re)framing the transitology literature to explain our insights, we have a way of accounting for the current disruptors of technological innovation and economic transformation in a post-2008 global recessionary period.

Our aim is not to apply Western concepts and practices of modernity to the study of education in Tunisia. Instead, we focus on the Tunisian story grounded in its own historical narrative. The political transition from one period to another requires new interpretations of old themes since previous education reforms and institutions are often perceived as being inadequate. Since transitions involve the confusion of flux and reflux through advances and retreat, there is often the perception that a break with the past is needed. However, the first set of reforms should not *throw the baby out with the bathwater, but instead, change the bathwater and keep the baby.* In this sense, the change in bathwater is an idiomatic expression to suggest there is a façade or veneer of reforms at the surface or discourse levels when in reality the institutional structures remain the same.

In what follows below, we present an overview of the social movement literature, paying attention to political opportunity structures to highlight how they can be used in studying transitory spaces in education. We then suggest that in reframing transitology literature to account for the escalation of new post-authoritarian spaces that have been developed in the post-Arabic Awakening. We by suggesting that studying the Tunisian transitions allows understanding of the wider post-Arab Awakening emphasis on the role of functional sectors, such as education (Breuer, Landman and Farquhar 2015; Foweraker 1989; 1995; Foweraker and Craig 1990; Foweraker and Landman 1997; Hawkins 2002; Landman 2008; Risse, Ropp and Sikkink 1999). As under many other authoritarian regimes, the national narrative in Tunisia was controlled by the state and its apparatuses. Also, that people could coordinate efficiently and mobilize in a climate of suppression contributed to the groundswell. As Breuer, Landman and Farquhar (2015) suggest, protest and mobilization under authoritarian regimes is only successful if individuals believe others will join the movement.

In Tunisia, social networks and online platforms provided a strategic enabling capacity that allowed individuals to calculate their "individual risk threshold" (Granovetter 1978) before determining whether to join the growing wave of discontent. In fact, it was Tunisia's education system, with its emphasis on expanded access to higher education and social media, which enabled individuals to perceive that their risk threshold for participation in the wake of Mohamed Bouazizi's death was advantageous. As Pena, Davies and Ryan (2016: 6) imply, it:

> . . . is rare to find a comment on the contentious events taking place worldwide since 2011 that does not establish a degree of continuity and inspiration with mobilizations triggered, according to the broad consensus, by the self-immolation of Mohamed Bouazizi in Tunisia in December 2010.

Since "thresholds are situation specific" (Granovetter 1978), it was the Bouazizi incident that created a catalyst for mass mobilization and not the Gafsa events of 2008. The current wave of research emphasizes the mobilizing aspects of social media as defined by its transnationalizing and empowering facets that allow for citizenry participation in the absence of open media (Breuer, Landman and Farquhar 2015; Khondker 2011; Lotan et al. 2014; Pena, Davies and Ryan 2016). In discussing the role of social media and other online platforms in the Tunisian *al-sahwa*, the role of education is often neglected. In fact, Twitter, Facebook, WhatsApp, and other online platforms that facilitated *al-sahwa* are part of the new "disruptive innovations" (Christensen et al. 2011) within education. Disruptive innovation is a technologically social movement theory that draws on the idea of "collective action" found in "resource mobilization theory" (McCarthy and Zald 1973; 1977). Opportunity structures focus on identifying the characteristics of the "political environment in which [social] movements operate" (Baumann 2007: 52; see also McAdam, McCarthy and Zald 1996) and have come to be defined as:

> . . . selective of strategy in the sense that, given a specific context, only certain courses of strategic action are likely to see actors realise their intentions. Social, political and economic contexts are densely structured and highly contoured. As such they present an unevenly distributed configuration of opportunity and constraint to actors. They are, in short, strategically selective, for whilst they may well facilitate the ability of resource- and knowledge-rich actors to further their strategic interests, they are equally likely to present significant obstacles to the realisation of the strategic intentions of those not similarly endowed.

Hay 2002: 380–381

Opportunity structures vary from field to field. The governance of educational activities in Tunisia is experienced through the ways in which opportunity structures frame different discourses.

More distinctive, but related, "political opportunity structure" ([POS] Koopmans and Muis 2009; Kriesi et al. 1995; McAdam 1982; Tarrow 1994) provides a broader paradigmatic parameter for us to explore the influence of political transitions upon national education development. In applying this to education, our aim is to comprehend how the opportunities and constraints within the current political-institutional characteristics affect the capacity to mobilize and frame new education reforms within the political space. Therefore, POS allows us to grasp the political milieu in which education reforms are undertaken. POS has four dimensions: "(i) the relative openness or closure of the institutionalized political system; (ii) the stability of that broad set of elite alignments that typically undergird a polity; (iii) the presence of elite allies; and (iv) the state's capacity and propensity for repression" (McAdam, McCarth and Zald 1996: 10) that collectively reflect the interaction between the movement and its environment. Tunisia's POS is framed around the discourse of unemployment and the ability to establish a competitive labor force using labor market information systems (see Chapter 7). We draw attention to how education is delivered and constructed and the power relations that arise during the coordination of activities, actors, and agents across different scales (Dale 2005; Robertson, Bonal and Dale 2002; Simons, Olssen and Peters 2009; Verger 2009). In examining the notion of scale in post-authoritarian spaces, we draw on the work of Robertson, Bonal and Dale (2002) who argue that scales are constructs that take place at different levels and are entwined and fixed through various processes. Education governance is multi-dimensional, multi-leveled, and multi-scalar and therefore governance in transitory spaces occurs at different levels. In analyzing governance in structures in transitory spaces, attention must be given to the "'politics of education' in capitalist societies and oriented to 'education politics' as specific events within governance structures" (Simons, Olssen and Peters 2009: 79). Thus, in looking at Tunisia's POS through the lens of pluri-scalar patterns of coordination in transitory spaces, we suggest that education is "... now being asked to do different things in different ways, rather than the same things in different ways ... [while on the systemic level] the constitution of education sectors may be in the process of changing, with a development of parallel sectors at different scales with different responsibilities" (Dale 2005: 117). We account for different scales vertically in POS by focusing on the controversies around the "educational restructuring" produced in various national contexts.

Second, scopic systems in education invite us to look at how education, historically and presently, has been projected globally as well as how education can be viewed as a project of globality (Sobe and Ortegón 2009: 59). For us, the notion of the projection of globality is taken further by suggesting that when coupled with POS, the "totality and reflexive comprehensiveness of projection and reality" (Sobe and Ortegón 2009: 59) is a *condition* and not a process since it is not a result of technological innovation. In this sense, we see POS in education as a new "condition or state in which things are global" and stem "from conscious and intentional actions of individuals and collective human actors" (Shaw 2000: 17–18). In locating the array of scopic systems that exist in transitory spaces, we focus on identifying how these systems have historically and in the present, projected the ideas of education as defined by dictatorial regimes. Educational scopic systems then represent a form of power that frames education challenges within the policy environment and tries to find solutions by employing mechanisms that ultimately reinforce social practices over time (Robertson 2011; 2012).

While scopic systems help us to understand the projectability of globality as constructed through the national lens, vertical comparisons allow us to "grasp the complexity of the relationships between the knowledge claims among actors with different social locations as an attempt to situate local action and interpretation within a broader cultural, historical and political investigation" (Bartlett and Vavrus 2014: 96). Vertical comparisons not only help us to understand how projected realities occur in the pre-*al-sahwa* and post-*al-sahwa* settings and spaces, but they also help us to focus on understanding how institutional forces shape social interactions. The vertical comparisons help us to understand how the multilevel dimensions ultimately allow for the construction and subsequent projection of a version of reality, which the authoritarian regimes strive to maintain in the form of performance legitimacy. At the end of the day, legitimacy matters in any transitory space under study and thus any empirical study of the post-*al-sahwa* or post-authoritarian spaces must consider the role of performance legitimacy in shaping and constructing a country's identity that is projected to the rest of the world. For us, vertical comparisons are a way of explaining the claims to legitimacy that exists, through the persuasive use of state propaganda, the illusion of political inclusiveness, the supply of standard public goods, and the dispensing patronage through client networks (Burnell 2006).

Third, in focusing on how POS favors certain strategies, actors, periods, places, and contexts, we employ the concept of policyscapes that suggest "... the spread of policy ideas and pedagogical practices across different national school systems" (Carney 2009: 68). For us, policyscape amounts to a "landscape densely laden with policies created in the past that have themselves become established institutions, bearing consequences for governing operations, the policy agenda and political behavior" (Mettler 2016: 369). However, in applying this notion to POS, the aim is to look at policy diffusion precipitously through different educational spaces (vertically and horizontally) to capture the ideological essences that remain after regime implosion and give rise to transitionary spaces focused on creating a new imagined community. As such, vertical comparisons of scales across transitionary spaces allow us to draw attention to the lived consequences of entanglement that exist within an imagined community. If we accept *al-sahwa* as commencing on December 17, 2010 with the self-immolation of the fruit vendor Tarek al-Tayeb Mohamed Bouazizi, then Tunisia represents a prime example of how we should study transitologies in post-spaces.

... From Studying, (Re)framing, and (Re)building Educational Transitologies

Tunisia's multifaceted history lends itself well to a theory that truly reads multiple dimensions of its educational past, while simultaneously offering insight into possible trajectories of its educational future. Within this context, we suggest that POS, which are embedded across different educational scales, scopic systems, and policyscapes, present a way for studying Tunisia's educational transitologies as a vertical site. In other words, we employ the transitologies literature to study Tunisia's pre-*al-sahwa* and post-*al-sahwa* education system since "educational reform itself helps to construct not sequential equilibrium conditions but more transitologies ..." (Cowen 2000a: 11).

Transitologies are not time bounded and "they occur at remarkable speed and often with stunning suddenness" (Cowen 2000b: 339). It is in times of disarray that "the educational patterns that are ordinarily, in ordinary daylight as it were, difficult to see" (Cowen 2000b: 339). These patterns are dependent on local conditions and assume a unique historical identity—adapting and diverging from perceived educational models (Rappleye 2010). Therefore, by historically analyzing the changes within Tunisia's education system, the aim is to unveil "educational codings" that are "the compression of political and economic power into educational forms" (Cowen 2000b: 339). The transitology framework accommodates: "(i) the historical contingency of particular forms of educational systems, (ii) the cultural variations within those forms and (iii) the various transitions from one major historical paradigm to the next" (Rappleye 2012: 52).

In focusing on POS within education, we illuminate the *motor nuclei* of education codings, where we "… situate [this study within the context of] local action and interpretation within broader cultural, historical and political investigation … [to grasp] … which historical trends, social structures and national and international forces shape local processes" (Vavrus and Bartlett 2006: 96). This is exemplified by the fact that Tunisia's education reforms resulted in creating an educated workforce coupled with the Ben Ali regime providing families with incentives to purchase computers. The two events, in turn, created a cadre of technologically literate educated Tunisians that turned against their government (Covatorta and Haugbølle 2012). Therefore, education is not divorced from other social, political, and economic occurrences: each domain is but a number needed in conjunction with other numbers to provide the entire code, which often appears in times of chaos. This exact process makes studying transitologies vital: "it simultaneously captures collective and socio-specific time, simultaneously allows for national context specificity and allows etic and emic perspectives to coexist" (Rappleye 2010: 15). Our aim is toward "reading the global," which "edges us toward reading the forces of history and the interplay of the domestic and the international in the construction of educational patterns," specifically by focusing on Tunisia's "educational codings" (Cowen 2000b: 339). Thus, educational codes are made most visible in transitologies, which often occur "when there is a collapse (and rapid redefinition) of international political boundary, of political regime and of political vision" (Cowen 2000b: 341). In studying Tunisia's educational codes, we look both historically and holistically at them across three educational paradigms, pre-modern, modern, and late-modern, to analyze "against major themes of political, economic and cultural formation" (Cowen 1996: 155).

Pre-modern educational patterns held political rather than economic purposes to high regard within the state. Education systems were either secular or focused on religious affairs and placed priority on the "stability in the social order and the education of carefully selected local elites" (Cowen 1996: 156). A central tenet within this paradigm is the absence of a concrete schooling system for the nation and the lack of concern for educating the entire populace. Rather, this paradigm "stressed the moral order and its maintenance by a selected and educated elite" (Cowen 1996: 156). Second, the modern educational paradigm is based on three dimensions: "the role and moral messages of the central state, educational content and structures and the international relations of the education system" (Cowen 1996: 168; see also Cowen 1982; 1994). Here, educational ideology shifts to focus on what is beneficial to the nation; this is where we see the organization of systems of mass schooling and a move toward centralization of the school system (Rappleye 2012). Education takes on a neoliberal structure, whereas choice becomes a prerogative for state and consumer. Thus, the purpose of using a transitology framework is to gage educational occurrences by examining these transitions or "turbulences"— uncovering "acts of rupture, conflict, tension and resistance" (Carney 2009: 69) that create post-*al-sahwa* models by examining the different educational paradigms, pre-modern, modern, and late-modern, that exist "against major themes of political, economic and cultural formation" (Cowen 1996: 155) that have come to be shaped by Tunisia's transition. Our theoretical starting point is based upon an unveiling of the "educational codings" that accompanied each of our three focus periods of reform. In applying the transitology literature to Tunisia, we sketch out a clear historical framework, focused on its developments and its processes as they interact with the power system at large and the people's forms of resistance to it. As we will argue in this book, education played an enabling role in incubating and facilitating *al-sahwa*.

As a project, transitory spaces structure the perceptions and scope through which educational challenges and solutions are framed. As a scale, transitory spaces allow actors to choose what ideas will be legitimized and which ones will be discouraged. Our vertical comparison draws attention to "politics of knowledge production" (Vavrus and Bartlett 2006), particularly in an era of regulated governance where the "... nation-states continue to be central players in a globalizing world, but partly as local agents of global forces, for the nation-state now operates within global economic constraints" (Marginson and Mollis 2001: 601). Such recognition of the changing role of the nation-state implies that we need to develop a different empirical approach to position the new geopolitical-educational architecture of power in a globalizing world.

Much of the transition literature has focused on the link between economics and political transitions (Cowen 2000a; Darvas and Tibbitts 1992; McLeish 1998; Pastuovic 1993). However, they do not draw attention to the distinctive educational spaces that are created and the opportunities that arise during transitions or in post-spaces. What truly sets transitologies apart from other research tools is their acuity to "tell us of the spirit of the battles still to come" (Cowen 2000b: 339). It challenges researchers to travel beyond the present, which is essential in making grounded policy decisions. Further, transitologies give us "new and meaningful insights into the interconnectivity of politics, history and culture across localities at a time when these three elements are often dismissed as outmoded" (Carney 2009: 69).

Concluding Thoughts—Studying Post-revolutionary Settings

To sum up and in returning to some of the slogans that we began this chapter with, it is evident that transitologies are extremely complex and this leads one to question whether such research can ever be successful. This historical study of educational change aims at deciphering educational patterns since it is grounded in comparative-historical approach. Additionally, as described, our "method of inquiry and as a frame of analysis" (Novóa and Yariv-Mashal 2003: 424) vertical sites illuminate the evolutionary dynamics that undergird education reforms as economic and political powers that become; the vertical case study allows us to "catch" the nuances of these reform developments, which might otherwise slip through the cracks.

Thus, the Tunisian transition represents a "set of interdependent economic, political and social reforms" (Birzea 1994: 12) across different scales that highlight different patterns. The rise of educational opportunity structures (the factors that constrain or empower educational actors) during different transitory periods across different spaces and governance structures helps to shed light on various dimensions of transitions and the role education plays. In following a structuralist orientation, we focus on endogenous and exogenous factors and structures that inhibit and foster opportunities to arise and how actors (the state in our case) use these opportunities to their, and, if imitation and replication are possible for, other systems.

To more thoroughly study the post-revolutionary and post-transitory educational spaces in Tunisia, or what has been called "post-spaces" (Jules and Barton 2014), we bring in the educational transitologies and opportunity structures. Our principal argument in this book is that scales help us to understand the rise of transitory spaces in education. In the next chapter, we present a brief overview of the first Tunisian situation (the pre-colonial and colonial period) and situate it within the wider Arab and Maghreb region. The theoretical framework in this book contributes to our understanding of educational transitologies in pre-*al-sahwa* and post-*al-sahwa* settings and spaces. The analysis of the historical chronology of educational transitologies in Chapters 3 and 4 explains the variation in different educational transitologies under authoritarian regimes. It also clarifies how different dictators and regimes use education and its ensuing institutions to deploy different authoritarian bargaining agreements. We support each of these arguments by using a vertical case study to comprehensively examine the different policy streams that frame educational transitions in Tunisia. Meanwhile, when we address the contemporary problems of the authoritarian bargaining agreement in Chapters 5, 6, and 7 we account for the recurrence of internal disruptions and how these shape the different educational transitions. Consistently with our arguments, we suggest that dictatorial regimes use authoritarian bargaining to shape educational transitologies.

The Birth of the Tunisian Republic, Colonialism, and Educational Expansion

Al-Jumhuriyyah at-Tunisiyyah (the Tunisian Republic), with its coastal capital, Tunis, is a society composed of several areas ranging from the Northern mountainous "Tell" region, to the barren areas of the South, to the "breadbasket" or "Sahel" coastal area, and to the phosphate mines in Gafsa, also known as the mining basin.[1] It consists of a landmass of 163,000 square kilometers and hosts an approximate population of 10,982,800 (INS 2014). The nation is situated between Algeria and Libya. Tunisia is an ethnically and religiously homogeneous nation of Muslim Sunnis with Arabic, Berber, Latin, and Punic ancestors. It was a former French Protectorate (from 1881 to 1956) and is the home of St. Augustine, the Carthaginian Empire, the Roman Empire, and numerous Arabic Kingdoms. From the date of its independence from France in 1956 to *al-sahwa,* Tunisia only had two presidents: Habib Ben Ali Bourguiba (from 1957 to 1987) and Zine El-Abidine Ben Ali (from 1987 to 2011).

Tunisia's youth population has grown up being shaped by several historical points. Tunisia became home to the headquarters of the Palestine Liberation Organization (from 1982 to 1991) after absconding from Israel's six-month invasion of Lebanon. Later, the African Development Bank (from 2000 to 2015) relocated to Tunisia after fleeing civil war in the Ivory Coast. Before *al-sahwa* (in 2011), there were two significant uprisings, in 1978 and 1984, and numerous riots to denounce inflation and the government in Tunisia. A bloodless *coup d'état* led by Ben Ali ousted Bourguiba in 1987. In 2005, at the zenith of the Ben Ali regime, Tunisia hosted the second part of the UN-sponsored World Summit on the Information Society (WSIS), which would push the country forwards to focus on accessing the knowledge economy.

Today, Tunisia continues to shape its identity as a nation committed to improving the lives of its people and the Arab region, and to understand Tunisia is to go back to its history. Tunisia has a very long history with successive and failed transitologies and transformations that have influenced its education system over the last three thousand years. Before Tunisia became the capital of several empires, its people had access to different forms of schooling, which were, for the most part, segregated and unequal. The transformation of that education system after *al-sahwa* is defined by Islamification, homogenization, revolution, radicalization, and contestation.

This chapter discusses the early beginnings of education in Tunisia across five major historical periods, covering its pre-colonial, colonial, and post-colonial era. The first historical state, the pre-historical or ancient period, includes the Caspian Civilization (until 900 BCE), the Phoenicians (from 900 BCE to 146 BCE), the Roman Empire (from 146 BCE to 435 CE), the Vandal Kingdom (from 435 to 534), and the Byzantine Empire (from 534 to 698). The second historical stage, the early Islamic period, consists of the Umayyad Caliphate (from 698 to 750), the Abbasid Caliphate (from 750 to 800), the Aghlabid Caliphate (from 800 to 909), and the Fatimid Caliphate (from 909 to 973). The third historical stage, the medieval period, incorporates the Zirid Dynasty (from 973 to 1146), the Norman Dynasty (from 1146 to 1160) followed by the Almohad Dynasty (from 1160 to 1229) and the Hafsid Dynasty (from 1229 to 1574). The fourth historical period, the early modern Islamic era, comprises the Ottoman Empire (from 1575 to 1705) and the Husainid Dynasty (from 1705 to 1881). The fifth historical stage, the modern period, began with the French Protectorate period (from 1881 to 1956) and continues to the present.

By examining this rich history, we show that education was of high priority in the North African country long before French rule in 1881. After briefly summarizing the major contributions of these five historical stages, we chronicle their different waves of education reform to show how education was consistently used as an elitist and political tool of the wealthy. Across these periods, we show how access to schooling was a luxury for the elites and used as a measure to suppress other groups within society. Importantly we show that, prior to independence, dictatorial regimes were ubiquitous and that authoritarian bargaining and relinquishing of political rights for social and economic freedoms were well-established practices that determined the pace and speed of political transitologies. Particularly from its early Phoenician foundations to the end of French rule, educational access was used to justify the status quo by creating education systems that were separate and unequal.

In the first half of this chapter, we discuss the rise of education in Tunisia beginning with pre-colonial education all the way through to the end of the French Protectorate period. The second half of the chapter details post-independence educational reform, from 1956 onwards. In doing this, we tell the chronological history of Tunisia's transition from one regime to another. We show how political and social events mobilized reforms to act in the interest of regimes or the elites and how these actions subsequently shaped Tunisia's current education system.

Berber Carthage: The "Free People"

The Berbers (circa 1100 BCE) were the first to settle in modern-day Tunisia coming from the south of the country up to the coast. The Berbers lived for centuries as a "free people," semi-pastoralists in the Maghreb region outside of Carthage (in the interior of the country in what was then called Numidia consisting of much of Tunisia and the adjacent regions) and were skilled in manufacturing, trade, and political organizing and later served as military recruits for the Phoenicians. Many Berbers were educated in the Punic language in temple schools run by Punic priestesses (Sadiqi 2014). Punic priestesses had paramount roles in Berber society and students received instruction in Latin language and literature in Carthage and, in some instances, they would go off to Alexandria in Egypt for additional studies (Sadiqi 2014). As Carthaginian power under the Phoenicians grew, so did the Berber civilization. However, by the second century, the Berbers had converted to the Phoenician culture and way of life.

The arrival of the Phoenicians in 814 BCE and their development of the city of Carthage made Tunisia a mecca for trade and the most prosperous port of its time. During the Punic Wars, the Carthaginians fought with the Romans. With the First Punic War (from 264 BCE to 241 BCE) behind them, the Carthaginians set out across the Alps with Hannibal's army and war elephants to conquer Rome in what became known as *Hannibal ante Portas* (Hannibal before the gates) before carnage would rain down. Carthage survived the first two Punic Wars, but it lost the third war after expansive losses in soldiers, machinery, and weaponry.

Phoenician Carthage: Forging a New City

The first authoritarian bargaining agreement can be dated to the Phoenicians of Tyre (or the Canaanites), under Queen Elissa (better known as *Dido*), who founded *Qart Hadasht* (or new city) as a maritime city-state on the ruins of

Carthage. Under the reign of the Phoenicians, the Berbers cultivated and transformed the farmland around Carthage into a world city (Appiah and Gates 2010). The Phoenicians brought their lifestyle and customs to the new maritime city-state of Carthage and used the Semitic language of Canaan. History tells us that the Phoenicians in Carthage had a strong literature, with several religious texts and an alphabet system (deciphered in 1758 by the French priest, Jean-Jacques Barthelemy). Scholars suggest that the Phoenician alphabet was the first alphabetic script that was commonly used, particularly for trade around the Mediterranean, and several alphabetic writing systems can be traced back to the Phoenician alphabet. While the Phoenicians did not document the development of their own education system, we know from other sources that "... Phoenician merchants were often philosophers, Carthaginian generals and statesmen, literary men and that Numidian kings, who received a Phoenician education and training, possessed libraries of Phoenician works" (Cory and Hodges 1876: xxxii). The education of Phoenicians was "... various and extensive: among Carthaginians, at least, that their children were practiced in reading, writing and arithmetic, in [addition to] religious duties; secondly in a trade; and finally in the use of arms" (Rosenkranz 1894: 215). Rosenkranz (1894: 206) claims that the Phoenicians had an active education system that was "outward [driven] with the brew to accomplish some new conquest" rather than a passive education system that was "conservative and aimed at crushing out individuality by imposing its burdensome codes of etiquette ceremonies and moral order" since Phoenicians were "educated for foreign commerce, the perils of the sea and hostile lands." Temple schools were responsible for educating children in basic reading and writing without any social class discrimination (AALAWA 2011). While some wealthy families sent their children to Sicily to learn science and philosophy, others preferred to bring teachers from abroad to educate their children (as was the case of Hannibal Barca, military commander and later elected as a *Suffete*). After studying at the temple school, selected students would continue their education at the Bitrogian School, where they might study medicine or agriculture.

As Carthage emerged into a metropolis, its influence stretched from North Africa to the Iberian Peninsula, Sardinia, and Sicily and, with time, the Jews brought monotheism to the region (Appiah and Gates 2010). When the Carthaginians conquered and settled new territories, one of the first things that they did was to establish new schools and impose the Latin language on the new inhabitants. The Carthaginians used education to achieve their political goals and the system was organized around three stages—"the first ... that of the teacher of letters, extricates us from illiteracy; the second, of the grammar teacher, instructs us in erudition; the third, or the teacher of rhetoric, arms us with eloquence" (Opeku 1993: 31)—that allowed the best students to continue their studies in the Greek centers of learning like Athens or Rhodes (Opeku 1993). Rosenkranz (1894) suggests that Phoenician education was a family responsibility, but also utilitarian in that it rooted out any affection that students possessed for home and parents. Even in 332 BCE, after Alexander the Great took the Phoenician cities on the East Coast of the Mediterranean, he left Carthage and its colonies on their own to continue to educate its citizens. However, after the Romans plundered Carthage, its libraries and archives were either given to Numidian kings or were destroyed.

Roman Carthage: The Romans are Coming

Carthaginian expansion under the Phoenicians brought it to Rome's attention, eventually leading to the First Punic War (from 264 BCE to 241 BCE) under the Punic general Hamilcar Barca (Hannibal Barca's father) after it seized Sicily from Rome. After the Second Punic War (from 218 BCE to 202 BCE), a new authoritarian bargaining agreement was struck. Roman dictators imposed sanctions on Carthage and as the *suffete* (judge), General Hannibal would enact unfavorable political and economic reforms that led to his self-imposed exile in 195 BCE. Under the Romans, Carthage would be rebuilt and become the second most populated city, after Rome, in the Western Mediterranean, as well as the center of early Christianity. Additionally, many of the earlier settlers, chiefly ex-service men, married Berber women and this would have given rise to a "Latin-seeking cultural upper class [that] developed, composed not only of Roman settlers and officials but also innumerable young African males who went to Rome for higher studies, preferabl[y] to become lawyers" (as cited in Mekonnen 2015: 338).

After the Third (and final) Punic War (from 149 BCE to 146 BCE) when Rome took control of Carthage, schooling consisted primarily of private family education. Roman parents would instruct their children in Roman beliefs, traditions, and ways of life through oratory teaching in the form of telling stories of Roman legends. Under the Carthaginian school system, boys and girls were taught differently and separately. Girls were taught to weave and sew and were usually married off by the time their educative learning had ended, around the age of eleven or twelve. Boys were educated to be citizens whereas girls were educated to be mothers and homemakers. Plutarch writing in the late first century and discussing the life of Marcus Porcius Cato or "Cato the Elder", a Roman senator, provides us with an insight into how wealthy Romans, in the Province of Africa, might have personally taken charge of the educative activities of their children in that:

> As soon as the boy showed signs of understanding, his father took him under his own charge and taught him to read, although he had an accomplished slave, Chilo by name, who ... taught many boys. Still, Cato thought it not right ... that he should be indebted to his slave for such a priceless thing as education.... He taught his son not merely to hurl the javelin and fight in armour and ride the horse, but also to box, to endure heat and cold and to swim lustily through the eddies and billows of the Tiber. His history of Rome ... he wrote out with his own hand and in large characters, that his son might have in his own home an aid to acquaintance with his country's ancient traditions.
>
> Perrin 1914: 360–366

As part of their formative training, boys also attended gymnasium because they were to be trained for war and peace. Wealthier boys had access to secondary education from age thirteen or fourteen and up. Much of Carthaginian education at the time was grounded in medical education, but privileged students were also exposed to grammar, rhetoric, law, literature, and philosophy.

Education was also used as a political tool for advancement and was organized in four steps that allowed the best students to continue their studies in Athens. At around age sixteen, particularly wealthy boys destined for careers as courtroom advocates and politicians, would become apprenticed to an older man. The work of the Roman historian Tacitus, in his Ciceronian Dialogue, provides us with a glimpse of what the relationship, in the Province of Africa, may have looked like between the master and apprentice. As he notes:

> The youth had to get the habit of following his patron about, of escorting him in public, of supporting him at all his appearances as a speaker, whether in the law courts or on the platform, hearing also his word-combats at first-hand, standing by him in his duelings and learning, as it were, to fight in the fighting-line. It was a method that secured at once for the young students a considerable amount of experience, great self-possession and a goodly store of sound judgment: for they carried on their studies in the light of open day and amid the shock of battle ...
>
> as cited in Peterson 2008: 113, [trans.]

After the apprenticeship, additional post-secondary education occurred in the form of military training (Wooten 1988). Under Roman rule, the Latin language was added to Greek, Punic, and Berber languages became the official medium of instruction. Additionally, the Latin language became the most prominently used language for writing. Even though family education was ubiquitous during this period, the schools that existed were public institutions. As Latin literature developed, students from wealthy families would have studied Rhetoric, a prerequisite to becoming a lawyer, in Carthage (as did Aurelius Augustinus Hipponensis—later called Saint Augustine) or in Rome (Götz 2010). Rhetoric in the Province of Africa would have focused on producing skilled orators who:

> ...learned the use of syllogism and induction and were taught how to appeal to an audience's reason (the logical proof) and to its passions (the pathetic proof) and how to inspire a favorable opinion (the ethical proof). The latter was especially attractive since Romans had so much respect for authority and hierarchy. A Roman orator would often attempt to convince his audience that his point of view should be accepted simply because of the trust that his own character inspired.
>
> Wooten 1988: 1114

Another source of public education was the libraries that the Romans built in Carthage. There were two kinds of libraries: (i) the Municipal Libraries in the cities open to the public; and (ii) the Libraries of the religious institutions (AALAWA 2011). Under the Romans, education was praised and celebrated by the wealthy and those of non-noble birth who could access it.

Vandal Carthage: Education in Africa Proconsularis

In 429, the Vandals (an East Germanic tribe that ruled from 429 to 533) left Spain after they were asked by Rome to intervene in the civil war in North Africa (Maas and Kihn 2003). In 439, the Vandals conquered the city of Carthage and in 474 Rome gave the Vandals the status of "... foederati with the right to rule North Africa in the imperial name" (Maas and Kihn 2003: 37). The transition from Roman rulership to Vandal dictatorship under a different authoritarian bargaining agreement effectively maintained Roman art, music, literature, traditions, and civilization. As such, Roman institutions of education were also maintained and embraced and the Roman school systems continued under the Vandals without interruption. While the Vandal and Roman citizens of this time had differences stemming from religious beliefs—the Vandals practiced Arian Christianity and the Romans Catholicism—the schools continued to educate many citizens in Latin, thus producing numerous poets, bureaucrats, lawyers, and churchmen (Maas and Kihn 2003). Although Latin was the most important instrument of instruction during this time, some children were instructed informally in Greek.

Under the Vandals, Carthage remained the "center of education and the hub of literacy activity" (Maas and Kihn 2003: 39) especially as Romans maintained their law courts under the Vandals. Thus, legal training was necessary for the lawyers working in this system. The *Codex Justinianus* (The Code of Justinian from 533 to 534) of Emperor Flavius Petrus Sabbatius Iustinianus Augustus (or Justinian I—reigned from 527 to 565) decreed that Carthage and nowhere else in the Kingdom, must upkeep two grammarians and two rhetors to provide lessons in the classical traditions (Conant 2012; Marrou 1956). In fact, it was normal for wealthy Carthaginians to study grammar and rhetoric in succession (Conant 2012). The classical school tradition of education survived through the Vandal period and students who moved beyond elementary schooling would pursue careers in medicine and law. Education continued to flourish and thrive under the Vandals until Emperor Justinian I re-conquered the North African Province of Carthage and began to administer it in Greek. The change from the Latin language to the Greek language ultimately led to the decline of the school system and by the time the Arabs took over Carthage in 698, "classical Latin literary culture had diminished almost to extinction during the Byzantine rule of North Africa" (Maas and Kihn 2003: 39).

Byzantine Carthage: Education in the "New" Eastern Roman Empire

In 533, General Belisarius entered Carthage unopposed after defeating the Vandals at the Battle of Ad Decimum (sixteen kilometers south of Carthage), thus changing dictatorial regime terms yet again. With the arrival of General Belisarius, Carthage educational traditions were restored since the city would eventually serve as the most important naval base for the Byzantines. As Lindberg (1992: 159) contends, Carthage:

> ...experienced so[me] of the same misfortunes ... as the [Western Roman Empire] – invasion, economic decline and social upheaval, it was less severe ...
> [and g]reater social and political stability meant greater continuity in schools.
> The tradition of classical studies in schools was fed by the steady copying of
> ancient works, as well as translations of new works; and of course, the East

never found itself separated from the original sources of Greek scholarship by a linguistic barrier.

Under the Byzantines, education operated across different levels of schooling and aimed at preserving the knowledge of ancient literary classics. Elementary education was widely available, usually private and it was organized around "... the traditional seven liberal arts – trivium (grammar, rhetoric and logic) and quadrivium (arithmetic, geometry, astronomy and music)" (Lindberg 1992: 159). Secondary and higher education were confined to the major cities, such as Carthage. At the tertiary level, students studied philosophy and theology. Theology became an important area of study in Carthage with the growth of Byzantine Christianity (it would later become the official religion of the Roman Empire by the end of the fourth century) (Lindberg 1992). The empire moved to Greek from Latin as its official lingua franca and medium of instruction for education. Additionally, the Byzantines became more oriented toward Greek culture and traditions and their religious beliefs became steeped in Orthodox Christianity. The early school system was established, survived, and thrived under the Eastern Roman Empire that lasted 977 years after the fall of the Western Roman Empire.

The Early Islamic Period: Education in the Caliphate

The Arab conquest from 647 to 690 under the Umayyad Caliphate, Sunni Muslims, brought Muslim Arabs to Tunisia. This transitology, both in terms of religion, culture, and politics brought with it a very different authoritarian bargaining agreement between the pluricultural and multi-ethnic citizenry and its new Arabic rulers. In 670, the city of Kairouan was built with the Great Mosque at its center. The Arabs named Kairouan as the capital of both Tunisia and the entire *Ifriqiya* (North African) region. Islam and Arabic culture spread as they created a new monetary and commercial system. Unlike the previous invaders, the Arabs introduced Islam and the Arabic language under their authoritarian agreement. With time, the Qur'an, the holy book of Islam, "... came to define all aspects of the Islamic faith and practices; it was the source of later Islamic theology, morality, law and cosmology and thus the centerpiece of Islamic education" (Lindberg 1992: 166). Therefore, when the Arabs finally arrived in Carthage in 674 they introduced their knowledge through educational institutions. Islamic primary schools taught the Qur'an, Islam, reading, and writing in courses where the pupils were divided by their ages. The role of the teacher was to make pupils, particularly boys, learn the Qur'an through memorization. At primary schools, "children sat on their haunches and learned the holy book by heart" (Ling 1979). The Mosque of *Okba Ibn Nafeaa* was the first educational institution. However, *Madrasat al-Zitouna* in Tunis, today called *Ez Zitouna* University, was founded as the school of the *Zitouna* mosque in 732 and was considered the principal center of Islamic scholarship, producing some of the region's foremost scholars of the time (Berry and Rinehart 1988). *Madrasat al-Zitouna's* curriculum principally focused on the Arabic language and the Qur'an with similar pedagogical methods as primary schools, albeit much more advanced (Green 1978). The Arabs also used knowledge councils or open schools (an idea taken from the Greeks), leagues (a military building, a kind of castle), and houses of wisdom (an institution that came from Baghdad and is defined as a place where one can find many books), to spread knowledge and educate people.

In 909, *Ifriqiya* was conquered by the Fatimids,[2] Shiite Muslims and the direct descendants of Prophet Mohamed. This transitology led to the founding of the capital of the Fatimid Caliphate (from 909 to 973) in Mahdia city (located in present day Tunisia). They also conquered Morocco and Egypt, where they moved to in 973. In the same year, the Zirids seized power. However, upon renouncing Shia Islam and becoming Sunnites and recognizing the Abbasid Caliphate, the Fatimids sent from Egypt to *Ifriqiya,* the people of Hilal (*Banu Hilal*) and the people of Sulaym (*Banu Sulaym*). After the Zirids had lost, their rule was limited to Mahdia.

The Fatimid's dictatorship built upon the educational achievements of their predecessors and made significant advances in the field of writing, notably the invention of the *Fahmpen* that stores ink, in the tenth century. In the same century, Tunis declined in importance when the Fatimids chose Mahdia (and later Mansuriy) as their new capital in their quest to escape the eleventh-century Hilalian invasion after the conquest in 1160 of Almohad North African.

The Medieval Islamic Period

In the twelfth-century, *Ifriqiya* came under the dictatorship of the Almohad Caliphate (from 1160 to 1229 also called the Monotheists or Unitarians), who were a Berber tribe and North African movement that reinforced strict Islamic practices. Then in the thirteenth century, another transitology occurred and the

Hafsid Dynasty began ruling Tunisia as a Sunni Muslim Caliphate (from 1229 to 1574) under dictators chosen from the people of Hafs (*Banu Hafs*), which were a powerful group within the Almohads Caliphate (a Berber tribal confederation based in the Atlas Mountains).

Under the Hafsid Dynasty's authoritarian bargaining agreement, trade flourished and the population tripled. As such, education witnessed a huge resurgence and several schools and libraries, including *Madrasat al-Zitouna*'s library, were built. Dictators paid special attention to the development of *al-zawya*, a place where people could learn and pray. There were different types of *al-zawayas* and they played a major role in educating people (AALAWA 2011). The next significant set of reforms in education took place during the Muradid dynasty (from 1613 to 1705). The Mouradites continued the path of construction and they played a significant role in building new schools (such as the Youssifi School, the Mouradi School, and the Achour School) and restoring other schools (such as the Chamaaya and Anakeya Schools). During the Husseiniyan dictatorial period, several new schools, such as *Madrasat al-Nakhla*, *Madrasat al-Djadida*, and *Madrasat al-Husainiya* were created in the capital (AALAWA 2011).

The Modern Islamic Period

In 1574, the Turks acquired Tunis and ruled the province through local tyrannical dictators called *Beys* (provincial governors) through to 1666. Two dynastic dictatorial regimes ruled the province of Tunis, namely, the Muradid (from 1631 to 1705) and the Husainid (from 1705 to 1957). The Muradid Caliphate was founded by Bey Murad of Corsican origin and a member of the Ottoman Sultan's *janissary* (he was an infantry soldier). The Husainid Caliphate, named after *al-Husayn Ibn Ali At-Turki* a Greek Muslim, ruled it under the title of *Beylerbeyi Pasha* for the Ottoman Empire. However, his allegiance to the empire was nominal and in 1710 he promulgated a law of succession. The Husainid Caliphate under Bey Ibn Ali's dictatorship developed given his ability to speak Turkish, and his concern for local issues as a Muslim gave him leverage with European partners on several diplomatic matters affecting both Tunisia and Europe.

The Ottoman emperor sought to replace him in 1715, when he almost failed to reinstate his authority. However, Ibn Ali garnered the support of local leaders and retained power. Bey Ibn Ali continued his reign without the interference of the Ottoman Empire and created treaties with France (from 1710 to 1728), Great

Britain (1716), Spain (1720), Austria (1725), and Holland (1728). He also built several *al-kuttabs* attached to mosques in the cities of Tunis (including *al-Jami al-Jadid Zitouna* [the Dyers or New School], *al-Nakhia Zitouna*, and *al-Husayniyya al-Sughra Zitouna*), Kairouan, Sfax, Sousse, and Nafta (Sebag 2007). In the nineteenth century, the Caliphate came under pressure from European forces to end the enslavement of and restrictions on Tunisian Jews, as well as from European suppression of Tunisia's privateering. At that time, Tunisia faced debt and an economic crisis due to Westernized reforms, such as taxes, modernization of the army, and the creation of monopolies. These pressures would eventually culminate in the establishment of the French Protectorate in 1881, the decades preceding French Tunisia demonstrate a record of significant development and reform under the watch of the Bey.

Bey Ahmed's Carthage: The Rise of Educational Militantism

Bey Ahmed (from 1837 to 1855), tenth ruler of the Husainid Dynasty, assumed power just after the French occupied Algeria in 1830 and the Ottomans occupied Libya in 1835. Given Tunisia's geography, both events posed risks to Tunisian sovereignty especially since the French supported the Bey during the Algerian War of Resistance (from 1830 to 1848). Upon becoming ruler in 1837, Bey Ahmed announced that he was commander of the army and requested assistance from France for military reforms. In Bey Ahmed's Bardo Palace of the eighteenth century, two types of slave existed: Black slaves and Christian slaves knows as *mamluks—mamluks al-sqifa* (those standing as guards at the entryways) and *mamluks al-bit* or *mamluks al-saray* (those serving inside) (Brown 2015; Kallander 2013). *Mamluks* were young boys and non-Muslim girls that were the personal property of the Bey, a male member of the Beylical family, or of a leading minister (Brown 2015). *Mamluks* were essentially elite palace slaves from the Italian peninsula, Sardinia, Malta, France, and Spain. *Mamluks* could attain positions in the government, hold political and military authority, and marry princesses since the Beys did not intermarry with the Tunisians. While Black slaves had no access to formal education, *mamluks* were raised alongside the princes and princesses in the palace and received the same education as members of the royal family. Each *mamluk* was expected to have rudimentary literacy skills consisting of a core knowledge of Islam.

The reforms in education under the modern Islamic periods began under the dictatorial regime of Hammuda Pasha (from 1782 to 1814) and continued under his successor, Bey Ahmed. In 1840, two historical events occurred that shaped the transition toward modernizing education. First, significant political, economic, and societal reforms were proposed and outright rejected, later resulting in the bloody riots and revolt from 1862 to 1864 (Abdeljaouad 2014). Second, with assistance from France, the first modern school was built in 1840. It was called the Bardo Military Academy, headed by Louis Calligaris, an Italian expatriate officer (from 1838 to 1850). The bilingual school was established as a military school with aspirations of educating a new generation of Tunisians in Western techniques and non-Islamic subjects. Abdeljaouad (2014: 493) in citing Ibn Abi al-Diyaf (1989: 41) articulates that:

> On the first of Muharram 1256 (March 5, 1840), Ahmed Bey set up a military school at the Bardo and installed it in his palace which he left for a new one. [The school] was intended for teaching all the sciences that Nizami [army] soldiers needed to know, such as fortification, geometry, arithmetic and the French language since most reference books were written in this language. Its Director was the competent and educated colonel Calligaris, who recruited a madrasa professor for teaching the Koran and religious subjects.

Over time, the curriculum of the Bardo Military Academy grew to include French and mathematics. Students were instructed in Turkish and Arabic in the art of war (Abdeljaouad 2014). While the Bardo was designed to educate the *mamluks* living in the palace, in time local Tunisians could attend the academy. In January 1846, Bey Ahmed promulgated a decree abolishing slavery in Tunisia regardless of parental origins, making Tunisia the first country in the Muslim world to do this.

In 1842, as part of the Beylical reforms and authoritarian bargaining agreement, Ahmed Bey constituted the School of War (or the New School of Military Services) with foreign teachers. However, when Bey Mohammed Sadiq succeeded Bey Ahmed in 1859, he officially replaced the Bardo Military Academy with the School of War. Under the direction of the Frenchman Capitaine de Taverne (from 1819 to 1865), it was required that all entering cadets be knowledgeable in reading and writing Arabic and that French be the language of instruction for mathematics and military sciences while Arabic could only be used for instruction in religious and literacy studies (Abdeljaouad 2014). As such, students spent six years being instructed by French teachers recruited to Tunisia. Students followed a strict schedule consisting of:

> First year: Qur'an and French language; Second year: Qur'an, Arabic syntax and French language; Third year: Arabic syntax, French language and Arithmetic; Fourth year: Arabic syntax, French language, Arithmetic,

Geometry and Algebra; and Fifth and Sixth years: Military sciences and their applications.

Abdeljaouad 2014: 416

During its tenure, which ended in 1869, the School of War had a mixed performance record. On the one hand, it trained several local Tunisians to take up military positions, but that training was substandard as compared to the Bardo Military Academy. Its graduates, having experienced a Western-style education, would be the champions of the era of Kheireddine Pacha's reforms (discussed later in this chapter).

Le Pacte Fondamental

In 1877, under *Le Pacte Fondamental* (the Basic Pact), Bey Ahmed issued his written authoritarian bargaining agreement that decreed the basic rights of subjects of the Bey including equality before the law and freedom of trade and worship. In 1861, still a province of the Ottoman Empire, the first written constitution in the Arab world was introduced in Tunisia. The 1861 Constitution was sanctioned by Europe and not promulgated until the Bey presented the French version to Napoleon III in April 1861. It was part of a broader set of reforms that followed the Ottomans' nineteenth-century political reforms, placing the outlying areas of the kingdom under greater control (Brown 2012; El-Mesawi 2008). The 1861 Constitution (which had thirteen sections and one hundred and fourteen articles), was enforced for three years and was rooted in Islamic terminology and traditions and European practices. While "the constitution dealt mainly with classical issues pertaining to the jurisdiction and relationship of the executive, the legislative and the judiciary bodies" (El-Mesawi 2008: 54), it did not specify education laws or reforms. The constitution gave Tunis a municipality government, created a constitutional monarchy module in the European tradition, and established a legislative body (Brown 2012; El-Mesawi 2008).

The proclamation of the constitution and rejection of the 1840 political, economic, and societal reforms were the catalysts for the bloody riots and revolt that commenced in the cities of Le Kef and Kairouan in 1862 and spread to the coastal areas, after taxes were raised and the Husaynid regime forged ahead with its statist-centered modernization project. While these reforms lacked the necessary institutional capacity, the constitution, which allowed foreigners to own property without discrimination, paved the way for European domination. On May 1, 1864, the 1861 Constitution was suspended and all institutions dissolved. By the time Bey Ahmed left office, his reforms would have influenced all levels of the educational system, thus creating the system that the French inherited and maintained up until independence.

Kheireddine Pacha's Carthage: The Great Reformer and *le Collège Sadiki*

Taking the advice of Prime Minister Kheireddine Pacha,[3] Bey Mohammed al-Sadiq founded *le Collège Sadiki* (the Sadiki High School) in 1875. *Le Collège Sadiki* was the first institution during the transition to the modern Islamic period to separate religion from education. Behind Pacha's ideology and approach to reform was the wish to:

> ... wake up the patriotism of the *Ulama* (savants) and of the Muslim statesmen and urge them to cooperate together in choosing the most effective ways to improve the State of the Islamic nation, to expand the circle of knowledge and increase public wealth, by the development of agriculture, trade and industry.
>
> Pacha 1876: 34 as cited in Abdeljaouad 2014: 406

In fact, Pacha requisitioned part of the army barracks of the Bardo Military Academy to house *le Collège Sadiki*. At the time of its opening in 1879, *le Collège Sadiki* was a pioneering institution first located on University Mosque Avenue and then in 1897 it was relocated to the Kasbah Square in the Medina in Tunis. Pacha's aim was to ensure that *le Collège Sadiki* was a reformist school that focused on opening the door for modern intellectual productions of knowledge and texts. His philosophy of education was that Western-inspired reforms were compatible with Islamic culture. Tunisia needed to "... forestall European imperialism by borrowing Western institutions which would strengthen Tunisia and at the same time eliminate such pretexts for direct European intervention as fiscal irresponsibility, administrative chaos and the absence of law and order" (Abdeljaouad 2014: 407). Thus, he saw education as contributing to modernization and social mobality. In his book, The Surest Path to Knowledge Concerning the Condition of Countries (*Aqwam al-Masalik fi Maarifat Ahwal al-Mamalik*) written in 1867, Pacha clearly articulates his views on the role of education in Tunisian society as:

> ... one of the most important duties imposed upon the princes of Islam, their ministers and the Ulama of the Sharia is their joining together in the establishment of Tanzimat resting on pillars of justice and consultation, which will secure education of the subjects, improve their circumstances in a manner

which will plant love of the homeland in their breasts and make them aware of
the benefit accruing to them both individually and collectively.

Pacha 1867: 129 as cited in Islahi 2012: 8

Upon opening, *le Collège Sadiki* enrolled one hundred and fifty pupils and had
three levels of courses. *Le Collège Sadiki* was underwritten through a special
fund and its curriculum was divided into three parts (*al-kuttab*, elementary or
intermediate, and secondary or high levels), which spanned eight years and used
traditional Islamic teachers to instruct students (Abdeljaouad 2014). The first
two sections, *al-kuttab* (two years) and elementary (four years), covered "the
Qu'ran, grammar, literature, rhetoric, logic, and jurisprudence. The third section,
early secondary [education (two years)] was optional and reserved for the most
gifted" (Sizer 1971: 7). Languages offered under the third section consisted of
Turkish, French, and Italian. *Le Collège Sadiki* also offered instruction in
mathematics, physical and natural sciences, social studies, and foreign languages,
albeit instructors (some foreign) were advised to "inculcate love of the Faith
and to discourage questioning from the students" (Sizer 1971: 7). The modern
le Collège Sadiki aimed to train young Tunisians for state service bureaucracies
and offered gifted Tunisians lessons in European languages and sciences, Arabic
language, and sound knowledge of Islam (Abdeljaouad 2014; Anderson 1986;
El-Mesawi 2008; Perkins 1986).

Le Collège Sadiki was unique in that it was the first school of the modern era
and "the instauration of a modern education provided in the establishments that
were conceived on the Occidental model was then the necessary lever"
(MOHESRT 2008: 25) to promote the creation of the unique Tunisian higher
education system—albeit one with some roots in the French system. *Le Collège
Sadiki's* design was an "early model of bilingual and bi-cultural education" and
became the standard for future educational endeavors under French rule (Sizer
1971: 7). In other words, "Pacha had intended Sadiqi College to prepare Tunisian
modern elites (teachers, engineers, architects, doctors, lawyers, and civil servants)
to be highly trained in all domains and capable of transforming the country into
a modern state, preserved from being devoured by other countries" (Abdeljaouad
2014: 417).

Pacha was involved in all the intricacies of his Western-inspired education
reforms at all levels, which led to trouble with the local oligarchy and his
dismissal. El-Mesawi (2008) suggests that Pacha's education reforms were
successful because he: (i) founded the national library with its first gift, eleven
hundred manuscripts donated by him; (ii) restructured the funding of Islamic

education under a new Religious Endowments Agency; and (iii) renewed the official government gazette (*al-Raid at-Tunisi*) and reactivated the Official Press, both of which had been neglected since being founded in 1860. In addition to numerous political and military reforms, Pacha encouraged the restoration and enlargement of schools across the major cities of Tunisia as he reorganized the education system (El-Mesawi 2008). In the end, the pre-colonial homegrown reforms that focused on developing a modern Tunisia based on European experiences would become instrumental in making Tunisia one of the most liberal Arab countries in its post-independence period.

The Modern Period: French Protectorate Rule and Post-Independence Reforms

On May 12, 1881, the dictator Bey Mohamed Sadok, signed the Treaty of Bardo to establish a French Protectorate and the French authoritarian bargaining agreement. The French colonization of Tunisia had not been communicated to the locals as a military occupancy, but rather as an effort to *protect* Tunisia from outside dangers. However, the occupancy took a military defense turn when the Bey grew uncomfortable with the content of the treaty claiming it was one-sided. Domestically, there were fears that Tunisia would be annexed to Algeria. Two years later, on June 8, 1883, another treaty, the Convention of La Marsa (*La Convention de la Marsa*), came into effect, thus increasing France's authority in the territory while reducing the Beylic's authority. Bey Ali, then in office and signatory of the binding document, was compelled to carry out certain administrative, legal, and financial reforms as "Paul Cambon [French diplomat in control of Tunisia] carefully kept the appearance of Tunisian sovereignty while reshaping the administrative structure to give France complete control of the country and render the *Beylical* government a hollow shell devoid of meaningful powers" (Perkins 1986: 86). Both agreements, the Treaty of Bardo and the Convention of La Marsa, opposed *Le Pacte Fondamental* of 1857 and the Constitution of 1861. France's intervention in the country alleviated some of its debt to international lending institutions, but it also started causing a disidentification and acculturation of the population. The Nationalist Movement that rose to defy the French colonization was rhetorically called the *Destour* Party (the Tunisian Liberal Constitutional Party).

French Carthage: *La Mission Civilisatrice* and Assimilative Education

By the nineteenth century, Tunisia had one of the most advanced Muslim education systems in the Maghreb region. Therefore, in 1881, when the French colonial regime took partial control of Tunisia, they found a religious education system that did not meet their administrative needs. These traditional Muslim institutions of education provided most of the talent for the marketplace of the time—clerks, judges, teachers, and clerics. In 1883, the education system came under the control of the Directorate of Public Education, with Louis Machuel becoming the Director of Education and Religious Institutions (Green 1978).

French officials originally stated that little change would be made to the Tunisian education system, but a growing European population from seventy-seven thousand in 1895 to one hundred and twenty-nine thousand in 1905 put pressure on the government to provide more European educational institutions (Sizer 1971). Under the French authoritarian bargaining agreement, the Muslim education institutions remained untouched while encouraging all non-Muslim students to study in French schools. By the turn of the century, Tunisia had "full-blown French primary and secondary education" that rivaled that of "metropolitan France with minor changes to fit the situation in Tunisia" (Coleman 1965: 147–148). Nevertheless, since Tunisia was a French Protectorate, it was subject to *la mission civilisatrice* (the civilizing mission). The Tunisian education system was not different from other French systems in Africa, and focused on assimilating the native populations through educative attainment, which had two aims: to "bring Africans into the modern world" and "bring Africans to a higher level of civilization and understanding" (White 1996: 15). The mission aimed to give Africans a "French consciousness" by supplanting the "village storyteller who captivated children with his heroic deeds of Islamic heroes [and replace it with] the village school" (Geyer 2003: 67). By the late 1800s, France allowed Tunisians to study in France in order to absorb French values, culture, and language to import to Tunisia. The education system was thus reformed to mirror the French school system and deeply entrenched in and defined by France's civilizing mission.

The commencement of Tunisia as a protectorate was accompanied by an influx of French civil servants and administrators creating "a colony of servants" who commanded a pay known as *"le tiers colonial"* (a colonial third)—more than the pay of Tunisians undertaking identical occupations (Borowiec 1988: 16). As France expanded its economic interest in the Middle East, its educational interest developed. Estimates suggest that by 1919, 5 percent or more of the Foreign Ministry's budget was devoted to supporting French schools, although it did not establish or build any schools across the Middle East (Burrows 1986). As France cemented control over Tunisian society, it "retained, strengthened and extended the bureaucratic administration of the local state" (Anderson 1999: 9), while at the same time laying the foundation for what ultimately became a robust centralized educational bureaucracy that still exists and was maintained under the Bourguiba and Ben Ali dictatorships.

Prior to the arrival of the French, the Islamic primary school was the most important educational institution. Director Machuel left the traditional Islamic school untouched but established new Franco-Arab schools to pragmatically teach both French and Tunisian students new subjects in French. Unlike the government primary schools that gave more weight to Arabic, the Franco-Arab schools emerged after French and modern subjects were introduced to the Islamic school curriculum (Abun-Nasr 1987). The Franco-Arab education system was established with the aim of instructing Tunisians in French and drew in the new Tunisian elites. These schools were loosely modeled after the bi-cultural *le Collège Sadiki* design, with Arabic and Italian language courses taught as second languages. The schools were intended to be open to all citizens (French and Tunisian), but many Tunisian Muslim students were excluded because of their low proficiency in French (Sizer 1971). Although the schools achieved some success in desegregating European and Tunisian students, the proportion of French students to Tunisian remained unequal throughout the protectorate period —with the schools never enrolling more than a fifth of the region's eligible students (Perkins 1986). The newly established school system closely resembled and was integrated with the school system in France (Sizer 1971).

A distinctive feature of francophone education was its focus on preparing the political and administrative elites to function in the colonial bureaucracy (Burrows 1986; Cowen 1996; Jules and Barton 2014; Rappleye 2012; White 1996). The administration also "hoped that a modern education would facilitate relations between France and the native people by fostering an understanding of the Arab–Islamic culture and the newly arrived European cultures" (DeGorge 2002: 580–581). Further, the government needed an educated Tunisian workforce to fill government positions. Over time, special high schools were created to train the children of the foreign community and Tunisians that came from the middle and the upper classes. From 1914 to 1942, student attendance and the number of schools established to educate both Tunisians and the French increased.

With time, a separate and unequal system of education emerged. Director Machuel left *le Collège Sadiki* untouched and it retained its place as the premier center of learning, where "its graduates were almost assured government positions by their advanced training in modern subjects and in the increasingly important French language" (Perkins 1986: 88–89). Over time, Machuel employed the twin objectives of: (i) downgrading *le Collège Sadiki* without rightly irritating the teachers and the administrative elite; and (ii) establishing a parallel non-religious system that functioned in French. However, unlike the Franco-Arab schools, *le Collège Sadiki's* curriculum did not prepare graduates for jobs beyond clerks and translators in the French administration.

Under Machuel, *le Collège Sadiki* had a revolving door of Tunisian directors between 1881 and 1889, after which he began to watch the financial, organizational, and pedagogical matters of the College closely (Abdeljaouad 2014). Then in 1897, Marius Delmas, a Frenchman, was appointed as director of *le Collège Sadiki*, where he introduced French laws and regulations. In 1897, under the stewardship of Delmas, for the first time in *le Collège Sadiki's* history, primary and secondary education were separated. With the separation of the different levels of schooling, Delmas created a system where:

> A vast room was used as a traditional *al-kuttab* where pupils collectively learned the Qur'an by heart and obtained some writing and reading skills in Arabic using clay tablets. Half of the study time during the first and second years, one fourth of the time in the third and fourth years and 1 h[our] per week in the fifth year were spent at the *al-kuttab*. The remaining time was devoted to the same curriculum offered in French primary schools, with Arabic language and grammar courses added and some training in translation between French and Arabic. In these courses, pupils used French textbooks for most subjects and a few strictly controlled Arabic books not published in Egypt.
>
> as cited in Abdeljaouad 2014: 420

Graduates from the College and the other modern educational establishments began to criticize the recently adopted education system. They argued for their own society's need "to make room for concepts and practices then current in the West but without discarding the Arabo-Islamic traditions in which it rested" (Perkins 1986: 92). In response to their concerns, the alumni began publishing *al-Hadira*, a newspaper that promoted societal change, while maintaining Islamic principles (Perkins 1986). In 1898, the French established a commission (comprised of the *Shaykh al-Islam*, the inspectors of education and seven *Madrasat al-Zitouna* professors) to reform *Madrasat al-Zitouna* at the behest of Director Machuel. This stimulated the opening of a new educational organization in 1896, entitled *al-Khaldunia* Association, which was designed to provide students attending *Madrasat al-Zitouna* with a European curriculum in addition to their Islamic education (Anderson 1986). *Al-Khaldunia* is the first modern school, established in 1896 by the Young Tunisians Movement, presided over by Béchir Sfar and named for the Turkish revolutionaries, the Young Turks (DeGorge 2002). In practice, *al-Khaldunia* and *le Collège Sadiki* functioned to undermine the position of *Madrasat al-Zitouna* and eventually it would serve as the incubator for the development of a new class of secularist/Westernized elites who would later establish the *Neo-Destour* Party in 1934, leading Tunisia to Independence (Lulat 2005). The French viewed *Madrasat al-Zitouna* as a bastion of cultural resistance against the French influence, yet they left it mostly untouched. Instead, the focus was on enhancing the system rather than weakening it (Lulat 2005).

Although *le Collège Sadiki* graduates worked in tandem with French officials to establish *al-Khaldunia* (Micaud 1964), the officials became concerned that the modern education system was "creating an educated elite who could cause political problems" (DeGorge 2002: 583). Their concerns were substantial; Tunisians became less passive and more concerned with maintaining their culture while simultaneously giving access to schools with modern curricula. One of the most salient demands of the Young Turks Movement was to make modern education more readily available to all Tunisians, in both urban and rural areas. As a result, the Department of Public Education began to deny access to European-style education for Tunisians (Anderson 1986). In 1898, Louis Machuel established a vocational school while ten Franco-Arab schools were closed due to low enrollments of Tunisian students (Perkins 1986). The resident governor, René Millet (from 1894 to 1900), opened the first school for girls in 1900, but it was not until 1908 that a school for Muslim girls, in Tunis, was opened.

Then, in 1906, Director Delmas supported the creation of the Perfectionist Council for *le Collège Sadiki*, made up of local Tunisians (including the president of *al-Khaldunia*—Ben Mustafa) that called for the upgrading of studies at *le Collège Sadiki* so that graduates could sit for the Baccalaureate examination (*le Bac*), which allowed admission to French universities. Eventually, students at *le Collège Sadiki* were prepared for the higher diploma of Arabic and translation, renamed "End of Studies Diploma" of *le Collège Sadiki*, which provided them with the ability to sit for the *le Bac* at the French *Lycée Saint-Louis,* discussed later (Abdeljaouad 2014). Then, in 1907, new regulations stipulated that only students receiving the primary school certificate be eligible to attend *le Collège Sadiki*. Under the 1907 regulations, *le Collège Sadiki* had the same curriculum and examinations as the French system, most of the teachers were French, and all subjects were taught in French (approximately twenty-two and a half hours per week). Students were given six hours per week of Arabic and one hour of calligraphy and at the end of the fourth year had to take the Arabic Elementary Exam (which was equivalent to *Le Brevet Élémentaire* in France). In the fifth and last year of studies, students could sit for the "end of studies" diploma after being trained in "French, Arabic, Islamic history, translation exercises, Islamic laws, Tunisian organizations and regulations and commercial and administrative accounting" (Abdeljaouad 2014: 421).

As the settler colony grew, in 1907 two significant events occurred. On the one hand, the French embarked upon a systematic policy of colonization, commandeering public and private lands and giving them to the European settlers. On the other hand, the Young Tunisians Movement and a new political newspaper, *Le Tunisien* (*The Tunisian*), were launched. *Le Tunisien* expounded the notion that education, justice, finance, agriculture, and administration were essential reforms that were needed and avowed: "in front rank of our preoccupations we shall place the question of instruction" (Abdeljaouad 2014: 407). The first editor of *Le Tunisien*, Ali Bach Hamba, a founding member of the Young Tunisians Movement, called for the end of segregation in education while encouraging the French to provide facilities for free and universal primary education for all children in Tunisia (Abdeljaouad 2014; Brown 1976). By 1914, Tunisia's education system consisted of thirty private schools and two hundred and eighty-eight public schools. Most of the schools were primary schools, along with one *lycée* for boys, a secondary school for girls, two colleges, two normal schools, and a professional school. From 1914 to 1942, student attendance and the number of schools established to educate both Tunisians and the French increased, however "... the establishment of a new school in the colonies required government permission, government-certified teachers, a state curriculum and the exclusive use of French as the language of instruction" (White 1996: 12). In 1942, in addition to new primary schools, technical and professional training institutes were opened. Finally, putting the educational processes in perspective, a conference was held in Tunis in April 1949, organized by the Directorate of Public Education to address educational issues. Members "called for teaching methods suitable for the Tunisian child, programs adapted to local realities and the use of Arabic as a vehicular language" (Sizer 1971: 12). The conference, along with a report commissioned by the French government, brought to fruition the twenty-year plan, entitled the Total Enrollment Plan, from 1949 to 1969. The Plan addressed demographic, economic, and cultural concerns within the education system, such as providing educational options for girls, preparing students to aid in the development of the country, and the need for Arab–Muslim elites to fulfill government positions. The Plan succeeded in increasing the population of children receiving an education, but "the proportion of eligible children in school remained between thirty and thirty-five percent" (Sizer 1971: 16). Education continued to be for the elite and wealthy.

Finally, in addition to government-run schools, several cultural associations flourished in Tunis and instituted different forms of education. Beginning in 1878, the *Alliance Israe'lite Universelle* (AIU), viewed as modern and perceived as second only in importance to the French Foreign Ministry, set up its first school in Tunis. The AIU taught using French methods and stressed "*l'instruction qu'on peut donner dans nos écoles est peu de choses, c'est l'éducation de l'esprit et du coeur qui est tout*"—the educational instruction that we may provide in our schools is not sufficient, education of the mind and heart is more important (as cited in Burrows 1986: 132; *author's translation*). These policies ultimately had the long-term consequence of creating the "francophone factor"—where "Tunisians are Arabs and the educated ones seem to be more at ease in France than in the Arabic countries" (Borowiec 1998: 9). Minority groups as well as Jews and Italians (arriving in 1896) maintained their own schools. Jews were instructed in French programs at the Jewish schools of the AIU and the consulate supported the Italian schools. The National Association for the Propagation of the French Language in the Colonies and Abroad (later renamed the *Alliance Française*) was founded by Paul Cambon (then resident general of Tunisia and future ambassador to Spain), Pierre Foncin (geographer, the Inspector General of Public Instruction and future Secretary General and President of the *Alliance Française*), and Paul Bert (former Minister of Public Instruction). The Association aimed at spreading French culture in Tunisia (Abadi 2013; Henry 2008). In fact, Pierre Foncin argued that "it is necessary to attach the colonies to the metropole by a very solid psychological bond[s], against the day when their progressive emancipation ends in a form of federation as is probable, that they be and they remain French in language, thought and spirit" (as cited in Rodney 1982: 259). In 1904, the Alumni Association of *le Collège Sadiki* was created with the aim of using the school's alumni to promote a bi-cultural society (Abdeljaouad 2014).

Concluding Thoughts—Marching Toward Independence and Dictatorial Transition

By the end of the French Protectorate in 1956, only 10 percent of the population in Tunisia was receiving an education (DeGorge 2002). Traditional Tunisian schools were identical to the Pre-Protectorate era and the "French system was merely juxtaposed to it, more modern in outlook, but transposed directly from France with little adaption to local needs" (Sizer 1971: 18). Although the reforms brought about during the French rule created more schools, these reforms also created an educational space that was highly complex and incongruous. Over time, power and the ensuing governance activities—funding, ownership, provision, and regulation—of education became centralized in the office of the Resident General and the French language replaced Arabic in the public sphere (Jules and Barton 2014). By the time the march toward independence commenced, three types of schooling existed: (i) the French and French–Arabic; (ii) the native modern, such as *le Collège Sadiki*; and (iii) the native traditional, such as the Qur'anic schools. We will return to the time compression chronology of transitologies in education—specifically, why education is often the last system to transition—in the final chapter.

4

Post-Colonialism and the Tale of Two Dictators

The fight for independence from France dates to the rise of early homegrown militancy and trade unionism in Tunisia under the auspices of the General Confederation of Tunisian Workers (CGTT), the first centralized federation in Tunisia, founded on January 19, 1925 by Mohamed Ali al-Hammi (1890–1928). After decades of leadership transition and turmoil, on January 20, 1946, the north and south branches of the CGTT merged to produce the Tunisian General Labor Union (UGTT) and elected Farhat Hached (1914–1952) as its general secretary. The creation of UGTT not only signaled the birth of an earlier form of home-grown Tunisian militancy, but its power to organize strengthened, developed by its years fighting Bourguiba's—"Father of the Nation," "Supreme Warrior," and *"Combatant Suprème"*—post-independence regime and the Ben Ali regime. Their new strength would allow the organization to mobilize its members at the dawning of *al-sahwa* in 2011. From its inception, UGTT has been politically involved in Tunisia and it has maintained and guarded its political voice vigorously both before and after *al-sahwa* (Omri 2014). UGTT's strategies and views on education have been crafted since its inception, as articulated by then president Farhat Hached, who clearly stipulated that "the Tunisian trade union movement ... is particularly interested in everything concerning social progress, the development of the family, health and future of young people, education of the popular classes in the fields to us" (Ennaceur 2000: 9 *author's translation*). In the pre- and post-independence periods, UGTT became the vanguard of the national education movement through the spreading of awareness, in the form of the right to education, among its workers. In the immediate post-independence period with demographic growth in the 1960s and 1970s, UGTT asked, and insisted, that Bourguiba's regime build schools and universities.

While the union was powerful in the pre-independence period, it would be the *Destour* Party, under the leadership of Ali Bash-Hamba (1876–1918) and Sheikh Abed Al-Aziz Athaalbi (1876–1944), who would fight French occupation while actively arousing the national consciousness of Tunisians. Destourian members were students, faculty members, and graduates from *le Collège Sadiki* and *Madrasat al-Zitouna* who wanted to *Tunisify* the country by scrubbing it of all French influences. While the *Destour* called for the equal distribution of resources between rural and urban governorates, its main goal was to achieve independence.

This chapter is organized chronologically and we draw on our comparative-historical approach to explore the intersection of education and authoritarian bargaining under two dictatorial regimes. In what follows, we will discuss the major reforms in education and the subsequent tweaks that took place under the authoritarian regimes of Bourguiba and Ben Ali. We begin by tracing Bourguiba's pre-independence vision for Tunisian education and the impact of the Tunisian socialist experiment, then discuss the infamous Bread Riots and suppression of extremist groups during the 1980s. In the second part of the chapter, we explore the stalling of education reform after the *coup de constitution*, in which Ben Ali replaced Bourguiba, and the effect of two major reforms—*le Changement* and *le Pacte National*—on the development of Tunisian education. We argue that under the Bourguiba and Ben Ali dictatorships, authoritarian bargaining was part of state corporatism that emerged in the post-independence period and promoted social policies, land reform, and jobs in state-owned enterprises with the aim of keeping workers and peasants happy and compliant. The promotion of education became the bedrock of these state corporatism policies. The policies were retained and tweaked only lightly once the Ben Ali regime came to power.

1956: The Education Revolution and the Road Toward the Decade of Al-Mesaâdi

At the birth of Tunisian independence, "several simultaneous social revolutions" (Tessler and Keppel 1976: 73) commenced, but it was the education revolution of 1956 that would be the catalyst for change. In 1956, the literacy rate in Tunisia stood at around 15 percent with less than one-quarter of young people attending schools and on average one in every thirty children receiving secondary or high school education (Berry and Rinehart 1988; Tessler and Keppel 1976). In 1956, the National Planning Board was created. Bourguiba's administration seemed to believe in the massification of education and increased capacity of its human capital as foundational to the creation of a modern Tunisian society. The defining characteristics of Tunisia's Post-Protectorate education spaces were Bourguibaism, Secularism, and Arabization[1] embodied in the hegemony of the state as tutelary (*l'État-patron*) and the state as a party (*l'État-parti*) (Belkhodja 1998; Sadiki 2002). The term "Bourguibaism" refers to the modernist policies of universal Arabization and francophone modernization, developed by the dominant socio-economic and political doctrine of the Bourguiba administration that eventually created a bicultural education system (Judy 2012). In fact, the National Association of Broadcasters (1968: 22) argues that:

> The focus of Bourguibaism in the broad educational realm has been on aggressive programs designed to weld Tunisia into conscious, modern, west-ward-looking nationhood and to give the Tunisian man-on-the-street fundamental coping skills, which will let him live and work effectively in the new, more complex socio-economic environment thus resulting. Various organs of government have been instructed to devise and operate educational programs and campaigns, which are roughly divisible into the following descriptive categories: (a) formal education (primary, secondary and higher); (b) vocational training for youth and adults; (c) homemaking training for girls and women; (d) community kindergarten programs; (e) agricultural training for youth and men; (f) literacy and cultural training for youth and adults; (g) health and family planning programs for adults.

However, it was Mahmoud Al-Masaâdi—the first Director of Education as well as the Secretary of Education, Youth and Sport and then General Inspector of Teaching, Minister of Culture (from 1973 to 1976), and later Speaker of Parliament (from 1981 to 1986)—who was the architect of the *Tunisification* of the old system and overseer of the bargaining agreement. As Allman (1979: 12–13) poignantly summarizes:

> In 1958, two years after independence, there was a basic educational reform that was implemented by a minister of education who had ten years to carry out his program under conditions of national political stability. Attempts were made to coordinate educational planning within the framework of comprehensive economic and social development plans. By the end of the first decade of education development, Tunisia was spending a proportion of its per capita gross domestic product on education exceeded by few other countries of the world.

Al-Masaâdi was tasked by Bourguiba with implementing the Project for Educational Reform (*le Projet de Réforme de l'Éducation*) in 1958 that focused on ensuring universal access to elementary school, the expansion of secondary education, and university reforms (Allman 1979; Omri 2006).[2] Al-Masaâdi stressed that reforms should be both vertical and horizontal to capture all aspects of society. On September 16, 1958, in a speech, Al-Masaâdi outlined the four pillars of his education vision: (i) unifying and standardizing education across the country; (ii) *Tunisifying*—conferring of national identity—in the curriculum (*al-Tawnasat*) and improving its national character; (iii) harmonizing education with the national needs for development; and (iv) publishing it horizontally and vertically to distribute it democratically. These core pillars stood the test of time and they eventually formed the foundation for Ben Ali's education reforms. Bourguiba argued that the mental structures (*les structures mentales*) of Tunisian people needed to change because part of the government's belief was in "a policy of horizontally broadened, and vertically extended, education is a fundamental precondition for the success of any plan for transforming the economic and social structure of the nation" (as cited in Allman 1979: 60). The authoritarian bargaining agreement produced the 1958 Ten-year Education Plan, the New Conception of Education in Tunisia (*la Nouvelle Conception de l'Éducation en Tunisie*), which not only addressed educational access, expansion, and re-nationalization, but aimed at unifying and *Tunisifying* the country while Arabizing the curriculum through vertical and horizontal expansion (Allman 1979; Jules and Barton 2014; Murphy 1999; Sizer 1971). With Al-Mesaâdi at the helm, on November 4, 1958, the Education Law (*Qanun al-Ttaelim*) was passed and for the first time, the education system split into three cycles; primary education, secondary education, and tertiary education. This three-level system of education is still active in Tunisia today. Article 1 stated the goals of Tunisian education and instruction as: (i) enabling all the children of both sexes, without any racial, religious, or social distinction, to develop their personality and natural skills; (ii) contributing to the development of scientific progress while ensuring that all benefit from these advances; (iii) promoting the development and the growth of the national culture; and (iv) preparing children for their role as citizens and humans and from the necessary executives for the development of the national activity in different aspects (Government of Tunisia 1958; MOE 1958).

Beginning from October 1958, the educational programs became fully unified and standardized in all of Tunisia's schools at all levels of education. In addition, these programs included the history and geography of Tunisia affirming its Arab–Muslim identity and placing it firmly in the Maghreb and the Arab world. Arabic was made the language of instruction for some subjects. These actions signaled the commencement of the *Tunisification* of the education system. However, the government continued to face several challenges, most notably high literacy rates and rapid demographic shifts. Soon after the national plan went into effect, overcrowding issues arose and the quality of education deteriorated (Allman 1979). In addition to the use of Arabic as the language of instruction, the age limits and hours of instruction changed. For example, at the primary level the age of enrollment decreased from seven years to six years. The hours of instruction decreased for the first and second grades from thirty to fifteen hours per week and the rest of the grades (four years) from thirty to twenty-five hours per week (AALAWA 2011). Coupled with this, the MOE mandated that, given the shortage of professionally trained teachers, students attend school for twenty-five hours a week for the remainder of the primary level and the seventh year of primary education was eliminated (Allman 1979; Sizer 1971).

Also in 1958, Tunisia signed the articles of agreement for the International Bank for Reconstruction and Development (IBRD—today the World Bank)—that provides loans at near-market interest rates to middle-income countries—and in 1960, it acceded to the International Development Association (IDA)—which gives grants and discounted loans to low-income countries. Then in 1962, Tunisia became the first country to receive a loan from the IDA for an education project. A US$5 million credit line, from the IDA, was given to Tunisia for the construction of six secondary and technical schools to accommodate approximately four thousand students and to extend the structure of the teacher training college in Tunis, *L'École Normale de Professeurs Adjoints* (IDA 1962). In line with the IDA's lending policies of the era, the credit line was given for bricks and mortar initiatives or manpower planning, and not for "soft" projects, such as teacher training or the purchase of textbooks. By the end of 1958, government spending on education also increased from 17.96 percent in 1958/59 to 24 percent in 1966, representing the largest share of the national budget. This dramatic restructuring of the system was done to accommodate: (i) the Decadal Perspective on Enrollment from 1959 to 1969 that sought to increase enrollments in primary and middle school education; (ii) the Decadal Plan for School Buildings that each governorate had to produce to account for how they planned on restructuring enrollment disparity between the different regions of Tunisia; and (iii) the Tunisian University Plan that was a twenty-year perspective for the development of the Tunisian university system (UNESCO 1966).

Under education Minister Al-Masaâdi, the enactment of these reforms collectively became known as the Decade of Al-Masaâd (*Achareyet Al-Masaâdi*). The 1960s in Tunisia were defined by its goals to establish a unified education system consistent with the Tunisian character. The reforms were twofold because they focused on: (i) expanding schooling to all Tunisians while creating a coherently unified system; and (ii) "training expeditiously the cadre that the ongoing state-building urgently needs" (MOET 2002: 9–10). The reforms gave the MOE opportunity to carry out its role in building a cultural system that linked education to the economic, social, and cultural development of a country. Its goal was for Tunisia to achieve total enrollment as quickly as possible. During the decade-long reforms, universal primary education was mandatory, access was expanded for both males and females, and secondary education was made open to all.

1960–1970: Socialism, Collectivism, and Cooperatives

A decade after the education revolution began in Tunisia, its second revolution— the cultural revolution—commenced. The cultural revolution sought to persuade the populace to abandon "outmoded beliefs" by emphasizing the education system be "designed to disengage the physiognomy of [Tunisia's] national culture" (as cited in Tessler and Keppel 1976: 74). Before independence, between 1958 and 1959, approximately thirty-two thousand three hundred and sixty-two students were enrolled in school. By 1967, 90 percent of school-aged boys and 50 percent of girls were receiving a primary education ("Le Système" 1962; Sizer 1971).

In 1960, Ahmed Ben Salah, a Soviet Union-oriented reformer, became Minister of Health and Social Affairs in Bourguiba's regime. One year later, after the economy collapsed, Bourguiba named him minister of the newly created Ministry of Planning, Commerce and Finance[3] and then Minister of Education in 1969. Ben Salah commenced with the decade-long socialist experiment that focused on accelerating the collectivization process through the development of the agriculture sector. Ben Salah adapted Jamal Abdel Nasser's ideas of Arab socialism based on Pan-Arabism and sought to implement them in Tunisia (Beinin 2015). During Ben Salah's tenure, the governing one-party, *Neo-Destour*, changed its name to the *Socialist Destourian* Party (PSD) to reflect the new economic module and path of that time. What was developing was "Tunisian Socialism," "peripheral Keynesianism," or "Tunisian Syndicalism"[4]—the idea that industries are organized into confederations or syndicates owned and controlled by workers. During this period, the government created and supported the institution of cooperatives in other sectors apart from education.

During the so-called period of "Tunisian Socialism," which relied on state planning, import substitution, industrialization, and high tariffs, the regime installed a quasi-socialist (collectivist) economic program of import substitution heavily dependent on the public sector. This statist-era development policy focused on providing free educational services and subsidized services in transportation, housing, health, and consumer goods. In 1962, the Ten-Year Development Plan (*Les Perspectives Décennales de Développement*), based on ideas adopted from UGTT's Congress of 1956, was passed. The Ten-Year Plan, started with Bourguiba's exploration of socialism and state control over the economy, aligned with the educational goals of the 1958-Education Plan. The plan called for agrarian reforms to facilitate economic decolonization, to increase livelihoods and self-sufficiency, and to create national markets.

During this era, Bourguiba and his government extended the social welfare project by giving access to university education, for the first time, to the urban working class, the lower-middle class and the children of peasants (Beinin 2015). This period also witnessed the rise of state-sponsored feminism (see Chapter 6). Under "Tunisian Socialism," education triumphed and resource allocations were the envy of third world countries (Dwyer 1991). Between 1962 and 1997, substantial investments in education gave rise to a doubling in enrollment for primary school students, a quadrupling for secondary level students, and a seven-fold increase for university education (Dwyer 1991). During this period, the tourism sector and infrastructure in cities, such as Sousse, Hammamet, and Djerba expanded and demand for new types of workers trained in hospitality increased exponentially (Dwyer 1991; Sayigh 2014).

By 1964, France canceled its financial assistance to Tunisia after the National Assembly enacted a policy for expropriation of all foreign-owned lands. The government responded by creating cooperatives in all sectors. Then, in 1967, a Commission on Education was established to evaluate the new challenges faced since the 1958-Education reforms. They were asked to focus their attention on the cost effectiveness of the education system. The Commission suggested the government readjust the amount of money it was spending on education at that time.

The 1969 riots in the *Sahel* region led to Ben Salah's dismissal by Bourguiba and he was eventually charged with treason and jailed, only to escape into exile several years later (Anderson 1990). However, by the 1969 riots, Bourguiba's education reforms appeared functional since the enrollment rate across all levels had increased between four and five times as compared to the immediate post-independence period (Allman 1979). Yet, by the end of the 1960s, Tunisia had not achieved the level of primary education it planned, evidenced by lower enrollment for girls, profound regional disparities, and high failure rates at the primary and secondary level (Bouraoui 1990).

1970–1980: From Socialism and Cooperatives to State Capitalism

As the 1970s began, with the socialist experiment firmly behind Bourguiba and Al-Masaâdi dismissed from the Ministry of Education, education reforms had a different tone. Bourguiba appointed the governor of the Tunisian Central Bank and architect of Tunisia's economic renewal in the 1960s, Hedi Nouira, as prime minister from 1970 to 1980 to create a new authoritarian agreement. From the outset, Nouira committed Tunisia to a five-point development strategy stipulating:

- The government had to maintain its control on the primary sector, while opening the rest of the economy to the private sector
- It was necessary to re-establish a free market economy
- Agriculture should become a priority for the development of the entire economy
- Within the industrial sector, priority should be given to the light industry and SMEs, giving preference to profitability and labor-intensity
- Foreign investment had to be actively supported.

Morrisson and Talbi 1996 as cited in Di Tommaso,
Lanzoni and Rubini 2001: 5

At its heart, the five-point plan was a semi-liberal *infitâh* policy that sought to combine import substitution and export promotion while encouraging the coexistence of the public and private sector (Ayadi and Mattoussi 2014).

In 1970, an Inter-Ministerial Commission was created and after two years of evaluation and reflection, it recommended rectifying qualitative deficiencies identified across the education system. Educational developments were quickly formulated to reflect the shift from collectivism and cooperatives to a more liberalized economy. Thus, the education reforms were responding to spillover effects of increased access to the system that caused enrollment rates to rise and repetition rates to grow (Pekkarinen and Pellicer 2013). In 1971, the secondary school cycle was changed to two cycles, comprised of four and seven years respectively, replacing the intermediate level designed to train middle-level technicians (Allman 1979). Then in 1972, the education system underwent minor reforms, after the Inter-Ministerial Commission released its report. The 1972 reforms mandated that schools concentrate on vocational training so that Tunisia would have a well-trained workforce. The reforms accommodated Nouira's new strategy of pursuing an industrial policy to open the Tunisian economy by liberalizing and privatizing key industries.

Prime Minister Nouira is credited with getting the economy back on track after the socialist experiment of the 1960s. The development of a skilled labor force was central to his policy of luring foreign direct investment (FDI) to Tunisia by playing up its educated population, low labor costs, and proximity to major European ports. His ideas would later be reinforced through the 1993 Investment Incentives Code that called for non-discriminatory treatment of FDI and the 1989 Legal Framework that restructured state enterprises. Moreover, during this time, there was a semantic shift in the internal movement of the Tunisian people from rural to coastal areas. In 1974, Bourguiba had the constitution revised and it named him as President for life and confirmed Nouira as his chosen successor.

By the early 1970s, the *Tunisification* of teaching texts and Arabic as the primary medium of instruction had occurred at the primary level. The reasons for *Tunisifying* the curriculum were stated as "provid[ing] our children with a linguistic background more close to our mother tongue to permit them [to] understand the subjects and avoid scholar failures and communication problems" (MONE 1981: 12). However, while enrollment rose, issues of quality, appropriate teacher development programs, and management were rampant. Moreover, Secretaries of State for Education were replaced so often that proposed reforms were never implemented. For example, between 1969 and 1976 there were five Secretaries of State for Education, with Mohammed Mzali serving thrice in that position. The reshuffling of the Secretaries of State for Education reflected the perceived importance of education to national development and Bourguiba's vision of what education was supposed to achieve. During Mohammed Mzali's first term, he accomplished nothing of significance. In his second term (from October 1971 to March 1973), Mzali added the seventh year, which had been deleted, back in to secondary education.

Mohammed Mzali returned as Secretary of State for Education in May 1976. He focused on a policy agenda of *al-taarib*, drawing lessons from other Arabic countries rather than Western nations as earlier reforms had done. The aim was to make the French language less relevant by demoting it to a second language taught in the fourth year, rather than the third, of primary school. At the secondary level, the goal was to make French an optional language at the Baccalaureate. In 1977, a post-primary cycle composed of two years of professional education was created for students who could not pass the primary school exit examination to attend secondary school (MONE 1981). There were quantitative shifts redirecting focus from primary education access to providing quality education that could contribute to national development (Allman 1979).

Between 1974 and 1975, secondary education was decentralized by creating four regional delegations with responsibility for the whole country. It would not be until 1981 (see later in this chapter) that primary education would be targeted for decentralization.

By the end of the 1970s, the age limit for access to primary schools was established at six years. Seventh and eighth years of school were added in 1977 to relieve the burden for students who were failing their sixth year. The two extra years of schooling sought to: (i) prepare students; (ii) decrease failure rates in the sixth grade; (iii) provide pupils with manual training to facilitate their integration into the economic system; (iv) transform the primary school not into a discriminatory institution but into an orientation one; (v) prepare pupils for secondary education; and (vi) prepare pupils to recognize the importance and value of manual work (MONE 1981).

In 1974, the last presidential elections were held under Bourguiba. In 1978, the government divided the Ministry of National Education into two ministries: (i) the Ministry of National Education became responsible for the management of primary and secondary education (as well as technical and professional education); and (ii) the Ministry of Higher Education and Scientific Research was given responsibility for higher education and fundamental and applied research. By the end of the 1970s, two more Commissions on Education (in 1977 and 1979 respectively) convened to discuss the state of education and to propose remedies to rectify the qualitative deficiencies stemming from the fallout of the 1958-Education reforms, even though educational expenditure was at 6 percent of the gross domestic product.

Under the Fifth Development Plan of 1977–1981, the government emphasized public investment to absorb the excess labor force and diversify the economy. In January 1978, UGTT broke the authoritarian bargaining agreement with the governing regime and called for a general strike, which included students from secondary schools and universities. A decree was issued on what later became known as "Black Thursday," since approximately four hundred people died. UGTT argued that high levels of unemployment, suppression of civil liberties, and economic discrimination frustrated its members. They called for political pluralism, democracy, extensive economic reform across all areas, and social equity (Clancy-Smith 2013). The state security forces responded ferociously, killing dozens and arresting and detaining thousands.

Black Thursday came shortly after Ben Ali's appointment as Director-General of National Security in December 1977. Additionally, as the decade came to a close, Prime Minister Nouira was handling the day-to-day running of the country as Bourguiba's health and alertness worsened. As the 1970s drew to a close, local Islamic groups began to gain momentum and heated battles between the development and incubation of deeper secular ideas and greater Islamification played out on university campuses across Tunisia. In fact, the *Islamic Tendency Movement* Party ([MTI] discussed later in this chapter) began its mobilization campaign, gaining traction and a following among university students in the 1970s.

1980–1987: From Bread Riots to a Medical *Coup d'état*

The 1980s began as usual for Tunisia: food prices rose and living standards declined as unemployment stood at 35 percent of the total labor force. The country, like the rest of the world, was recovering from the global energy crisis (defined by the 1973 oil crisis—driven by the oil embargo—and the 1979 energy crisis—sparked by the Yom Kippur War and the Iranian Revolution). The country experienced: (i) the rise of militant Islam and fundamentalism and its suppression; (ii) the imposition of the Structural Adjustment Program (SAP) under the IMF and the backlash in the form of "Bread Riots" in 1984; and (iii) the deposing of Bourguiba, ruler for life, under a medical *coup d'état* by Ben Ali.

The reform of the education system at the beginning of the 1980s coincided with the emerging indigenous Islamist movement that claimed it would be a better economic and political alternative to Bourguiba's authoritarian rule. The arrival of militant Islam in Tunisia coincided with the "triple 'scares' of 1979—the siege of the Grand Mosque in Mecca, the Iranian Islamic revolution and the rise of the *Mujahideen* against the Soviet occupation in Afghanistan" (Hudson 2015: 38) that allowed Bourguiba to reassert his authoritarian rule. Tunisia's homegrown Islamist movement commenced in 1981, when *Ennahdha* (*Hizb al-Nadha* or the *Islamic Tendency Movement* Party, later renamed the *Renaissance* Party), was founded by Rachid al-Ghannouchi and Abdelfattah Mourou. Though moderate in its foundation, it quickly grew in popularity and was considered the biggest opposition to the government. After applying for official recognition as an Islamic political party, approximately one hundred of its members were arrested; this sparked unrest, specifically on university campuses. The government sought to ease tensions by releasing the leaders of the organization and allowing them to be recognized as a cultural society instead of granting them legal recognition. The unrest overshadowed national reforms, and was a catalyst in creating the Ben Ali palace coup in 1987. Internally, in February 1980, Prime Minister Nouira suffered a stroke. In April 1980, Mohammed Mzali, then Minister of National Education, replaced him as prime minister and heir apparent to Bourguiba until his dismissal and self-imposed exile to France in July 1986. Under Mzali's tenure, the economy continued to struggle and he was not able to reinvigorate it even with the Sixth Development Plan of 1982–1986. By:

> ... the mid–1980s, the government put in place the Economic Recovery and Structural Adjustment Programme (ERSAP) that focused on tariffs reduction, facilitating quantitative restrictions on imports, the introduction of a value added tax, the reduction of personal income taxes, the devaluation of the Tunisian Dinar and negotiations with creditors that extended the maturity on the country's foreign debt.
>
> Ayadi and Mattoussi 2014: 1

The education reforms of the 1980s were done against the backdrop of a declining economy and rising Islamic insurgency. Thus in 1980, another Commission on Education was convened, which made similar recommendations to those made by the previous Commission. After the 1978 splitting of the Ministry of Education between higher education and national education (comprising pre-primary, primary, and secondary education), the 1980 national education policy further divided the Ministry of National Education into a central administration and a regional administration. The central government was tasked with managing programs, training, and regulation of primary, secondary, technical, and professional education, curriculum content, and examinations. In addition, the central administration was given responsibility for implementing duties and common services. The regional administrations took responsibility for the administrative, pedagogical, and financial aspects of primary and secondary education.

The first part of the 1980s focused on decentralizing the primary education system by creating regional delegations in all governorates in 1981. In addition to the *Tunisification* of secondary education in the early 1980s, reforms focused on the continued decentralization of the administrative activities and the organization of regional services related to primary and secondary education: (i) the development of teachers' conditions through different measures; indemnity for the rural zone; (ii) the promulgation of a particular statute for teachers; (iii) the creation of the accommodation office, which permitted the development of their living conditions; and (iv) the development of teaching quality (MONE 1981). Numerous challenges remained in primary and secondary schools including the imbalance in enrollment rates for girls across the different governorates; teachers highlighting the mechanical acquisition of knowledge; and infrastructural disparities in rural schools (UNESCO 1980).

In 1982, yet another Commission on the state of education was established to problematize the consequences of inaction across the national system. Every commission on education established under Bourguiba's tenure invested in solving Tunisia's educational crisis and critically reflecting on whether education was enabling his vision of a modern and secular Tunisia. By contrast, in 1983, Prime Minister Mzali began to look at the Gulf countries for inspiration and refocused on Arabizing the curriculum, rupturing the system, and breaking from the 1981 reforms. In 1983, Tunisia signed educational cooperation agreements with Algeria and Morocco to coordinate education policy in all three countries through the unifying of programs in all specialties, including the creation of mixed committees in the fields of human sciences and languages; technical sciences and esthetic education; training of education officers; and the harmonization and reinforcement of the use of didactic means (MONE 1981).[5]

The "Bread Riots" begun after citizens protested a 100 percent increase in the price of bread and were Tunisia's first mass mobilization since independence. By 1984, the global recession and plunging prices of crude oil had cost Bourguiba's government an estimated US$236 million for food subsidies alone. Disturbances started in the peripheral states and quickly spread to the wealthy coastal areas. The riots led to restructuring of food subsidies after Bourguiba's government had allowed wages to increase to keep pace with inflation (Alam 2011). The bloody Bread Riots brought Tunisia to its feet and a state of emergency was declared:

> While gunfire sounded, police and army troops in Jeeps and armored personnel carriers fanned out through the city to quell the "bread riot." The show of force finally brought an uneasy calm, but only after more than 50 demonstrators and bystanders were killed. Then, in a dramatic five-minute radio and television broadcast, Bourguiba announced that he was reversing the price hike. The cost of bread would drop immediately from 18¢ to 8¢, he declared, while previous increases for such staples as pasta and flour would be reduced as well. "We are going back to where we were," he said, fervently hoping that was so. Once again, thousands took to the streets, this time in frantic celebration. Waving baguettes, Tunisian flags and portraits of the President, the exuberant crowds shouted, "Long live Bourguiba".

> Time Magazine 1984: 44

The Bread Riots cemented the legacy of a new form of militantism. Young people taking to the streets did not view Bourguiba and his regime as the "savior" or "hero" of the nation who had won independence from France but instead, saw him as "the paramount symbol of the status quo and they can curse him one day and cheer him the next" (Time Magazine 1984: 44)

Between 1984 and 1989, Tunisia increased its allocation of foreign investment in education, despite the rising political tide. In 1984, Tunisia obtained seven loans for education from the African Bank of Development, amounting to over US$27 million to support primary and secondary education. In 1985, just over US$7 million was obtained for the construction of dormitories for eight hundred boys and girls at the Higher Institute of Technical Training for instructors in Nabeul. Then, in 1986, the Ministries of National Education and of Higher Education were merged to create a new centralized Ministry of Basic and Higher Education and Scientific Research. That same year, significant economic reforms were put in place, which were intended to stimulate employment. By 1986, the government believed that investment in education would improve income levels and employment and boost economic growth for the country. Tunisia began to implement World Bank and IMF-backed SAPs aimed at: "(i) preserving the stability of the macroeconomic framework and financial balances, (ii) integrating Tunisia into the world economy, (iii) redistributing income by reconciling social and economic policies and (iv) widening the middle class and reducing poverty" (Chemingui and Sánchez 2011: 6). These reform priorities, led by Bourguiba's appointee Rachid Sfar[6] who later became prime minister, outlined his vision in the Seventh Economic and Social Plan (*le Septieme Plan Économique et Social*) from 1987 to 1991 that called for a three-pronged development program: "(i) creating jobs; (ii) protecting the equilibrium of the balance of payments and (iii) sharing the wealth of the country more equitably among the regions" (U.S. Department of Commerce 1988: 6). Even under SAPs reforms, Tunisia continued to spend between 6 and 7.5 percent of its GDP on education.

During the rest of the 1980s until the 1987 *coup d'état* that replaced Bourguiba, there was a revolving door of Secretaries of State for Education. In fact, between 1980 and 1986, no actions concerning the regulation of education took place except a few minor administrative changes. However, after Bourguiba's replacement, education policy came to a quick, and lasting, halt. On November 7, 1987, Zine El Abidine Ben Ali took office in the bloodless, silent "*palace coup*" or "*coup de constitution*" (Reich 1990); the event was also referred to as the "medical *coup d'état*" or "*changement de palais*"—an internal transition via "Palace Revolt"

(Logan 2012). Five weeks after his ascension to Tunisia's prime ministership, Ben Ali, a military man and former Interior Minister from April 28, 1986 to October 2, 1987, used Article 57 of the 1959 Tunisian Constitution[7] that stated a president's "death [or] resignation due to permanent inability" are grounds for the prime minister to ascend to the presidency. Many of Bourguiba's policies were kept and maintained during the first four years of Ben Ali's regime. Ben Ali focused on courting the West for financial and legitimacy support and preparing for the 1989 election where Ben Ali appeared alone on the ballot. No significant improvements took place in education or any other sector during this time.

The Soft Landing: Not too "French," not too "Arabic," just *"Tunisified"*

In coming to power in 1987, Ben Ali inherited an education system where "the first two decades of independence were devoted to the spread of education [1960s] then to Arabization and Tunisification [1970s] ... the present decade [1980] is that of making choices for the future. The critical issue [as Ben Ali saw it, was] how to form the generation of the year 2000" (as cited in Daoud 1991: 4). Ben Ali's first political, economic, and social reforms or what might be called his social pact and authoritarian bargaining agreement with Tunisians were based on *le Changement* (the Change) and all government activates became dominated by *le Pacte National* (the National Pact)—political and economic reforms to encourage foreign investment (Borowiec 1998). *Le Pacte National* drew heavily upon the Spanish model that "brought together political actors with independent bases of power in the society and economy and institutionalized and symbolized the compromise that had been brokered among them" (Anderson 1999: 4).

The road toward *le Pacte National* commenced immediately after Ben Ali took power and began to discuss national identity, the political system, economic development, and foreign policy with opposition forces, including the Islamists *Ennahdha*. This process of *Conseil Supérieur du Plan* (consultations and dialogues) led to the eventual negotiating and signing of an agreement between the six legal opposition parties of the time and several civil society organizations (Alam 2011). *Le Pacte National* was Ben Ali's breaking away from Bourguibaism, by proposing guaranteed democratic openness, multiparty politics, and respect for human rights (Alam 2011; Shillington 2013). As Anderson (1999: 4) suggests, "virtually all the signatories of the [national] pact represented dependencies of the perennial ruling party; far from a compromise or bargain among equals, the pact was an effort to create the appearance of political pluralism in the absence of political actors with autonomous social and economic power."

At this time, in 1987, the Tunisian economy was out of control due to its balance of payment crisis. The Seventh Five-Year Development Plan of 1987–1991 and the Eighth Five-Year Development Plan of 1992–1996, both implemented under Ben Ali, promoted structural adjustment reforms aimed at liberalizing the economic sector, privatizing state assets (hotels and commercial establishments followed by textiles, foodstuffs, transport, chemicals, building materials, and suppliers of electric and mechanical equipment), and trimming the state's role in competitive sectors (El Jorshi 2003; Di Tommaso, Lanzoni and Rubini 2001). The goal was to "... encourage foreign investment, accelerate privatization, develop the stock market and deepen integration with the European market" (Di Tommaso, Lanzoni and Rubini 2001: 11). Both plans had disastrous consequences for education since they restricted public expenditure in its sector.

Bourguiba's rule gave rise to three myths—the economic miracle, democratic gradualism, and *laicity*—which provided fertile ground for the rise of Ben Ali. In 1987, his administration reinstituted Arabic as the language of instruction for primary and secondary schooling under the Seventh Economic and Social Plan of 1987–1991. In a speech in November 1988, Ben Ali stated that:

> [...] Because we believe that the schools have to prepare our children on the basis of good morals (manners), teach them to appreciate the work and finally to learn about our Arabic and Islamic identity, we have decided to improve the educational system with the assistance of a big number of people from the civil society, teachers and experts. Thus, we have decided to create the elementary school from the next school year, so that we can guarantee to our children an education of at least nine continuous years of studies and that we can decrease the number of pupils that leave the school at an early age. We have also decided that the Arabic language will be the official language of teaching sciences in all the different levels and that we will support scientific and technical education in the first cycle (9 years), which constitutes the elementary school. The higher council of education, higher education and scientific research that we have re-constituted will give its opinion in the big directions of this corrective project.

During the immediate post-Bourguiba era, Ben Ali begun to focus education reforms on cultivating skills in: (i) practical (mathematics, science, computer science, and technology); (ii) strategic (organize, analyze and find correct info); (iii) initiative (spirit of creativity); and (iv) behavioral (senses of responsibility, self-reliance, and cooperation) (MOHESRT 2008). He made no major reforms in education during his first two years in office and as Sadiki (2002: 65) poignantly asserts, "Ben Ali took over the reign [sic] of power to change the status quo. Up [until his overthrow] his reforms have offered more or less the '*status quo*' in that he continued to link state and party together as Bourguiba did." His regime continued to recognize free and compulsory schooling, but it "redefined the mission and finalities of education [and] restructured secondary education" due to evaluations that "revealed gaps and modest student performance," which highlighted "persistent weakness of the system's efficiency and payoff" (MOET 2002: 10–11).

The 1991 "Grand Education Reforms": *Les Lois de Mohamed Charfi* and the Neo-corporatist State

At the beginning of the 1990s, Ben Ali began courting the World Bank and the IMF. He wanted to be perceived as a "democratic" reformer who broke away from the tyranny, dictatorship, and failures of the Bourguiba era and its associated policies and reforms. As Chossudovsky (2011) observes:

> Barely a few months following Ben Ali's installment as the country's president, a major agreement was signed with the IMF. An agreement had also been reached with Brussels pertaining to the establishment of a free trade regime with the EU. A massive privatization program under the supervision of the IMF-World Bank was also launched. With hourly wages on the order of €75 an hour, Tunisia had also become a cheap labor haven for the European Union.

Ben Ali would use the military coup in Algeria, which led to *La Sale Guerre* (the Dirty War) in 1991, to justify his continued crackdowns on Islamists by unleashing the state security apparatus on them. As Schraeder and Redissi (2011: 5–6) comment, the political role of the "*Mukhabarat* (the intelligence-based) police state [was based on a] 'strong neo-corporatist state' or the 'force of obedience' or an 'authoritarian syndrome.'" Ben Ali drew upon his experience of quashing Islamists in 1987 by drawing a line in the sand between Islam, the religion of many Tunisians, and the distortions of Islam made by local fundamentalist and terrorist movements. His central argument was that homegrown fundamentalists, such as the *Ennahdha* Party, were using "double-talk" to exploit the religion of Islam for political means while using terrorism and violence.

In his crackdown on Islamists, either through submission or exile, he found backing among Western allies. Violent confrontations between Ben Ali's government and *Ennahdha* escalated and eventually led to an alleged Islamic attack on his party offices, in Bab Souika, on February 17, 1991. *Ennahdha* was accused of the offensive by Ben Ali, but they refuted the claims. Nonetheless, Ben Ali believed that *Ennahdha* was conspiring against him, exposing a plot for his assassination. In 1992, because of these accusations, two hundred and sixty-five *Ennahdha* members were arrested by the Tunisian military. To quell the militant threat and reinforce secularism, Ben Ali and his government began to tinker with their authoritarian bargaining agreement and he chose education as his focus to widen his social agreement with Tunisia.

In a speech on July 10, 1989, to celebrate national education day, Ben Ali reiterated the relationship between education and democracy by arguing that free will and an enlightened mind would provide the population with the power needed to create a modern history that would preserve Tunisian civilization and support its Arabic-Islamic culture. Under these broad canons, he sought to institute broad regulatory, institutional, financial, and pedagogical reforms across the education system to give the illusion to the rest of the world that Tunisia was continuing to transition to a full-fledged democracy. Ben Ali's education reforms of 1991, led by Minister of Basic and Higher Education and Scientific Research, Mohamed Charfi (from 1989–1994), under the Education Act, aimed at: (i) constructing more schools in rural areas; (ii) increasing school enrollment especially for girls; and (iii) introducing human rights and tolerance in the education programs (MOET 2002). In international documents, Ben Ali's government described the discourse of the 1991 Laws as:

> [...] the fruit of broad consultations affecting, in addition to teachers, educators and their representatives in the various pedagogic and trade-union structures, all the living components of the nation: political parties, national organizations, associations, etc. to the extent of undoubtedly constituting today one of the major achievements of the work of change carried out in Tunisia since 1987.
>
> UN Committee on the Rights of the Child 1994: 7–8

Collectively, the 1991-Education reforms became known as *les lois de Mohamed Charfi* (the laws of Mohamed Charfi), and came on the heels of Ben Ali's regime finally accepting that the promises of the 1958-Education reforms, which sought to provide access to adequate schooling, had not been fully realized despite the changes in economic and social structures that had taken place in the previous three decades. Ben Ali's movement toward completely overhauling the national education system in 1991 fixated on: (i) creating the perception of encouraging human rights; (ii) rooting out homegrown militant Islam; and (iii) expanding literacy. Ben Ali focused on reforming national education laws and promoting his image in the West as a democratic reformer, however Cavatorta and Haugbølle (2012) suggest his projection of embracing modernization and education reforms was a myth.

The 1991-Education reforms were a way for Ben Ali to suggest to the international community that Tunisia was equally invested in fixing its educational deficits as it was in embracing modernity and democratic governances in the education space, i.e., expanding schooling in rural areas, increasing enrollment among girls, and introducing human rights and tolerance programs into curricula. The aim of Ben Ali's education plan was to reduce dropout rates at the primary level and improve the quality of teachers. The 1991 Laws focused on "reshap[ing educational] structures according to a rational approach that takes into account the national reality, inspired of success instances worldwide" (MOHERST 2008: 71). It also added an end to primary cycle examinations to gain access to secondary school and promulgated education as part of the inclusive and the sustainable development of the country. It made education obligatory for all citizens until the age of sixteen and stipulated "the state guarantees, free of charge, to all school-age children, the right to schooling and the maximum equal opportunity to enjoy this right for as long as they [can] regularly attend their schools according to the regulations in force" (Chemingui and Sánchez 2011: 23). Thus, "education aims at cultivating ... fidelity and loyalty in students to Tunisia" (MOET 2002: 5) while increasing their "capacity for self-education and to prepare them for access to the educated community" (MOET 2002: 9). The 1991 Laws were unique in that they paid particular attention to the right to education for children with special needs.

The 1991 Laws also focused on scrutinizing school textbooks to ensure all statements encouraging intolerance of different religions and groups were deleted while he sought to retain the liberal aspects of Muslim thought in religious education (Faour 2012). For example, science curricula was revised to include non-Islamic ideas, such as Darwinian evolution and the Big Bang theory. Islamists argued that these changes were "de-Islamizing" Tunisian society (Faour 2012). In a speech in November 1992, Ben Ali stated that:

> ... Because we believe that the future is about education and intelligence, we have decided to revise the whole methodology of the educational system in order to overcome the negative impacts of the past. By orientating the educational institutions in the right way, we have begun to gain the fruits of this national

effort ... we are following the updates of the technologies in the world, we began, in the framework of a whole overview that contains the adaptation and the complicity between the educational system and the training system and also the demand in the market place, to build a modern and advanced system ... The purpose of this revision is to make the training system more effective by exploiting the energies that we have and to double the outcome of the training system of the country by modernizing the programs, the manners of training and prepare the trainers.

as cited in UNESCO 1992

In a speech in 1995, Ben Ali called for "a methodical and thorough renewal of the mission of the school ... in a world known to undergo profound changes affecting the organization of societies, the structure of knowledge, the methods of work and the means of production, in order to prepare us properly for the future" (as cited in Jemni 2010: 34). This call cemented the beginning of the structural reforms of vocational education. After winning a third term in the first multiparty presidential elections of 1999, Ben Ali's government established the National Employment Fund to fight underemployment and promote labor market integration for unemployed youth "whose level of education does not give them access to official vocational training provided by official establishments and those with higher education qualifications, who have acquired initial training in certain areas but have very few employment opportunities outside teaching" (Dridi 2006: 1). The Ministry of Vocational Training and Employment became responsible for Vocational Employment Training (VET) in over one hundred and thirty training centers in Tunisia, covering some two hundred specializations. VET was divided into three two-year cycles and certification was issued after successful completion of each cycle. After completing the second year of basic secondary education, students could enroll in the first two-year program and be awarded a *Certificat d'Aptitude Professionnelle* (a vocational training certificate) upon successful completion. Once students completed the first cycle, they could enroll for two additional years of vocational programs and be awarded a *Brevet de Technicien Professionnel* (a technical school certificate) at the end. Upon finishing the second cycle, students could work toward the completion of a diploma.

In preparation for the African Development Bank Group's funding of the Scientific and Technical Education Reinforcement Project (STERP) and the Secondary Education Support Project (SESP) in 1995,[9] in 1994 the regime again split the Ministry of Basic and Higher Education and Scientific Research into two separate ministries by creating the Ministry of Education and Science and the Ministry of Higher Education and Scientific Research. Almost no major reforms were undertaken until 2001 when the national end-of-secondary examination, *le Bac*, was restructured. Students could earn 25 percent of their final grade during the school year and the other 75 percent through written and oral examinations. Their total grade would be used for ranking examinees for university placement. In January 2002, a ministerial decree established a new method for calculating *le Bac*'s annual average. Students who failed their fourth year of secondary schooling could pass because they were able to count 25 percent of their pre-examination course work. The last major change to the *le Bac* was in 2004, when the Sport Baccalaureate was created.[10]

The 2002-Education Reforms: The Rouissi Plan, The School of Tomorrow, and Social Liberalism

In January of 1988 the National Commission on Reflection (*le Commission Nationale de Réflexion*), tasked with defining the contours of the "School of Tomorrow," released its report entitled "*The Big Orientations of the Reforms of the Educational System.*" The report noted that, after thirty years of experience initiated by the education laws of 1958, the Commission's role was to undertake a major revision of Tunisia's education policy. The Tunisian education system, weighted by heterogenic and inappropriate regulations, needed to face its new challenges due to the scientific and technological mutations and requirements of the economic, social, and cultural developments of the coming decades. The Commission made it clear that four fundamental tenets should guide any education reforms: (i) promote the Tunisian national culture by focusing on its authenticity and modernity; (ii) confirm the democratic character of the education system; (iii) guarantee social justice by ensuring every child has access to an education system appropriate to their skill-set as well as to social promotion; and (iv) allow the continuous adaptation of the educational policy to focus on the actual and anticipated needs of the country. The Committee went on to recommend specific reforms later adopted by the Ben Ali regime, namely, decentralization at the primary and secondary levels through use of "academies" and restructuring accountability and reporting mechanisms. At the same time, the Commission was cautious in its recommendations since it recognized the implementation of its proposals required a profound transformation in the actual structures of primary schools, colleges, and high schools and the redistribution of human and material means.

At the beginning of the 2000s, several multilateral donors funded Ben Ali's education project, commencing with SESP Phase I. In 2001, the World Bank lent Tunisia US$90 million for the Education System Quality Improvement Project (PAQSET I) aimed at promoting excellence in teaching and learning and greater inclusion and improved quality for children at all levels of the basic education system. In 2004, an additional US$130.34 million was provided for PAQSET II, which focused on improving the quality of basic education through the modernization of the management of school sectors, strengthening the systems of training, assessment, and infrastructure and boosting completion and enrollment rates for boys and girls aged six to eighteen years. In 2005, the African Development Bank financed €60 million for the Secondary Education Support Project (SESP Phase II) aimed at increasing the intake capacity and improving the quality of basic and secondary education through the promotion of the second cycle. At the time of its launching, this ambitious reform intended to train one hundred and fifty pedagogical instructors—inspectors, pedagogical advisers, teacher trainers—and four thousand teachers in different areas of secondary education reform, as well as to construct fifty new junior secondary schools and twenty high schools and to rehabilitate other schools ("AfDB Supports" 2005). In 2006, the European Commission support program contributed €36 million to fund improvement in the quality of secondary education.

In July 2002, Ben Ali was re-elected president and began the second round, and the most comprehensive set, of education reforms in the post-Bourguiba era, based on "social liberalism" (Mbougueng 1999). These reforms adopted aspects of neo-liberal market reforms in conjunction with massive state intervention in the social sector. The education reforms of 2002 aimed to fill the gaps left by the 1991 Laws by focusing on developing Tunisia's information society by ending school dropouts, mandating the Preparatory year (*année Préparatoire*) across the country, and generalizing physical education. The 2002 Laws emphasized:

- Putting education at the top of national priorities
- Working hard to make education more open to different cultures without neglecting Tunisian identity and historical traditions
- Operationalizing a student-centered approach to education
- Financial support for all the educational operations and literacy programs in order to achieve the national goals
- Giving importance to the quality of education

The main goal of the 2002-Education reforms was to decentralize the education system while encouraging local initiatives across its different levels.

Additionally, the regime placed emphasis on adding new programs that facilitated the learning of new technologies. As Ben Ali sought to develop an educated populace and project his image as a democratic leader:

> [a] Tunisian economic miracle [took place] ... [where the leadership sought] to tackle the most pressing problems of the country and then generate sufficient growth to be able to defuse social tensions in order to open up the political system without risking the growth of Islamic extremism (read Islamism), as economic success could be used to undermine the attraction of political Islam.
>
> Cavatorta and Haugbølle 2012: 183

The 2002 Laws regulated early childhood education (nurseries, kindergartens and/or *al-kuttabs*, and the Preparatory year), six years of primary education (basic education and lower secondary), four years of secondary education (upper secondary—general academic and specialized), and higher education (at any of the thirteen public universities). It stipulated education as a fundamental right guaranteed to all Tunisians without discrimination based on sex, social origin, color, or religion. The law aimed to strengthen awareness of national identity and a sense of belonging to a civilization with national dimensions, including Maghreb, Arab, Islamic, African, and Mediterranean histories, while reinforcing the country's openness to universal culture.

Building the School of Tomorrow into the Tunisia of Tomorrow

Under the Presidential Program *Tounes al-Ghad* (Tunisia of Tomorrow), from 2004 to 2009, education reforms coalesced around the idea of developing "a school for all in which each has a chance" (Ben Ali 2004: 15). In outlining his manifesto for the 2004 elections, Ben Ali placed education at the center of his platform by suggesting an expansion of democratic pluralism while rejecting fanaticism, extremism, and hatred and an interest in building an efficient Maghreb network, a strong joint-Arab action, and an efficient pan-African cooperation. The proposed reforms for primary and secondary education were comprehensive in that Ben Ali articulated his government would develop and implement curriculum programs that incorporated information and communication technologies into the teaching of various subjects of study, reduce class sizes, provide greater options for cultural education and arts, and develop better partnerships between schools and the environment. The presidential program also championed a focus on reducing dropouts, improving school quality, and establishing an information society by 2009.

On March 31, 2004, the World Bank approved a US$130 million loan for the second phase of the Education Quality Improvement Program (EQIP II), from 2004 to 2007. The project aimed to boost enrollment and completion rates for basic education. EQIP II was expected to complement the government's education plan by expanding access and developing stronger transition links between primary and secondary schooling. Also in 2004, the Minister of Education, Ahmed Raouf Najjar, made an executive order mandating that all school inspectors, who are responsible for implementing and controlling courses, had to take courses at the National Center of Training the Trainers in Education (CENAFF). However, by 2010, the OECD (2015a) reported that Tunisia's student performance on the Program for International Student Assessment (PISA) test remained low despite the reforms passed in preceding years. In fact, the OECD (2015a) concluded that Tunisia's education expenditure as a portion of the GDP shrank from an average of around 5 percent between 1990 and 2005 to approximately 4.6 percent between 2006 and 2010. In 2010,[11] under the regime's proposed decentralization plan for education, regional education commissions with fixed administrative and financial responsibilities were created to address the low student test scores.

A Word on Early Childhood Education

The literature on Early Childhood Education, or pre-primary or preschool education, before the French occupation, is scant since *le Collège Sadiki* provided preschool education in its *al-kuttabs*. Before the development of modern primary and secondary schools during the French Protectorate period (from 1881 to 1956), historically, *al-kuttabs* were defined as traditional Qur'anic schools. *Al-kuttabs* often referred to a religious school with a small learning unit (a single classroom) for young children, connected to a mosque (Akkari 2004: 2). The French established private kindergartens for the children of French colonialists, foreigners, wealthy elite, and people who worked with the French authorities (MOE 2015). These schools were often affiliated with the church. As part of preschool reforms, the *Madrasat al-Usfuriyya* training school (from 1894 to 1908) was open for the training of *muaddibs* (pre-school teachers), but it was disastrous because trained teachers ended up teaching in public primary schools

(Abdeljaouad 2014). In 1900, the first elementary school, the School of Pasha Street for Muslim girls, was opened with the aim of "ameliorat[ing] the lot of [Tunisian women] and provid[ing]Tunisian independence in 1956". Abdeljaouad (2014: 408–409) in citing Khairallah Ben Mustapha, one of the leaders of the Young Tunisian movement, notes that:

> In summer as in winter, children arrive at the sunrise... They drop out their tablets hanged on nails against the wall and sit in their respective places. After a first collective prayer, they start the individual dictation, which consists in continuation of the last verse written the day before by each student. Once the dictation is completed, the master takes the tablets one after the other to fix errors. Woe to the student who made mistakes! The hand of the *muaddib* is quick to slap his head and pull his ears ... Then comes the recitation, still in a very loud voice, then washing tablets ... The most advanced students rewrite with red ink letters or words already shaped with a non-cut reed pen on a tablet coated with clay. Then they learn them by repeating each letter or each word after the monitors, imitating his movements made by swinging the top of the body, until they learn them well ... Later all the students recite very loudly the first Qur'an surat (*al-Fatiha*) and a prayer.

By the time the march toward independence commenced, three types of schooling existed: (i) the French and French-Arabic, such as the Franco-Arabic schools; (ii) the native modern, such as *le Collège Sadiki*; and (iii) the native traditional, such as the Qur'anic schools. After independence, *al-kuttabs* were left to the discretion of local communities and private citizens. Alternative pre-primary education was available through modern schools, but at the age of six, all children went to public primary schools. In *al-kuttabs*, the teachers received some religious education but no formalized instruction (Abdeljaouad 2014). However, in the immediate independence period, preschool education facilities would be developed as part of the broader post-independence 1958-Education reforms, under Habib Bourguiba, which aimed at setting Tunisia along a path of secular modernization or *Tunisification*.

Concluding Thoughts—The Curtain Falls on *Tunisification*

Education reforms can be categorized as beginning after independence with the decade of Al Mesaadi (from 1958 to 1970). This was followed by two decades (the 1960s and 1970s) where no significant reforms took place until 1981. The next major improvements were in 1991 and 2002 under Ben Ali. The development of the post-Bourguiba space movement moved from *Tunisification* toward expanding access for Tunisians to the global market and financial capital.

Leila Ben Ali (formerly Trabelsi) married Ben Ali in 1992. After the marriage, the Trabelsi clan rose to prominence in Tunisia and eventually owned and controlled major interests in a majority of the most profitable sectors, such as retail, telecommunications, media, construction, car dealerships, and property. After Ben Ali took power in 1987, he promised that free market capitalism, under the auspices of IMF and World Bank-backed SAPs, would provide jobs through the privatization of several state industries. However, the forced march toward secular modernization in the form of state privatization was not fruitful. Instead, we see the rise of crony capitalism as Ben Ali and other regime loyalists took advantage of the economic openings provided by neo-liberalism. The Ben Ali clan and other blessed oligopolistic families mobilized their collective influence to regulate, dominate, and exploit every aspect of the economy that had or showed developmental potential. Therefore, it was no coincidence that the clan had its hands in education through the rigging of the national Baccalaureate examination by using bribery, nepotism, and blackmail. This was a drastic change from the implicit social pack and authoritarian bargaining that Bourguiba and his regime had developed with the Tunisian people.

In theory, the Ben Ali regime sought to buy off the population by promising them employment guarantees and first world social services in health care and education while subsidizing consumer goods. By the 1990s, many Tunisians identified themselves as being middle class. Ascribing to the middle class became linked to a university education based on merit and elitism, something that would change under the Ben Ali regime. Thus, Tunisians came to honor the implicit social pact, linking mobility to education, that the Bourguiba regime made with them. This "Faustian pact" (Clancy-Smith 2013) meant that middle-class existence was achieved mainly through education and access to consumer culture while accepting that open political dissent would not be tolerated by the regime. In return for obeying the Faustian pact, the Bourguiba regime refrained from interfering with the Baccalaureate examinations. Ultimately, the authoritarian bargaining of both the Bourguiba and Ben Ali regimes failed and the Tunisian response to the dysfunctional/low-performing/suffering state of government-mandated education would become the rallying call for uprisings in the interior regions of Tunisia in the 2008, 2010, and 2011 uprisings.

Higher Education and the Labor Market Information System

Higher education in Tunisia has always been a central component of the Tunisian authoritarian bargaining process under different dictatorial regimes. Nevertheless, the core focus of higher education reform has always concentrated on developing talent for the local job market, a practice dating back to the founding of *Madrasat al-Zitouna* (today *Ez Zitouna* University) in 732 BCE with its Arabic language and the Qur'an curriculum, which attracted both local and international students.[1] A small number of graduates from *Madrasat al-Zitouna* often took positions as Islamic teachers, judges in Sharia courts, or became members of the *Ulama* ranks (an exclusive group of religious leaders) (Green 1978; Jules and Barton 2014; Micaud 1964). In seeking to understand how discursive policymaking and policy practices informed Tunisia's education across different historical periods, this chapter focuses on the link between the weaning authoritarian bargaining established under different dictatorial regimes and the role of education in creating employment opportunities.

We argue that the rise in access to higher education created an expansion boom in the construction of new universities. Significant investments were placed on creating large "brick and mortar" universities, but limited monies were spent on professional development, hiring and retention of top faculty, and bureaucratic restructuring at universities. In this chapter, we draw on the analysis of our comparative-historical approach to historicize Tunisia's higher education system in the context of labor market mobility. We mostly discuss the reforms of Tunisia's public universities since they have dominated and continue to dominate the tertiary education sector.

Next, we chronicle the historical evolutionary dynamics of higher education in Tunisia. We then turn to higher education reforms during the different dynastic empires that ruled Tunisia, including the reforms under the last Bey of Tunisia. The second half of the chapter covers the major post-independence reforms in 1958, 1987, 1991, and 2008 that significantly restructured the tertiary system. We conclude the chapter by discussing the rise of religious education after *al-sahwa*.

Tunisian Labor Market Dynamics

Access to higher education is free at any of the one hundred and ninety-two public institutions of higher education. The higher education system, supervised by the Ministry of Higher Education, Scientific Research and Technology (MOHESRT), consists of thirteen state universities (including the Virtual University) and four main types of institutions of higher education in Tunisia: (i) universities (*universités*); (ii) faculties (*facultés*); (iii) *institutes* (*instituts*); and (iv) specialized schools (*écoles*).[2] Across the public university system, there are twenty-four Higher Institutes of Technological Studies (*Instituts Supérieurs D'études Technologiques* [ISETs]) created in 1992 and six higher institutes of teacher training (*Instituts Supérieurs de Formation des Maîtres*). Additionally, there is the network of ISETs that is governed by the Directorate-General for Technological Studies and the Virtual University of Tunis, which is responsible for providing distance learning and the management and digitization of courses for all public universities. Both public and private higher education institutions are open to all students who have completed their secondary education and have been awarded the *Diplôme du Baccalauréat*.

The demand for higher education far outstrips the available capacity and space since more students are passing *le Bac*, considered the gatekeeper to accessing higher education (Gyimah-Brempong and Ondiege 2011). Upon completing their *Diplôme du Baccalauréat*, students apply to public universities through the centrally controlled system, the National University Orientation System (*Système National d'Orientation Universitaire*),[3] which uses an algorithm to compute student preference, scores, and program of instruction at the secondary level. While admission to tertiary institutions is contingent on performance in *le Bac*, secondary school grades, coursework and enrollment quotas placed on specific programs, in recent years more and more students who get lower grades in their *le Bac* will write their *Concours de Ré-orientation*[4] (the Re-specialization Examination) that allows them to change their proposed field of study. In fact, attendance and completion of a higher education degree are viewed as a rite of passage for the middle class and elites. Tunisia's higher education system is decentralized in theory, but in practice is centralized, wherein MOHESRT sets a yearly quota for each field of study and institution.

The so-called decentralization of the Tunisian system raises questions as to whether the governorates truly had power or if it was policy-on-paper only.

MOHESRT is regulated under the Higher Educational Framework of 1989 and Law No. 4 of 2008, allowing MOHESRT to accredit private and public universities. Tunisia has defined the goal of its education system as that of preparing its youth to compete on the global stage. As such, Tunisian officials compare its education system to those of the European Union, Finland, North America, Asia, Australia, and New Zealand (MOET 2003). Yet, from a quality perspective, Tunisia's higher education system is ranked first regionally (Africa) and high in the top quartile globally (Gyimah-Brempong and Ondiege 2011; UNESCO 2007). When Tunisia is compared to its closest counterparts in the region (South Africa and Kenya), it spends almost twice as much, about 2 percent of GDP, on higher education. When compared to OECD countries that spend on average 1.5 percent of their budgets on university research and laboratories, Tunisia spends 2.5 percent on improving its facilities, which are outdated and dilapidated. Tunisia does not see its higher education system competing with other African higher education systems, which may potentially set up the nation for future lending purposes to other African countries. Overall, the Tunisian aim has always been to design a system that has worldwide recognition and is the "standard bearer of sciences, knowledge and research" (MOHESRT 2008: 15). Gyimah-Brempong and Ondiege (2011) in a World Bank study note that 0.05 percent is the global average of the adult population that completes tertiary education while 0.2 is the African average. However, in Tunisia, 6.2 percent of the adult population has completed tertiary education. They further argue that enrollments in tertiary education in Tunisia between 2000 and 2007 increased by 102 percent resulting in a 32 percent gross enrollment rate,[5] which is very high by African standards. However, the percentage of young people seeking access to higher education is expected to rise drastically since *al-sahwa*. The current government has expressed interest in deepening existing public-private partnerships and developing new ones (through subsidies, land grants, and other incentives) in higher education.

Labor market information is defined as "any information concerning the size and composition of the labor market or any part of the labor market, the way it or any part of it functions, its problems, the opportunities which may be available to it and the employment related intentions or aspirations of those who are part of it" (Thuy, Hansen and Price 2001: 57). Historically, not enough information has been collected from the school-to-work transition in Tunisia. The African Union (2004), in its Ouagadougou Declaration and *Plan of Action on Employment and Poverty Alleviation*, called for the development and bolstering of labor market information systems criteria and prioritized the elimination of unemployment. In fact, the Tunisian labor market transformed profoundly under the tutelage of Ben Ali's administration, due to internal threats of the early 1980s (demographic, political, and economic developments) and external realignment with the implementation of SAPs aimed at privatization, deregulation, and the liberalization of the economy. Other contributory factors for lack of adequate labor market gathering techniques included the efficacy of SAPs, increased unemployment among university graduates and the liberalization of the educational service as Tunisia opened its economy for entry into the Free Trade Area with the European Union.

While it is arduous to observe the labor market directly and to ascertain its volume, Ben Ali's regime did not collect any information to support new reform in education that would have rectified labor market policies and programs. In line with its implicit authoritarian bargaining agreement, rather than paying attention to the needs of the Tunisian labor market, which had changed drastically since access to higher education was expanded in the early 1980s, the Ben Ali regime undertook higher education reforms in a haphazard way to: (i) fulfill the conditionalities external donors placed upon borrowed monies; and (ii) buy time, as the regime hoped jobs would eventually materialize. The challenge was that the transition from the steering economy dominated by state-owned enterprises and developed under Bourguiba's regime, to an open economy driven by private sector growth was an ill-conceived reform that was externally driven. The biggest problem was that the skills of university graduates did not match what the market needed. The Tunisian university system continued to produce bureaucrats for post-colonial French posts that no longer existed. The push toward a private sector growth model under Ben Ali and his regime only benefited him, the ruling families, and party affiliates as investments first went into the tourism industry. These investments sparked a construction boom aimed only at establishing service industry training facilities for the emergent sector so did not benefit other sectors.

Tunisia's size allowed for a rapid dispersal of education efforts throughout the nation "progressively through and starting from the sixties; the university institutions have spread out to the towns of the interior. With this impetus came the setting up of the research structures and the Tunisification of the teaching staff" (MOHESRT 2008: 18). The 1969 Education Law "stipulates that the council of the university presidency would be headed by the state secretary of the national education" thus ending the independence of the university. Higher education came directly under state control. In the 1970s, the higher education system was essentially dissolved, "putting an end to the structure as defined by the decree of 1960" (MOHESRT 2008: 48). A key component of policy is to give to each governorate control of its higher education system; an example of this is the University of Tunis.

In 2003, MOET suggested, "it's time for the university level institutions to proliferate in all regions. Rarely would you find a governorate that does not have a faculty, a college or a technological institute" (MOET 2003: 15), relating the importance of decentralization. The movement from the autonomous University of Tunis to the decentralized faculties overseen by the governorates locally and MOHESRT nationally let the policymakers consolidate the power of the university to combat globalization, as "externally, profound and rapid 'mutations' [had upset their] world vision and affected all the fields of social and individual life" (MOET 2003: 11). The shift of the university was meant to be a major force in Tunisia's grappling with the consequences of economic globalization. As far as education policy, it meant that practices amongst the universities in Tunis would be the same, as they would all come from the central office in Tunis. The convergence led to changes in curriculum and pedagogy and removed the freedom of individual professors and school administrators to guide the development of the institutions. Therefore, convergence and consolidation of the education system led to a restriction of academic freedom within higher education, particularly given that up until *al-sahwa* Directors and Deans in universities were appointed by MOHESRT (something that only changed after 2011).

Historicizing Higher Education

While there is no accurate description of higher education practices and patterns in ancient Tunisia based on how higher education is viewed today, we know from historical evidence that the Phoenicians were maritime traders and intermediaries who eventually founded colonies in Cyprus, Sicily, Sardinia, Southern Spain, and along the shores of North Africa. We know that they had a written language, an alphabet, and probably some form of a post-primary education system. The arrival of the Romans led to the eventual Romanization of North Africa and the adoption of the Roman system of higher education. Roman education was based upon the Greek system and with time evolved from an informal familial system to one based on tuition. The education system was exported to all Roman provinces, thus allowing it to eventually become the foundation of Western Civilization. As Clark (2005) points out, Romanization was achieved through a "symbolic means" since basic education was readily available in several provincial schools (see Chapter 3). However, a student with sufficient means would have journeyed from *Ifriqiya* (the name of the former Roman Province of Africa) to Rome to complete their studies in higher education.

We know that in 370 Roman officials passed a law that sought to curb the number of North Africans entering the city of Rome. However, those North Africans who had an opportunity to partake in higher levels of education would have been exposed to the Latin classics. Since Rome's unofficial policy was one of "cooperation" and not "warfare" in North Africa, it is important to note that North Africans had access to Roman higher education, which emphasized that Roman rulership of the civilized world would be by divine providence (Clark 2005). The Roman system with its different tiers (moral education, litterator, grammaticus, and rhetor) would have been replicated in some form or the other in *Ifriqiya*. We know that the famous Tunisian, *Aurelius Augustinus Hipponensis* (Saint Augustine), attained his higher education studies in Carthage and eventually moved and taught Rhetoric there as well.

Rhetoric (the Art of Discourse) was the final stage of Roman education that an *Ingenium* (Gifted) student could attain. Students studying and using *Rhetoric* in *Ifriqiya* focused on the "faculty of observing in any given case the available means of persuasion" (Aristotle Book 1, *trans.* W. Rhys Roberts 1991). Thus, the focus on higher education of the time was on the means of persuasion that aimed at being able: "(i) to reason logically; (ii) to understand human character and goodness in their various forms; and (iii) to understand the emotions, that is, to name them and describe them, to know their causes and the way in which they are excited" (Aristotle Book 1, *trans.* W. Rhys Roberts 1991). More important, *Rhetor* was the art of shaping public discussion and opinions.

Higher Education under the Dynastic Empires of *Ifriqiya*

Of all the Arabic Caliphates that inhabited *Ifriqiya*, two of them – the Aghlabid Caliphate from 800 to 909 and the Husainid Caliphate from 1705 to 1881 – and the French from 1881 to 1956 contributed significantly to the development and expansion of the system of higher education. The Great Mosque of Kairouan

(*Masjid Okba Ibn Nafaa*) was the first educational institution of higher learning in what is modern-day Tunisia, founded in 670 BCE[6] by the General Uqbah ibn Nafi.[7] The great mosque was destroyed in 690 BCE and finally rebuilt in 703 BCE. Both the Umayyad Caliphate (from 661 to 750 it ruled from Damascus) and the Abbasid Caliphate (from 750 to 800, founded by Ibrahim Ibn al-Aghlab after he restored stability in 797) paid little attention to the development of higher education in *Ifriqiya*. Because the Umayyad Caliphate ruled out of Damascus, it had no reason to invest in libraries and colleges of higher learning in *Ifriqiya*. Although the Umayyad Caliphate fell in 750, the Abbasid Caliphate was not created until almost fifty years later due to instability in *Ifriqiya* and constant Berber *Kharijite* revolts, which meant that Caliphs from East of them could not control the region. During the rise of these two Caliphates, students from North Africa would undertake studies in higher education in the intellectual centers of Damascus (Umayyad Caliphate), Baghdad (Abbasid Caliphate), and later Cairo (the Fatimid Caliphate).

Early students traveled to Tunisia from all over the Muslim Occident to attend *Madrasat al-Zitouna*, the Mosque of *al-Zitouna* in La Kasbah Tunis,[8] founded in 734 BCE and recognized worldwide as one of the oldest institutions of higher education for traditional Islamic learning and scholarship (DeGorge 2002; Sizer 1971). In fact, *Madrasat al-Zitouna's* "impact spread beyond the boundaries of the country thanks to the great culture and aura of its scientists who taught there" (MOHESRT 2008: 24). *Madrasat al-Zitounas* were small institutions of learning connected to local mosques (*masjids*) and were privately funded. The most promising students advanced their religious studies by attending *Madrasat al-Zitouna* in the major cities. However, during its heyday, *Madrasat al-Zitouna's* curriculum focused on instructing students in the Arabic language and the Qur'an, using similar pedagogical instructions to those of *al-kuttabs* (see Chapter 3), albeit much more advanced and based on rote memorization (Green 1978; Jules and Barton 2014). It was not until the rise of the Aghlabid dynasty and the designation of *al-Kairouan* (*stronghold*) as its capital that higher education flourished in the different *madares* attached to *masjids al-Zitouna*. The expansion of higher education occurred under the "Islamic golden age" (from the eighth century to the thirteenth century) that was a period of stability and prosperity as trade flourished and tremendous advances were made in mathematics, arts, and medicine. *Madrasat al-Zitouna's* of Tunis (hereinafter *Madrasat al-Zitouna*) role expanded in 864 when a new wing was added to the mosque. In addition to learning the Qur'an, *Madrasat al-Zitouna* provided students with basic reading, writing, and arithmetic skills. Gaining acceptance into *Madrasat al-Zitouna* was difficult, with only eight to nine hundred students enrolled annually (Green 1978). Students had to have graduated with high standing from *al-kuttab*, be at least twelve years old, able to read and write and have a significant portion of the Qur'an memorized (Sizer 1971).

Under the Fatimid Caliphate, a Shia sect, which ruled from 909 to 973, education reforms were incorporated into the expansion of the dynasty as it expanded, and the Caliphate eventually conquered Egypt and established Cairo (*al-Qahirah*) as its capital. After the Fatimid Caliph moved its capital from Tunisia, no new institutions of higher learning were established in Tunisia, but students benefited tremendously from the establishment of libraries and colleges in Cairo,[9] whose main purpose was to spread Islam. As noted above, students wishing to pursue higher education would do so in the intellectual capital of Fatimid's Caliphate, Cairo. With the fall of the Fatimid Caliphate, four Berber dynasties (whose rulers had converted to Islam by the eighth century) rose to power between 973 and 1574: they were (i) the Zirid dynasty from 973 to 1148/1152; (ii) the Norman dynasty from 1148 to 1160; (iii) the Almohad dynasty from 1160 to 1229; and (iv) the Hafsid dynasty from 1229 to 1574. These dynasties did not make any drastic improvements to higher education in *Ifriqiya*.

It was not until the ascendancy of the dictator Ahmed Ibn Mustafa (from 1837 to 1855) of the Husainid dynasty (hereinafter referred to as Bey Ahmed and his government as the Bey; also, called the great reformer, modernizer, and abolisher),[10] and his authoritarian bargaining of *Le Pacte Fondamental* of 1857 that higher education reforms began in earnest as part of a system-wide effort of nation building. Bey Ahmed came to power in an independent and autonomous province that was still part of the Ottoman Empire. In higher education, Bey Ahmed concentrated his efforts on "introducing administrative, staff, teaching and financial measures designed to make the pursuit of Islamic knowledge more systematic and stable" (El-Mesawi 2008: 50). The Suspended Decree (*al-Mu'allaqah*) of 1842 established "a supervisory body consisting of the two shaykhs and the two chief judges of both schools" (El-Mesawi 2008: 50). Additionally, the Bey donated thousands of books to *Madrasat al-Zitouna* to create a permanent and cataloged library and appointed "two officers in the library to look after its management, thereby facilitating 'the pursuit of knowledge for the poor and the rich alike'" (as cited in El-Mesawi 2008: 51).

In 1842, the Bey and other religious hardliners of the time called for the restructuring of *Madrasat al-Zitouna* through the introduction of new disciplines and incentives for teachers in Tunisia. As Tibi (1974) observes:

Thus the reforms of the Zaitounian educational system, the efforts deployed by Sheikh Ibrahim al-Raiahi for renewing traditional teaching methods, the encouragements by Ahmed Bey or other Tunisian dignitaries to educational institutions, traditional and modern, the frequency visits to *al-Zitouna* and the Polytechnic of Bardo by Ahmed Bey and his ministers, among other facts were preparing the mutation of Tunisian society and consequently the creation of a new social group in favor of the adaptation of the traditional social systems to new requirements of change.

as cited in Bsaies 1989: 276

With the dawn of the nineteenth century, higher education reforms were gradual, unrelenting and fixated on the "non-conducive internal and external environment" (El-Mesawi 2008: 52).

In the 1870s, Prime Minister Pacha (from 1873 to 1877), who had lived in Europe in the 1860s, began to focus his attention on modernizing Tunisian educational institutions, especially *Madrasat al-Zitouna*. Subsequently, his Minister of Education and Public Works, General Muhammad Hussein, instituted higher education reforms that sought to reorganize Islamic education in *Madrasat al-Zitouna* by dividing studies into high, intermediate, and elementary levels. Since graduates of the university often held bureaucratic positions, Pacha aimed to reform the university to match the needs of contemporary Tunisians (Perkins 1986). In the end, *Madrasat al-Zitouna* remained conservative, with little change to the curriculum and after the arrival of the French in 1881, kept the "Islamic tradition alive by carrying out its ritual and legal duties" (Sizer 1971: 6).

In 1883, *Madrasat al-Zitouna* came under the Directorate of Public Education, with Louis Machuel as the Director of Education, as well as several religious institutions (Green 1978). Graduates from *le Collège Sadiki* and the other modern educational establishments began to criticize this new form of adopted education system. They argued for their own society's need "to make room for concepts and practices then current in the West but without discarding the Arab–Islamic traditions in which it rested" (Perkins 1986: 92). In response to their concerns, the alumni began publishing *al Hadira*, which promoted societal change while maintaining Islamic principles (Perkins 1986). In 1898, at the behest of Director Machuel, a commission comprising *Shaykh al-Islam* (education inspectors) and seven university professors was established to reform *Madrasat al-Zitouna*. This led to the opening of a new educational organization on December 22, 1896, entitled *Al-Jam'iyyah Al-Khalduniyyah*, (named after a famous Tunisian philosopher and historian Ibn Khaldun),[11] which was designed to provide students attending *Madrasat al-Zitouna* with a European curriculum in addition to their Islamic education (Anderson 1986).

Al-Jam'iyyah al-Khaldouniyah, as a new educational institution, was founded in response to the dominant renewal tendency that kept resisting the mainly religious educational patterns at that time. The new institution's educational orientations were considered pivotal and fundamental for the advancement of profound reforms to an archaic system that had *Masjid al-Zitouna* at its center. This movement was led by the Tunisian reformist and militant Béchir Sfar who fought for the establishment of the first modern public school in Tunisia, *Madrasat al-khaldouniyah*. *Al-Jam'iyyah Al-Khalduniyah* was the first modern school, established in 1896, aimed at providing students with a scientific education, which was viewed as a modern education. In fact, *Al-Jam'iyyah Al-Khalduniyah* planned to spread a trend of science, geography, mathematics, and law and to destroy the residual stereotypes from exclusively religious schools/ curricula by developing critical thinking and analyzing skills among the *adherent* students (Latrech 2007).

Al-Jam'iyyah Al-Khalduniyah promoted the need for progressive reforms in education and the family. In practice, *Al-Jam'iyyah Al-Khalduniyah* (and *le Collège Sadiki*) functioned to undermine the position of *Madrasat al-Zitouna*. Eventually, they would serve as the incubator for the development of a new class of secularist/Westernist elites who would later establish the *Neo-Destour* Party and lead Tunisia to independence (Lulat 2005). *Al-Jam'iyyah Al-Khalduniyah* aimed at familiarizing Tunisians from a different educational background with each other and therefore attracted students from *Madrasat al-Zitouna* and other educational experiences.

The French viewed *Madrasat al-Zitouna* as a bastion of cultural resistance against French influence. Unlike other colonies, France's policy position toward *Madrasat al-Zitouna* was, for the most part, one of isolation; they focused on incorporating the system rather than weakening it (Lulat 2005). Although the *le Collège Sadiki* graduates worked in tandem with French officials to establish *Al-Jam'iyyah Al-Khalduniyah* (Lulat 2005; Micaud 1964), the officials became concerned that the modern education system was "creating an educated elite who could cause political problems" (DeGorge 2002: 583). Their concerns were substantial; Tunisians became less passive and more concerned with maintaining their culture as they were simultaneously given more access to schools with advanced curricula.

The reformers, who began to act politically, became known as *Les Jeunes Tunisiens*, named after the Turkish revolutionaries, the Young Turks (DeGorge

2002). One of their most salient demands was to make modern education more readily available to all Tunisians, in both urban and rural areas. As a result, the Department of Public Education began to deny access to the European-style education system for Tunisians (Anderson 1986). On December 16, 1912, a statute organizing the education system at the *Madrasat al-Zitouna* decreed that the institution should have three cycles: (i) *al-Ahlya* (a primary cycle leading to an Aptitude Degree); (ii) *al-Tahcil* (an intermediate cycle resulting in the Proficiency Degree); and (iii) *al-Alimy* (a higher education cycle leading to the Scholarship Degree).

In 1933, reforms were undertaken to revise the syllabuses and create an "*al-Tatwii*" degree to become the "*al-Tahcil*" (comparable to the Baccalaureate or "A" levels) (Ez Zitouna 2005). In 1944, the French established the Higher Education Institute of Tunis, the Tunisian School of Management, and the Law Institute. In April 1951, a modern branch was created and a two-stage *al-Tahcil* degree was instituted. However, this modern branch experienced a period of decline from the late 1950s onwards, following the rise of the unified secondary education system whose syllabuses had been gradually introduced by the Tunisian government starting in October 1958.

The Last Beylic Reforms

Outside of *Madrasat al-Zitouna,* "the Institute of Higher Studies ... which depends on the University of Paris may be considered as the matrix and cornerstone to modern Tunisian higher education" (MOHESRT 2008: 25) and therefore, in the 1950s, the Bey sought to modernize *Madrasat al-Zitouna* after the student sit-ins. The problem was that *le Collège Sadiki* had undergone reforms to modernize, while students at *Madrasat al-Zitouna* could not pass the national examination. In 1955, the management of the Public Education Department was transferred to Tunisian officials. Then, on March 20, 1956, after signing the "Internal Autonomy Agreement," Habib Bourguiba returned to Tunisia to take up the positions of president of the National Constituent Assembly (NCA)[12] and designated prime minister. On March 29, 1956, Muhammad VIII Bey al-Amin, issued Decree No. 96[13] that sought, for the first time, to organize and modernize the teaching in *Madrasat al-Zitouna* and its annexes.

This Decree not only tweaked the authoritarian bargaining agreement between the *Bey* and the people, but it argued the purpose of education in *Madrasat al-Zitouna* and its branches is preserving the Sharia and the Arabic language and teaching modern sciences to the students of these institutes.

Article 2 of the Decree made *Madrasat al-Zitouna* public institutes, with a civil personality—directed by an appointed dean directly attached to the Ministry of Knowledge. Article 3 stated that *Madrasat al-Zitouna* are institutes of higher education responsible for preparing students to obtain diplomas in language, Arab literature, and the Sharia. Article 20 stipulates the purpose of education in *Madrasat al-Zitouna* and its branches is the preservation of Sharia and the Arabic language and educating students in these institutes in modern sciences. Article 21 recognized the different divisions of *Madrasat al-Zitouna*, comprising secondary education (with its three divisions: readings, religious studies, and modern division) and higher education (with its five divisions: readings, the origins of religion, the religious judiciary, morals, and language).

However, this Decree left the curriculum content and examination structure of *Madrasat al-Zitouna* under the purview of the Ministry of Education, adding responsibilities for educational programs and materials to the Ministry's portfolio. The Beylical Decree No. 116[14] of April 26, 1956 nullified the *Madrasat al-Zitouna* that was created as an institute of secondary and higher education as well as an organization of the Great Mosque of Tunis (*Al Jamii Al Ahdham* of Tunis) and its annexes. The 1956 Beylical Decree also added the title of *Jamiat* (university) to *Madrasat al-Zitouna*, giving it the name *Jamiat al-Zitouna* (*al-Zitouna University*) (El Ayechi 2012). Between 1956 and 1957, many new higher educational institution were created, such as the Higher House of Teachers and the College of Arts.

The 1958-Education Reforms and the *Tunisification* of Higher Education

At independence, Tunisia did not have a well-established higher education system by Western benchmarks, just a few agricultural research centers and colonial outposts, such as France's *Pasteur Institute* in Tunis. It is critical to note here that the higher education system that already existed in Tunisia only achieved modern status when it was linked to, or built upon, the system imported and transferred by the French. Indeed, "the stage was prepared by the creation of the *École Normale Supérieure* (Higher Normal School) in 1956, the first institution of higher education in independent Tunisia" (MOHESRT 2008: 27). Therefore, in the immediate post-independence period, higher education reforms "... had to respond to the needs of an independent and modern nation that has the ambition to maintain sovereignty and its own personality and to beam both on the regional and worldly environment" (MOHESRT 2008: 18).

These higher education reforms sought to provide greater access to "training consonant with demands and needs of a society that aspires to progress and is resolutely open onto modernity" (MOET 2003: 9). These reforms would, ideally, provide a new generation of workers to fill the colonial bureaucracies that had been developed and would deliver training consistent with Bourguiba's vision of building a modern secular Tunisia. On November 4, 1958, Law on Education No. 58–118, a ten-year plan, (hereinafter the 1958-Education reforms) was passed and for the first time, the education system was divided into three cycles: (i) primary school cycle (covered in section one); secondary school cycle (covered in section two); and higher education (covered in section three). Section three of the 1958-Education reforms identified the conditions and regulations of higher education and Article 25 outlined the fundamental roles of higher education as:

(a) To exempt, in the various domain of sciences, techniques, literature and arts, a culture of the highest level.
(b) To contribute in these same domains, to the development and to the continuous progress of the science, conceptions, means and scientific research's methods.
(c) To form the researchers and the scholars and to provide the ways and the means in order to enhance the vitality of their creative scientific activity.
(d) Ensure the training of the senior executives, scientists, techniques, and non-techniques, necessary for the life of the nation and the teachers of the second degree and to beneficiate the education in its various degrees of the science of progress and knowledge.

MOE 1958: 8

After independence, the authoritarian bargaining changed and with the centralization of governance activities under the state, religious institutions lost their appeal and were considered impractical (Micaud 1964). Bourguiba was a staunch supporter of *Madrasat al-Zitouna* and he often emphasized the role of *Madrasat al-Zitouna* in resisting the colonial system in both Tunisia and Algeria. Therefore, when the education system was unified under Mahmoud Al Mesaadi, the branches of *Madrasat al-Zitouna* became middle schools instead of high schools through the removal of the fifth and sixth grade classes. These changes in the branches of *Madrasat al-Zitouna* led to critics arguing that this change could endanger the integrity of Islam and the Arab–Islamic personality of *Madrasat al-Zitouna*.

In addition to restructuring *Madrasat al-Zitouna*, Bourguiba and his regime embarked upon a process of *Tunisification* as "the post-independence Tunisian government's desire to use education to create citizen-subjects ... in which Westernization and Tunisian Islamic culture would be 'synthesized'" (Champagne 2007: 204). The development of higher education in Tunisia "... relied in 1958 on institutions and schools that already existed during colonization and which were adapted to be converted into national institutions" (MOHESRT 2008: 17). The process of *Tunisification* began with the Beylic Decree No. 98[15] that created the University of Tunis (*Université de Tunis*) by combining the School of Fine Arts, the Higher School of Commerce and the Classes of Higher Letters, and Special Mathematics of *Lycée Carnot* (Bourguiba's High School) (Siino 2004). The new university began with six faculties: Natural Sciences, Physics, Mathematics and Science; Medicine and Pharmacy; Law, Political Science and Economic Science; Letters and Human Sciences; Theology; and *École Normale Supériure.*

With this Beylic Decree, "the Tunisian university, a major link in the process of the *Tunisification* of education was created by the finance law promulgated on [March 31, 1960]" (MOHESRT 2008: 32). The goals of the *Tunisification* process were two-fold: (i) to create a new cadre of professors at the University of Tunis; and (ii) to keep Tunisian students in the country through three core elements (a) evoking history, (b) enhancing culture and religion, and (c) promoting gender equity. Then, the complementary Beylic Decree No. 110[16] of March 1, 1961 expanded the University of Tunis to include the Faculty of Sharia and the Origins of Religion[17] (that was later incorporated into *Ez al-Zitouna* University in 1987) by stripping *Jamiat al-Zitouna* of its independent status. In the post-independence period, the religious education offered by *Jamiat al-Zitouna* was not a significant contributor to the economic development of the country. There was a desire to keep *Jamiat al-Zitouna* going, most likely because of its significance within religious circles in the Arab world.

The reforms to *Jamiat al-Zitouna* aimed at providing education in one language, Arabic, so that students would be able to complete their studies and proceed to university. In October 1961, the curricula for the Bachelor's degree in Sharia, sciences, and theology were finalized. Bourguiba's government integrated the teachers of *Jamiat al-Zitouna* into the public service sector, something that was in stark contrast to colonial times. The National School of Engineers and the Higher Institute of Enterprise Management were created in 1969 at the University of Tunis, and with time, other institutions, such as teacher training colleges were added to the university.

The University of Tunis was created to educate a new crop of post-independence students wishing to fill the bureaucratic positions held by former French residents (Rossi 1967). However, upon opening its doors, the University of Tunis faced a shortage of local Tunisian professional staff and most of the teachers across the faculties were foreigners (MOHESRT 2008). During the experimentation with "Tunisian cooperative socialism" in the 1960s, no significant reforms were undertaken. The next higher education reform occurred on January 24, 1969 and stipulated that "the council of the university presidency would be headed by the state secretary of the national education" (MOHESRT 2008: 48), moving the system under the direct control of the government. Finally, in 1969, a higher education law was passed and it decreed that government-recognized institutions of higher learning would be placed under the University of Tunis. The institutes, faculties, and schools were separated and, after some time, several of them were transformed into new universities.

In 1971, after Mohammed Mzali was appointed as Minister of Education, he decentralized the faculties of medicine in Sousse and Sfax and modified the relationship between the University of Tunis and the Center for Studies, Economic and Social Relations (Allman 1979). The Education Law of July 12, 1976 not only reinforced Bourguiba's vision of free access to higher education, it "defined the mission of higher education and scientific research and directed orientations (MOHESRT 2008: 58)." The Law stipulated the conditions of eligibility to attend university and the organization of higher education. The Law also called for "the preservation and reinforcement of humanity and civilization values so as to consolidate and perpetuate the national and cultural identity through the systematic teaching of the Arabic language" (MOHESRT 2008: 58). The law did not make a distinction between public and private provision and supply of higher education.

Finally, in 1978, the government divided the Ministry of National Education into two ministries. The Ministry of National Education became responsible for the management of primary and secondary education (technical and professional) and the Ministry of Higher Education and Scientific Research was placed in charge of higher education and fundamental and applied research. By the early 1980s, the *Tunisification* of the teaching personnel was achieved as the large crop of foreign faculty members were replaced by Tunisians who had been trained at the University of Tunis (MOHESRT 2008).

Throughout Bourguiba's era, the number of enrollees in higher education and the number of teachers grew. The expansion of enrollment led to the government borrowing monies for infrastructural projects, as exemplified in the construction of dormitories for eight hundrad boys and girls at the Higher

Institute of Technical Training Instructors in Nabeul. From the time Ben Ali and his new regime ascended to power on November 7, 1987, after the medical *coup d'état* until his demise on January 14, 2011, higher education underwent three intensive reform periods: the 1987 reforms; the 1991 reforms; and the 2008 reforms.

The 1987-Education Reforms: Infrastructural Expansionism to Alleviate Unemployment

With the medical *coup d'état* that peacefully transferred power from Bourguiba to Ben Ali, the authoritarian bargaining changed as the Ben Ali regime promised sweeping reforms based on free markets, choice, and democratic governance in return for obedience to the regime. With the growing number of students seeking higher education, by the mid-1980s, several new universities[18] were created under Law No. 80 of August 9, 1986—the University of Tunis for the North (*Université de Tunis Pour le Nord*), the University of Monastir for the Center (*Université de Monastir Pour le Centre*), and the University of Sfax for the South (*Université de Sfax*[19] *Pour le Sud*). Additionally, in 1986, the Ministry of National Education and the Ministry of Higher Education were merged to create a new centralized Ministry of Basic and Higher Education and Scientific Research. It was the Finance Law of December 31, 1986 that paved the way for a massive infrastructural expansion plan in higher education. Ben Ali's rush to restructure higher education across the country focused on reshaping educational "structures according to a rational approach that considers the national reality, inspired of success instances worldwide" (MOHERST 2008: 71).

In return for loyalty to the regime, the fundamental reforms under the 1987 Finance Law aimed at delaying the provision of jobs for an over-educated booming middle class and curbing the number of students who were seeking degrees in higher education given the lack of employment in the economy at the time. Thus, the 1987 reforms were Band-Aid solutions to temporarily reduce youth unemployment. The higher education reforms were incorporated under Article 97 of the 1987 Finance Law that called for the organization of the University of Tunis into three separate institutions of higher education—Tunis University I (Faculty of Sciences, Techniques and Medicine—founded in 1988); Tunis University II (Faculty of Law, Economics and Management); and Tunis University III (Faculty of Letters, Arts and Human Sciences)—Article 96 of the same law made provisions for the establishment of *Jamiat al-Zitouna*[20] (today called *Ez Zitouna* University) and replacing the Faculty of Sharia at the University of Tunis, which included three institutions: (i) the Institute of Sharia; (ii) the Institute of Religion's Origins; and (iii) the Institute of Religious Guidance)[21] (*Journal Officiel de la République Tunisienne* [JORT] 1987).

In 1988, with the change of the *Destourian* Socialist Party to the Democratic Constitutional Rally and presidential elections firmly behind him, Ben Ali and his regime commenced with a new expansionist phase in higher education anchored by two events. First, in January 1988, the National Commission on Reflection was established to consider the contours of the "School of Tomorrow" (*l'école de Demain*). In its report entitled the Big Orientations of the Reforms of the Educational System (*les Grandes Orientations des Réformes du Système educatif*), the Commission's recommendation was clear. It called for the consolidation and organizing of institutions of higher learning and universities to make them more efficient at the national level. The Commission further stipulated that a reduction in the failure rate of first-year university students could be reversed through the implementation of a one-year "preparatory year" training program organized by the universities, or by a group of institutions from neighbors' disciplines. Its recommendation fell within the purview of the overall 1989 reforms that called for "... the university decentralization and the autonomy of the universities in the fields of the administrative, financial and pedagogical management ..." to "... reduce pressure on the north-east pole of the capital" through the establishment of centers in Bizerte and Gafsa (MOHESRT 2008: 71–74).

Second, 1988 was the beginning of the building boom for new universities commencing with Tunis el Manar University (*Université de Tunis El Manar*)[22] and the University of Carthage (*Université de Carthage*).[23] This infrastructural expansion of building public universities to accommodate the fledgling numbers of Tunisians leaving secondary schooling and now unemployed continued through 2004. In 2000, the Manouba University (*Université de la Manouba*) expanded,[24] and in 2003 the University of Gabes (*Université de Gabès*)[25] and the University of Jendouba (*Université de Jendouba*)[26] came on stream. Then, on July 16, 2004, the "Day of Knowledge," the University of the Centre was split into four different universities: Monastir University (*Université de Monastir*),[27] Kairouan University (*Université de Kairouan*),[28] the University of Sousse (*Université de Sousse*),[29] and Gafsa University (*Université de Gafsa*).[30]

In these new universities and even after *al-sahwa*, the language of instruction for the sciences continued to be French, and the Arts and Letters were dominated by a type of Francophone–Arabic (Tunisian Arabic or Tunisian) more French-based (Lulat 2005). The universities had facilities, institutes, and *école supérieures* (specialized colleges). Before *al-sahwa*, Deans, who oversee faculties and Directors who are responsible for institutes and *écoles supérieures*, were appointed under the Ben Ali regime by the Ministry of Higher Education. However, in the immediate aftermath, appointments to the positions of Deans and Directors are now conducted through faculty elections in each of the public universities.

The 1991-Education Reforms: Striving for Everything Under the Sun

Even though Ben Ali took until 1991 to enact major reforms, upon taking office in 1987 his administration re-instituted Arabic as the language of instruction for primary and secondary schooling under the Seventh Plan of the Economic and Social Development Recommendations of 1987 to 1991. In a speech in November 1988, Ben Ali stated that:

> ... Because we believe that the schools have to prepare our children on the basis of good morals (manners), teach them to appreciate the work and finally to learn about our Arabic and Islamic identity, we have decided to improve the educational system with the assistance of a big number of people from the civil society, teachers and experts. Thus, we have decided to create the elementary school from the next school year, so that we can guarantee to our children an education of at least [nine] continuous years of studies and that we can decrease the number of pupils that leave the school in an early age. We have also decided that the Arabic language will be the official language of teaching sciences in all the different levels and that we will support the scientific and technique education in the first cycle [nine years], which constitutes the elementary school. The higher council of education, higher education and scientific research that we have re-constituted will give its opinion in the big directions of this corrective project.

Ben's Ali's performance legitimation in higher education reforms suggests "the university will ... boost the comprehensive process of economic development. It will remain an inexhaustible source of creation and innovation ... So that Tunisia remains forever, the symbol of science, culture and civilization which it has always been throughout history" (MOHESRT 2008: 15). Even with these lofty measures, the MOET (2003: 37) writes that education is "still far behind what has been achieved in the European Union."

General higher education reforms began in 1989 and were managed by Law No. 89-70 of July 26, 1989. The aim of the reforms was to ensure that higher education (including post-secondary training) was linked to scientific research in such a manner that the one encourages the development of the other. The reforms also stipulated that access to higher education is open to those who have obtained their Baccalaureate diploma in secondary education or an equivalent diploma. In this way, higher education and the scientific education it was aiming for, were seen as contributing to the nation's development toward the production sector and openness of the economic, social, and cultural environment (UNESCO 1992).

Privatizing Higher Education

The reconstitution of the higher council of education paved the way for the opening up of market choice in education by allowing private suppliers to provide selective educational services. It is important to note that private suppliers of higher education in Tunisia enroll less than 5 percent of the total number of students in programs in higher education. Within the private sector, in 1973, Mr. Mohamed Boussairi Bouebdelli established the Free University of Tunis (*L'Université Libre de Tunis*) [ULT]) as the first private university. However, ULT, which began from humble origins as the School of Electronics and Automation, did not offer higher education studies until 1992. During the 1990s, several incentives were provided by the Ben Ali regime to entice new suppliers to enter the higher education market in order to accommodate the overflow capacity in public universities, which stemmed from expanded access to higher education. In addition to universities brimming beyond capacity, during this period dropout rates hovered at 7.1 percent and would eventually be reversed to 5.2 percent by 2001 (World Bank 2006). These inducements included providing state land, state funding up to 25 percent of permanent teaching staff salaries, ten years' commitment to state contributions to national social security systems and tax reduction for their first ten years (Abdessalem 2010).

Education Law No. 2000–73 of July 25, 2000, the Private Higher Education Law (*Loi sur l'Enseignement Supérieur Privé*), reorganized the private university.[31] However, some private suppliers were operating at that time and students paid market rates to attend those institutions. In instances where students needed to pay for aspects of their higher education, the Tunisian government subsidized about 85 percent of tuition and provided scholarships, grants, and loans to cover additional costs where necessary. The provisions of Law No. 2000–2125 of September 24, 2000 identified the instruments that govern and regulate Private Higher Education Institutions (PHEIs), while a Higher Education Ministerial Decree of September 28, 2000 stipulated the approval of the specification note governing the organization and the functioning of the private universities.

Law No. 2000–73 instructs that tertiary diplomas from all private schools must be recognized by public universities for further study and by public sector institutions for employment purposes. The Law regulates private institutions of higher education as corporations and mandates that certain licensing procedure is strictly enforced (Ben Othman 2010). The Law also provides the necessary steps (for the filing of a detailed description of the project, a comprehensive profile of the director, and a pedagogical dossier related to the planned educational program) that persons or institutions wishing to establish a private university must undertake. Unlike Western institutions, Law No. 2000–73 notes that private suppliers are not entitled to receive gifts and endowments from abroad and local donations and endowments from Tunisian citizens are subject to approval from MOHESRT. Private institutions are responsible for yearly reporting of their student enrollments and this must be categorized by years of studies and specializations and a list of their permanent and adjunct faculty members.

Unlike other countries and entrenched in the authoritarian bargaining agreement, private universities in Tunisia are not viewed as being as prestigious as the public universities and they usually fall into three categories: (i) those that offer a Bachelor degree in English; (ii) those that attract students who did poorly in their *le Bac* and do not wish to undertake *le Concours de Ré-orientation* (the Reorientation Examination); and (iii) international students coming from other African countries. Given the proliferation of private universities in recent times, the verdict is still out as to whether or not they have mastered the competency of providing the skills needed for the labor market, since this data is unavailable. As of 2016, sixty-six private universities are operating and regulated by the MOHESRT, primarily within Tunis, with the rest spread across Tunisia.

As part of Ben Ali's projection of democratic values and authoritarian agreement, the post-Bourguiba era continued with "promotion of absolute equality among the sexes … [which] has become the best means of social promotion" (MOET 2003: 17). Therefore, the ideas of competition internally and externally permeated the post-Bourguiba space as education was expected to generate a "link between training and the labor market at the regional and national level" (MOET 2008: 19). With the ending in 1995 of the *Scientific and Technical Education Reinforcement Project* funded by the African Development

Bank Group, the discussion commenced on the funding of the *Secondary Education Support Project* (SESP). Finally funded in 2005, the Ministry of Basic and Higher Education and Scientific Research was split into two separate ministries, thus creating the Ministry of Education and Science and the Ministry of Higher Education and Scientific Research. After this split, approximately 4 percent of Tunisia's national budget was spent on tertiary education.

ICT and Higher Education

The main instrument of *al-sahwa* was the use of social media and its different apparatuses by the middle-class elites. In 1978, the Tunisian University established the first computer science department in North Africa "in order to train engineers in this specialty" (MOHESRT 2008: 39). This history is so important to show that early on the Tunisian government connected development with technology. The Tunisian government realized that the largest portion of advancement in the sciences included English as a common language (Altbach 2004). They did allude to the idea that "modern exact sciences and new technologies" are "the effective agents of building of a knowledge society and sustainable development" (MOHESRT 2008: 15). The 1970s saw planned movement of students away from humanities toward sciences, and included the necessity of English. Finally, access to and the promotion of technology led to an increase in access to computers and the Internet.

After Ben Ali took power in 1987, one of the first things that he did in 1989 in higher education was to create the National Foundation of Scientific Research that transformed in 1996 to become the Secretariat of State for Scientific Research and Technology (SERST), with reporting duties to the prime minister's office (JORT 1996). This new scientific field restructured national research and development systems in public research institutions, public health institutions, and higher education (MSRTCD 2006). Its additional responsibilities included directing the government's policy on scientific research across all areas of higher education to ensure consistency in Tunisia's national development plans and implementation of strategic priorities. The aim was to facilitate horizontal coordination between several ministries concerned with scientific research and research on technology.

Information Communication Technologies (ICT) was expanded publicly in a speech Ben Ali gave on November 7, 2000 and then formally at the university level with the establishment of the Virtual University of Tunis (*Université Virtuelle de Tunis* [UVT]), which formally began in 2003.[32] In his speech, he announced measures to promote the Internet by giving the opportunity to middle-class families to acquire high quality "family computers" at a competitive price of fewer than 1,000 dinars (approximately US$500 today). He also launched the "Seven-November Internet Bus"[33] project for the popularization of the Internet among young people and children in rural areas and at the end of the year he stated that his regime had secured a reduction in Internet service tariffs starting from 2001. As 2001 drew to a close, the regime investment in computer literacy could be summed up under four acts: (i) permission for banks to grant loans for the purchase of personal computers—some fifteen thousand seven hundred and fifty-five personal computers were financed at a cost of 15.6 million dinars ("Tunisie: PC Familial" 2001); (ii) the hosting of Arab Ministers of Communications that year, which led to the creation of the Arab Organization of Communication Technologies and of Information that made Tunisia its permanent headquarters; (iii) permission for an increasing number of Tunisians to complete basic education graduation diplomas online; and (iv) celebration of the hosting of the third iteration of the National Week of the Internet (*la Semaine Nationale de L'internet*). Then in 2002, domain fees for the name "dot.TN" were decreased to allow the proliferation of its usage.

In establishing the UVT in 2000, Ben Ali's regime combined the fields of ICT and higher education to prepare Tunisia for the knowledge economy. The development of UVT was a lofty project that boasted about its high-tech physical spaces that facilitate education through access centers and online content; digital production laboratories where faculty members can digitalize their course content and video lectures; and video conferencing centers that allow educators and students to be in varying locations. In 2003, in conjunction with the Higher Institutes of Technological Studies, UVT piloted two distance modules—General Introduction to Management and French—of its Business Administration program. In 2005, UVT presented its then objective[34] to increase access to distance education, particularly in rural areas, through the provision of higher education content virtually.

While, in 2002, the Education Act made the Ministry of Education and Training and the Ministry of Higher Education responsible, in principle, for the integration of ICT into education, in practice, Ben Ali presided over which initiatives and opportunities were to go into effect. Each ministry is allocated funds to carry out the proposed duties inclusive of training and paying employees. The integration of technology through the Education Act also requires the inclusion of computer science courses available at the Basic Education level. Today, UVT is organized under the Department of Virtual Education (DEV),[35] which is headed by a faculty member who is appointed by each university and comprised of three levels (pedagogical coordinators, course designers, and evaluators).[36]

In addition to a focus on ICT, the Education Act of July 23, 2002 identifies the national education goals and the functions of schools, stating "education aims at cultivating ... fidelity and loyalty in students to Tunisia" (MOET 2002: 5) while increasing their "capacity for self-education and to prepare them for access to the educated community" (MOET 2002: 9). The Education Act further details the set of skills students were to acquire in school: (i) practical (math, science, computer science, and technology); (ii) strategic (organize, analyze and find correct information); (iii) initiative (spirit of creativity); and (iv) behavioral (sense of responsibility, self-reliance, and cooperation). Article 29 of the 2002 Education Act also enshrines the idea of the development of entrepreneurial skills and suggests a pedagogical approach to ensure that it is implemented in every course in the entire education system. This initiative was not properly implemented, although several technology parks to spur business incubation were established. In the end, access to and promotion of technology under the Education Act would increase once again, as it had in the 1970s, Tunisian's access to computers and the Internet. As students became familiar with social media, the already *Tunisified* population most likely became smaller and more intimate, thus cementing the fruits of the forthcoming *al-shawa* of 2011.

Finally, in 2004, the Ministry of Scientific Research, Technology and Competency Development (MSRTCD) was established with independent power, but reporting and regulation remain under the office of the prime minister. This ministry maintains all the mandates of SERST, but its portfolio has been expanded to include the development of competencies that encourage technological innovation. Its objectives are intertwined with the president's program Tunisia of Tomorrow (*la Tunisie de Demain*), implemented from 2004 to 2009. In higher education, Tunisia of Tomorrow eventually created a network of technological parks (Borj Cédria, El Ghazala, Monastir, Sousse, Sidi Thabet, and Sfax) to promote the development of a knowledge-based economy and boost innovation. In 2004, the World Bank, as part of the *Education Quality Improvement Program* (EQIP) II education loan package, insisted on a component that focused on strengthening higher education institutions and other levels of education.

The 2008-Education Reforms and the Commencement of the *Licence–Maîtrise–Doctorat* (LMD) System

Over time, Tunisian reforms became constructed along cycles. With the ending of the Tunisia of Tomorrow reforms in 2009 and not enough jobs materializing from the knowledge-based economy and tourism and manufacturing sectors, the regime, with external pressure from international financial institutions, undertook a systematic overhaul of higher education that concluded with the adoption of the French degree credentials, *Licence–Maîtrise–Doctorat* ([LMD] Bachelor–Master–PhD) in 2008. The movement to this new system was the Ben Ali regime's way of controlling the narrative of the authoritarian bargaining agreement, which Ben Ali feared was slipping as unemployment rose and youth became agitated since they could not find work.

Prior to 2008, as shown in Table 2, studies in Tunisia's higher education universities commenced with the "first cycle" that lasted for two years and resulted in the granting of a *Diplôme d'Etudes Universitaires de Premier Cycle* (Diploma of University Studies of the First Cycle) (DEUPC) for students in technical fields. The DEUPC was considered as the "preparation phase" in technical fields for entry into the second cycle, which lasted an additional two years. Students not in the technical fields studied for four years after which they were awarded the *Maîtrise* (Bachelor Degree)—this was the first actual degree of the Tunisian higher education system. The *Diplôme d'Études Approfondies* (DEA) (Master's degree) was awarded at the Master's level after two years of studies that ended with a thesis defense—that was either open or closed based upon the field of study. Holding a *Diplôme d'Etudes Approfondies* was a prerequisite for admission into a doctoral program that lasted for three years (World Bank 2008).

In 2006, Tunisia formally adopted the LMD system of degree classifications by copying the French model. This adoption and subsequent implementation of LMD reforms by Ben Ali's government was in response to the creation of the European Higher Education Area in 1999 under the Bologna Declaration, which was adopted by twenty-nine European countries. Ben Ali's copying of the French Module of Bologna was expected since Tunisians have maintained the French bureaucratic structuring of the pre-independence state. The university system in Tunisia, though reformed, has been almost holistically borrowed from Europe but with the push toward internationalizing, Tunisian policymakers admit their mission is to "spot the most convincing experiences in the field and to profit from them" (MOET 2003: 12), signifying a direct method of borrowing that tops their strategy and agenda.

Table 2 Comparison of the old Tunisian Diplomas and Anglo-Saxon Diplomas

Old Tunisian Diplomas	Anglo-Saxon Diplomas
Diplôme de fin d'Études Secondaires / High School Diploma	
Baccalauréat	General Certificate of Education advanced-level (GCE "A" level). General Certificate of Secondary Education (GCSE)
Diplômes du 1er Cycle / First Degrees	
Diplôme de Technicien Supérieur	Bachelor of Technology Higher National Diploma (HND)
Course length: 3 years	Course length: 2 years
Diplôme d'Études Universitaires de Premier Cycle (DEUPC)	Diploma of Higher Education (DHE)
Course length: 2 years	Course length: 2 years
Diplômes du 2ème Cycle / Master's Degrees	
Maîtrise	Bachelor's Degree BA: Bachelor of Arts BCom: Bachelor of Commerce BSc: Bachelor of Science
Course length: 4 years	Course length: 3–4 years
Diplômes du 3ème Cycle / Research Degrees	
Mastère–Mastère spécialisé—Diplômes d'Études Supérieures Spécialisées (DESS)	Master's Degree MA: Master of Art MSc: Master of Science BPhil: Bachelor of Philosophy
Course length: 3 semesters after the Bachelor's Degree	Course length: 1–2 years after the Bachelor's Degree
Diplôme d'Études Approfondies (DEA)	Master's Degree (with thesis) MA: Master of Art
Course length: 3–4 semesters after the Bachelor's Degree	Course length: 2 years after the Bachelor's Degree
Doctorat	DLitt: Doctor of Letters PhD: Doctor of Philosophy DSc: Doctor of Science
Course length: 3 years or more after the Master's Degree or DEA	Course length: 3 years after Master's Degree

Source: Tunisian Agency for Technical Cooperation (2015)

In 2005, Ben Ali introduced another set of reforms under the title "Tunisia Tomorrow," which calls for "a large scientific and technological partnership with the overseas" (MOHESRT 2008: 155). Thus, the aim of the Higher Education Act of February 25, 2008 is to "boost the confidence of students and parents, answer societal expectations and employers' needs and confirm the credibility of national degrees abroad" (MOET 2008: 1). It also "intends to metamorphose higher education in the sole aim at the improvement of the quality of its teaching and research services, a better adaptation of the training to the local, regional, and world mutations and a greater enhancement of the students, teachers and researchers' initiative" (MOHESRT 2008: 191). These reforms were designed to "fulfill the convergence with the university teaching at the EU countries" (MOHESRT 2008: 207).

In 2007, the government began to revise the higher education curriculum that sought to better prepare students for the labor market by developing a system of applied diplomas (applied Bachelor's degree and professional Master's degree). The LMD system is governed today by the Act of February 25, 2008, wherein Degrees or Diplomas are referred to as "Cycles." The First Cycle or *la Licence* (the *Baccalauréat + 3 years)—Diplôme d'Études Universitaires du Premier Cycle*—consists of undergraduate studies for three years (two of which are general studies and one year is professional specialization) after passing *le Bac.* The Second Cycle or *la Maîtrise* (the *Baccalauréat + 5 years*) is equivalent to a Master's degree, where the first year is focused on general studies and the second year on either research or professional specialization. The Third Cycle or *Doctorat* (the *Baccalauréat + 8 years)—Diplôme d'Études Approfondies* (DEA)—is a master of advanced studies for three years after *la Maîtrise* leading to a doctorate.

At that time, the MOHESRT outlined seven main objectives for the LMD reforms that would regulate both private and public universities, citing: (i) the adoption of a system of easily readable and comparable degrees; (ii) the implementation of an academic credit–hour system; (iii) a focus on applied and professional degrees; (iv) encouragement of labor mobility through credit comparability; (v) internationalization of higher education; (vi) greater institutional autonomy; and (vii) defined state standards for the awarding of all degrees. Finally, the old system was abandoned by the Act of February 25, 2008, which introduced a major reform in facilities of Tunisian universities. However, the school and facilities of medicine, engineering, and architecture are still excluded from the 2008 reforms. Since there are no longer any university courses that are shorter than the three-year Bachelor course model, the exemption of these schools and facilities are based upon the rule that:

> ... (8 years of postsecondary study in medical studies and 6 years in dentist studies, pharmacy and architecture) 5 years of engineering courses, are based on

the structure of Bachelor degrees, awarded on accumulation of 180 credits, Master degrees, awarded after a further 120 credits have been accumulated and Doctorates. Engineering students attend two years of preparatory classes, culminating in a national competitive examination and are then assigned to "les écoles d'ingénieurs" [schools of engineering] on the basis of their grading and their wishes. Specialised training in "les écoles d'ingénieurs" takes three years, bringing the total length of engineer training to five years. In medical subjects, the number of places is limited to about 200 first-year students in each institution and studies last for five years, followed by one year of clinical training. Courses in paramedical subjects, i.e. health science and technology and nursing, have switched to the Bachelor, Master and Doctorate system.

European Commission TEMPUS 2010: 2

In the 1990s, there was a push toward increasing enrollment in the science and technology faculties while shortening the period for completing technical degrees. This led to a drastic increase between 2000 and 2008 where enrollment doubled in these fields (Abdessalem 2010). The switch to the LMD system was both a strategic choice and based upon lingering notions that the higher education system was failing to provide the necessary talent pool for the labor market.

In fact, "the LMD system is a choice made by the State to develop higher education and raise it to the standards of most developed countries as well as to achieve the strategic objectives of the country" (MOET 2008: 18). A part of the general philosophy of this reform was a push toward "devolution of spending authority" by decentralizing, in theory, universities and departments, while at the same time encouraging the "assessment grounded upon clear criteria: internal efficiency, external efficiency, pedagogy innovation and pedagogic skills of teachers, scientific output, relationship and partnership with economic environment as well as foreign universities" (Abdessalem 2010: 10).

Therefore, the university has been placed in a specific space and time and it has been charged with the following: to lead the country out of economic trials by aiming to catch up rapidly with the university system in Europe; and to "enhance Tunisia's place in the world" (TECA 1992: 6). In the end, the LMD system was phased in simultaneously with the old system and no major institutional investment or expansions were made. Owing to these innovations offered by the Act of 2008, which introduced the three-cycle degree system, the various types of institutions no longer differ in terms of course structure and duration.

The Constant Pestilence: The Youth Bulge and Labor Market Dynamics

Under the Ben Ali authoritarian bargaining agreement, Tunisia's social challenge was that there were too many university graduates who were not trained to meet the demands of the labor market and not enough jobs were being created. This problem became endemic under Ben Ali's leadership and his regime proposed Band-Aid solutions. As was the case during his regime and remains a feature of the post-*al-sahwa* environment, the average Tunisian university graduate can take up to sixty months securing a job (that is, if they do not withdraw from their employment search). It is hard to tabulate accurately how many Tunisians stop looking for work altogether or become underemployed. Tunisia has always had a problem finding adequate employment for its burdened educated middle class.

In 1991, higher education enrollments increased some 500 percent. In December 1999 under Law No. 99–101, Ben Ali's government established the National Employment Fund (*le Fonds National pour l'Emploi 21/21*) to fight underemployment and promote labor market integration for unemployed youth in "those whose level of education does not give them access to official vocational training provided by official establishments; and those with higher education qualifications, who have acquired initial training in certain areas but have very few employment opportunities outside teaching" (Dridi 2006: 1).

As the seeds for *al-sahwa* began to grow, the prospect of work opportunities for college-educated individuals seemed dismal "... high unemployment rates among higher education graduates *represent a dead loss of the resources invested by both government and households*" (El-Araby 2011: 14, *emphasis added*). The broken economy was a consistent theme of the Ben Ali government: yet higher levels of employment existed in the areas in which most students sought their education—the humanities and languages—which received less attention yet remained popular. The regime never acknowledged the shortcomings of the *traditional economy* or how the job opportunities would be generated for the new graduates. The changes proposed in the education policies came too late to counteract the sentiments that catalyzed *al-sahwa*; the turn toward applying external fixes to internal problems could not fix the deepening rift between policy and reality.

Tunisia suffers from a unique phenomenon in that there is a very high unemployment rate for university graduates, which make up a significant proportion of the middle class. This phenomenon suggests there is a mismatch between the demands of the economy and the skills offered by the recent university graduate. For example, Ben Ali's earlier investment in ICT and higher education was laid out in the Tenth Development Plan from 2002 to 2006 that called for the ICT sector to increase its revenues in GDP from 3.3 percent to about 8 percent through the creation of thirty-one thousand jobs (World Bank 2002). The problem was that Ben Ali's regime was disconnected from the contrast between the grand vision they intended and what really happened on the ground; the universities were responsible for educating a wide range and growing number of people and the government was not doing anything outside the system to create jobs for these highly-educated citizens. The official rhetoric of the regime for years was that "university training has also become an important factor in the process of development ... in the dynamics of the new economy" (MOHESRT 2008: 18), situating the university and its students as primary vanguards and propagators of the economy, particularly the global knowledge economy in the areas of research and technology.

However, unemployment after graduation in Tunisia persisted given "the poor quality of higher education is the most important challenge for almost all Arab countries. They all face a mismatch between the needs of the competitive open labor markets and the skills that students gain in schools and universities" (El-Araby 2011: 17–18). The reality of the university degree fell short of the results its scope seemed to promise. Additionally, higher education reforms did not closely reflect the changes that occurred at the secondary school level. At that time, there were two tracks for students: science or humanities. Now high schools are focusing on a liberal arts education, including a heavy focus on the arts and foreign languages. Yet the policy of higher education still stresses science, technology, and vocational training—the disconnect remains static.

Concluding Thoughts—The Return of Religious Education

With all the reforms that have been undertaken in higher education, one thing has remained consistent: both Bourguiba and Ben Ali during their dictatorships maintained strong connections between Islam and higher education, while pursuing a secular vision, so that "Tunisia [would] remain what it has always been, one of the centers of Islamic influence" (TECA 1992: 10). While both Bourguiba and Ben Ali viewed the education offered by *al-Zitouna* as backward and insisted that religious education should be delivered within the university and not *al-Masjid*, both embraced the historical significance of the institution within Tunisia's cultural heritage. The maintenance of *al-Zitouna* and its incorporation into the university structure enabled the government to show

how "Islam is vital and open to the requirements of the modern age and of evolution" (TECA 1992: 11). The connection to Islam points to a desire for Tunisia to remain connected to the Arab world and for Tunisia to maintain its influence with its Islamic neighbors, despite the secularist declarations of the government. In this way, students who graduate from *al-Zitouna* can carry their Tunisian identity and religious knowledge throughout the Arab world, perpetuating the significance of the Tunisian university system as a place where religion and contemporary secular curricula can co-exist.

The absence of reforms aimed specifically at religious education speaks to the distance the governments of both regimes wanted to establish between themselves and religion. The education reform of both regimes dealt with secular issues, despite the use of the history of *al-Zitouna*, by both regimes, to highlight its appeal to foreign students and faculty. This disconnection, combined with the suppression of religious expression during the 1980s, simmered within higher education institutions. In the Maghreb, religion and culture are intricately entwined; the goal of the university is to "preserve national culture and endeavor to promote it by furthering qualitative and ongoing creations in the domains of science, letters and fine arts" (MOHESRT 2008: 33), effectively ignoring this interconnection and paving the way for religious counterculture to enter the revolutionary fray.

In fact, in the post-*al-sahwa* period, one of the first acts of the new government elected in December 2011 was the reversal of the politics of *tajfif al-manabi'* (the policy of drying up the sources of religion) by unsealing the administrative offices of *al-hay'a-al-ilmiyya* (the scientific committee) on March 19, 2012. This act allowed *Ulama* (the savants) to teach in *Masjid al-Zitouna*. During the 2014–2015 academic year, there were five hundred and twenty students enrolled as reported by the UVT website. Of these, one hundred and eighty-eight students were enrolled in the Master's program and three hundred and thirty-two in the *Licence* program. However, today most universities, research centers, and technology parks (techno-parks) are located along the country's coastline and in wealthy cities (Brisson and Kronfris 2012; Jelassi, Bouzguenda and Malzy 2015a; 2015b).

State Feminism and *Le Code du Statut Personnel*

In the preceding chapters, we detailed how the authoritarian bargaining agreements under different dictatorial regimes and personalities shaped the historical and pre-revolutionary transitologies and education reforms in Tunisia. In this chapter, applying our comparative-historical framework, we focus on the role of women in shaping educational transitologies in the post-independence period. Unlike other Arabic dictatorships, in the immediate post-independence period, women in Tunisia were given a tremendous amount of personal and political freedoms under the Tunisian authoritarian bargaining agreement in the form of the Code of Personal Status (*le Code du Statut Personnel*). The *Code* created a unique relationship between Bourguiba's government and Tunisia's citizens. Bourguiba facilitated the establishment of the National Union of Tunisian Women (UNFT) in 1957, which supported women by sponsoring conferences, facilitating welfare projects, and establishing kindergartens (Moore 1965).

On August 13, 1956,[1] five months after independence, *le Code du Statut Personnel* came into effect, granting women new rights that included receiving the custody of children in cases of divorce and the right to request and initiate divorce proceedings. Bourguiba's authoritarian bargaining agreement saw him using a gradualist approach during the transition period to self-rule, with his early education reforms setting out to establish that "the principle of equality is no less important than the principle of freedom: equality between citizens, between men and women, there must be no discrimination" (TECA 1992: 16–17). In referring to the *Code*, Bourguiba championed free compulsory primary schooling for all Tunisian men and women. Part of Bourguiba's secularization vision and the first part of his *Tunisification* process, the *Code* also gave Tunisian women the right to vote and is considered one of the most progressive civil codes in the Arab world. For Bourguiba, women were essential in codifying the central tenets of the social authoritarian bargaining under his regime; his support of women would be promulgated under his successor and his regime. Bourguiba sought to give and provide protection for different forms of social freedoms to allow women to retain elements of French secularism and Tunisian nationalism.

Significantly, Bourguiba advocated against Tunisian women veiling themselves in classrooms, schools, and government offices, and later prohibited the practice, which had begun to unravel during the French colonial era. The ban on the veil was later extended to prayer rooms in offices, factories, and educational institutions (Adjibolosoo 1995; Boulby 1988). On one occasion, he outrightly described the "veil" as an odious rag. In 1981, *hijabs* (traditional Islamic veil covering part of the face) were banned from being worn by women in public offices and in 1985, *hijabs*[2] were banned in educational establishments.[3] Today, women outnumber men in the higher education workforce in Tunisia by a significant margin and represent some of the voices in *al-sahwa* as well. Bourguiba's uncontestable *chef-d'oeuvre* remains in education and women's rights. However, after *al-sahwa*, *hijabs*, and *niqabs* (full body dress that only leaves the eyes clear) began to appear in public offices, schools, and universities. In 2015, the Ministry of Education announced that teachers and students were prohibited from wearing both *hijabs* and *niqabs* in schools after President Beji Caid Essebsi (from 2014) called for a law restricting these garments.

Tunisia has often been lauded as one of the most progressive countries in the Middle East and North African region (MENA) due to its longstanding tradition in enacting policies promoting gender equality. Even prior to Tunisia's status as a protectorate under France, Tunisian officials prioritized education under the authoritarian bargaining agreement of its resident governor. Tunisia's commitment to an educated and equal population seemingly has paid off, with literacy rates in 2008 reaching 96.1 percent for young women and 98.2 percent for young men (UNICEF 2013). Along with high literacy rates, school enrollment numbers in primary school are near universal with 99 percent of girls and 98 percent of boys attending school (UNICEF 2011). Further, more women are now attending university in Tunisia than men. Despite these impressive numbers, this chapter demonstrates that looking at statistics alone does not tell the whole story. While Tunisia has made exponential gains in education and women's rights throughout the country's short history, top-down policies, described as "state feminism," have created an environment where the advancement of women is tied more closely to state interests than grassroots feminist efforts. The push for an educated populace in Tunisia, however, has proved highly effective in mobilizing women as active agents in their quest for change.

Using women's rights as a political platform to garner support both intra-nationally and internationally, both pre-*al-sahwa* presidents Bourguiba and Ben Ali, created opportunities for women, but in doing so marginalized the large population of rural Islamic women and women from a lower socio-economic class (Khalil 2014). Through Tunisia's arduous struggle to gain independence and moreover a uniquely Tunisian identity, gender relations have become not only intertwined with politics, but women have been "functioning as a symbol of the struggle between a secularist and an Islamist Tunisian future" (El Masry 2014: 107). By discussing the history of women's rights and gender relations in Tunisia, this chapter frames the different political opportunity structures that have altered the state of gender relations in Tunisia by highlighting how initial top-down policies have created a highly educated populace willing to fight for change from the bottom-up. Taking a holistic approach, this chapter will first briefly discuss state feminism and the background of women's rights and education prior the nation's independence. Next, we will highlight schooling and gender policies under the presidencies of Bourguiba and Ben Ali, with special attention to Tunisia's *le Code du Statut Personnel* enacted in 1956. Our comparative-historical approach highlights the shifts in policy under Bourguiba and Ben Ali, focusing on the move towards state feminism, also known as a "masculine feminism" (Naciri 2003: 23). Finally, this chapter will discuss the role of women in *al-sahwa* and the subsequent gender and educational issues and developments that have arisen after the overthrow of the government. The chapter will end with the transition from state feminism to autonomous action that has led to current debates on gender politics and the role of women in a newly established democracy.

State Feminism and Gender Relations

The state has historically played a predominant role in gender relations and policy formation in Tunisia. Describing the development of women's rights in Tunisia as in the "shadow of the state," Hatem (2005: 24) highlights Tunisia's "complete nationalization of women's rights as a sign of its commitment to modernization," which has resulted in fundamental reforms, particularly an educated female population determined to further women's rights. While research often points to the state enacting "women friendly" policies in a quest to modernize and look appealing to the West (Daniele 2014; Jomier 2011; Suleiman 1993), it is important not to dismiss the pivotal role these policies have played in the advancement of women's rights. Charrad (2007: 157) asserts, the Tunisian experience of state feminism "suggests that 'women friendly' reforms matter a great deal, even when they are top-down and even when they are initiated by power holders in the absence of feminist pressures." Top-down policies that put political interests above all else have created a space for women to advance their cause.

Although state feminism may have been beneficial for the more secular-oriented segments of the female population, state feminism also had detrimental effects, particularly through the isolation and persecution of women in ways that did not fit the state's progressive agenda. With the state having clear nationalist goals, officials made little room for alternative ideologies. International organizations, such as Human Rights Watch and Amnesty International, have both issued reports highlighting the imprisonment, forced exile and torture of Islamists mostly associated with *Ennahdha* (the Renaissance) party under the regimes of both Bourguiba and Ben Ali (Arfaoui 2014; Gray 2012). While the number of women jailed throughout these regimes for their political affiliation is unavailable, the wives of Islamists, often connected through their families' persecution, have been vocal since *al-sahwa*, stressing the need for women's rights in Tunisia to reach beyond state-imposed binaries (Gray 2012).

In this chapter, we argue that while the state may have been "the chief agent of change," (Murphy 2003: 169) women in Tunisia have benefited from *le Code du Statut Personnel* through educational opportunities and equality and the increased availability of jobs outside of the home (Madi 2013). While research varies as to when exactly women began to rise up and become agents of their own change, new segments of an educated female populace began to collectively emerge and organize in the 1970s. Further, *al-sahwa* enabled women from both the Islamist and the secular sectors of society to debate what feminism means from below, instead of above. While disparities about gender rights continue to be an ongoing debate within post-*al-sahwa* Tunisia, women from all backgrounds took to the streets during the revolution to voice their concerns. As Khalil (2015: 57) asserts, "when political crowds are diverse and inclusive, they deconstruct state-imposed binaries." It was finally when the public sphere opened that women could collectively fight for the commonality of independence (Arfaoui 2007). To fully understand the scope of state feminism and its impact not only on gender-specific policies within Tunisia, but on its relevance to current structures of schooling, the chapter will begin with a background of women's rights and common practices during French colonization.

Historicizing Gender Relations

As in any attempt of a collective history of a nation, it is important to note that women's activism in Tunisia under different authoritarian bargaining agreements "cannot be defined through an unequivocal picture, but must rather be seen as a diverse and fluid movement linked with the everyday reality of the country" (Daniele 2014: 20). With an history of major transitions in governance, the progression of women's rights and schooling in Tunisia is tied deeply to the political climate. Acknowledging the heterogeneity of both the political structures and sectors of women in Tunisia, the call for gender reform began much earlier than in its Maghreb counterparts. Tunisians believed in the power of a good education, which was placed at the forefront of the country's agenda even before becoming a protectorate. As noted earlier, the first school for Muslim women was founded in 1900. While the school taught an array of "traditional" subjects, such as hygiene and child rearing, women were also taught academic subjects and Islam (Clancy-Smith 2000; Hawkins 2001). It was only privileged women through private tutoring who gained access to a more thoroughly academic curriculum. By the 1920s, only 10 percent of women in Tunisia were literate. This early school model, nonetheless, set the precedent for modernization (Hawkins 2001).

Despite low literacy rates and the expectation for women to partake in traditional domestic duties, education was promoted through a small number of women's organizations, which focused on both the educational and social affairs of women (Afraoui 2007; Hatem 2005). In the 1920s, a women's organization, the Young Female Muslims of Tunisia (*Les Jeunes Femmes Musulmans de Tunisie*), stated their primary concern was to teach Tunisian girls the tenets of Islam. Early feminists were concerned with preparing women for the home as a wife and mother. They raised money to establish schools that taught the Qur'an and domesticity (Arfaoui 2007). Religious leaders were also concerned that French-colonization would impact education in Tunisia, believing that a French influenced education system was "against God and the nation" and would result in a loss of Tunisian identity (Naciri 2003: 21). As a result, *al-Ulama* (Muslim scholars) pushed for free Islamic education and, to lead by example, sent their daughters to school. However, these schools had a strict religious curriculum and great care was taken not to lead the girls astray of their familial duties (Naciri 2003). Overall, during this early period in history, Tunisian women, due to societal expectations and some pressure from colonial leaders, were driven to the home sphere, while the public sphere was strictly for men (Arfaoui 2007).

Initial efforts to mobilize women consisted primarily of members of the urban middle class concerned with assisting poor rural women or came from religious organizations teaching Islam. These early associations of women championing altruistic causes shortly gave way to the nationalists' struggle for independence (Naciri 2003). A small number of males from the reformist movement during the 1930s called for equal rights for women. Tahar Haddad, a legal scholar and *Madrasat al-Zitouna* graduate, authored a highly controversial book in 1930, entitled *Nos Femmes dans Shari'a et la Société* (Our Women in Shari'a and Society). Haddad condemned the treatment of women in Tunisian society, stating that women were treated no better than dogs. Articulating how the mistreatment of women was detrimental to society, Haddad championed changes in family law, particularly regarding marriage and divorce (Charrad 1997). Looking beyond the use of women for political purposes, Haddad urged for gender reform "and improvements in women's education as a way of making women better citizens, better wives and better mothers" (Charrad 2001: 216).

Preaching progressive values that were ahead of his time, Haddad's work sparked outrage from the Islamic community. Facing sharp criticism, fellow reformers sided with the Islamists and Haddad became marginalized (Labidi 2007); at the time of his death he was isolated from society. The activist was later revered for his commitment to women's rights and became a "symbol for those who questioned the paternalist political discourse and took it upon themselves to construct a new discourse" (Labidi 2007: 10). Haddad laid the foundations for later work on feminist thought, but his revolutionary work on gender reform was overshadowed by the nationalists' struggle for independence.

At the beginning of the independence movement, the traditional home/public sphere divide began to dissolve and the shift toward state-defined feminism took hold. As Charrad (1997: 289) asserts, "Tunisian nationalists treated gender as a resource for power in the nationalist struggle and 'The Woman' as a sacred repository of national values." Women began to mobilize and fight for their country outside of the home, joining male nationalists in the public sphere, collectively calling for independence. Reformists wanted to present both a unified affection for the French while simultaneously highlighting their distinct Islamic heritage; the responsibility for the latter was assigned to women (Charrad 2007). This meant, while women took to the streets in solidarity, nationalists insisted they remained veiled to show their sharp distinction from the French. Even future president Bourguiba called on women in 1929 to wear the veil as a "symbol of Tunisian personality" (Hawkins 2011: 39). Addressing gender issues and equality would have to wait until the fight for independence was over.

Bourguibaism and the New Feminist Movement

When Tunisia finally became an independent nation in 1956, two competing nationalist groups, the modernist group led by Bourguiba and the traditionalist group led by Salah Ben Youssef, began vying for the leadership position with the country. Constituents from urban areas, labor unions, and the French supported Bourguiba, while Youssef found support within religious communities (Baliamoune 2011). In the end, Bourguiba prevailed and put modernization at the forefront of his agenda, utilizing Tunisian law to suppress the opposing Islamist faction and to promulgate "an ideology based on the ideal of a homogenous, united, modern, Francophile and secular national body" (Marzouki 2011: 17). This was evident in the 1956 and 1958 decrees that disbanded *al-Zitouna* University, which was the leading institution of Islamic higher education in the Maghreb (Jomier 2011). Further, Bourguiba wasted no time expanding women's rights and made education a top priority for the sake of modernization. At the advent of Bourguiba's presidency, he immediately focused on gender equality and educational expansion. Overall, "Bourguiba bet on women, through family planning, education and women's liberation to create a new state with modern and progressive identity that would serve as an example in the Arab world" (Joline 2012: 8). Under colonial rule for more than seventy years, it was essential for Tunisia to reestablish itself and Bourguiba looked to women and educational establishments to lead the way.

On August 13, 1956, the monumental law, *le Code du Statut Personnel*, was passed. In direct opposition to traditional Sharia law, the *Code* reformed marriage laws, divorce, custody, and inheritance laws. Most importantly, the law abolished some of the most patriarchal elements of traditional laws; the *Code* "abolished polygamy, eliminated the husband's right to repudiate his wife, allowed women to file for divorce and increased women's custody rights" (Charrad 1997: 295). While the law was revolutionary, there was no feminist movement to speak of at that time calling for such reforms; Bourguiba's policymakers, mostly male, utilized the highly politicized, then-hot topic of gender equality to "create a new Tunisian identity, to transform women into more efficient citizens and to cement women's popular support for his authoritarian rule" (El Masry 2014: 116). The *Code* coincided with Bourguiba's authoritarian bargaining interests and was used as a way to strengthen the government, while simultaneously weakening traditional kin-based groups. Charrad (2007: 1518–1519) argues that the *Code* was "not a victory for feminism, but rather of the government strong enough to place a claim on Islam and enforce a reformist interpretation of the Islamic tradition." Regardless of intention, the state-imposed measure opened the doors for grassroots feminism later in the century and led to a series of other female-friendly reforms that have given women in Tunisia an independent voice (Charrad 2001).

Following the passing of the *Code*, Bourguiba was quick to enact other pivotal dictatorial reforms under his authoritarian bargaining, including compulsory education for girls, employment rights, child adoption, and family planning laws later in the 1970s, including the right to contraception and abortion (El Masry 2014). In 1957, women were given the right to vote and the Education Reform Law of 1958 called for the elementary enrollment of all six year olds by the year 1967 and the enrollment of all primary school students by 1972 (Jones 1980). The call for widespread education to include boys and girls was viewed as a necessary component to the *Code* and further equality measures. In line with Bourguiba's authoritarian vision, he not only wanted women to be educated, but he also wanted them to appear "modern." Reversing his earlier stance during colonial rule that women should wear the *hijab*, he spoke out against them, calling them "odious rags" and even outlawed them in the classroom (Boulby 1988).

Enrollment in school sharply increased for both boys and girls. Coeducation spread quickly throughout the country, despite opposition from parents and teachers in some traditional communities. Despite parental illiteracy and their apprehension of sending their daughters to school, parents enrolled their daughters in such high numbers that the public demand for schooling exceeded the amount of space in schools (Jones 1980). To accompany the increasing demand, the Ministry of Education increased the national budget for schooling from 18 percent in 1959 to 34.5 percent in 1971. Despite the growing budget, enrollment grew more quickly than the infrastructure. In 1958, there was a shortage of teachers, which led to less-qualified teachers and shorter school days. In addition, secondary schooling was cut by one year (Jones 1980). While the quality of education in Tunisia may have deteriorated, the demand and drive for education was more prevalent than ever.

It was also during these early years that Bourguiba set out to gain collective support by combining the factions of female nationalists into one state-sponsored *Neo-Destour* affiliated women's association. The National Union of Tunisian Women Entitled (UNFT) appealed to female nationalists looking to further their activism into modernizing the state (Mulrine 2011). The UNFT became the only recognized women's organization under the Bourguiba regime and the association was a way for women to represent the state's "generous" stance on women. Overall, UNFT was Bourguiba's organization and women were still not granted the rights to independently organize (Arfaoui 2007; Mulrine 2011).

As Bourguiba's initial reforms began to transform the independent state, new policies and grassroots causes began to take hold. The state enacted very few women and family related laws throughout the 1970s and 1980s (Charrad 1997), except for the passing (with reservations) of the Convention on the Elimination of All Forms of Discrimination Against Women (CEDAW), ratified in 1985. The United Nations General Assembly-backed committee called for the end of discrimination, particularly in relation to property, family, employment, and citizenship (Stetter and Reuter 2014). While the passing of CEDAW was important, the Tunisian government expressed reservations with clauses that addressed equal rights on marriage and family life (Daniele 2014: 17), which caused concern over the state's commitment to equality. Despite the lack of government-sponsored reform, however, a growing cadre of educated women led to the beginnings of a feminist movement. A group of students in 1978 started an organization entitled *Club Tahar al Haddad* after the late feminist scholar. The Club's main objectives included: to show fellow women that despite advances, gender equality was still an issue; to establish a support system for women interested in furthering the development of the country; "and to direct women's struggle not against men as such, but against social practices that place power in the hands of men" (Charrad 2007: 1524). The club became a platform for highly educated women, including lawyers and academics, to discuss prevailing social issues.

Arfaoui (2007) describes this period from 1970 to 2000 as *Le Nouveau Mouvement Féministe* (the New Feminist Movement), whereas women pushed forward the work of early twentieth-century feminists, instead of viewing feminism solely through the state. In 1985, the magazine *Nissaa* (Women) a feminist bilingual (Arabic and French) platform was launched to discuss general equality and various modes of feminism, particularly how feminism was conceptualized locally. Divorcing itself from any particular institution, organization, or the State, *Nissaa* placed issues associated with women's rights in the hands of its writers and readers.

It would be incorrect to say that women's causes and the advancement of education did not make great gains during Bourguiba's presidency, but it is fair to assert that women's causes were an instrument of the State's push toward modernization. The expansion of female rights, most notably the *Code* and education, brought a breadth of opportunities for women that were not available to previous generations. Educational issues continued to persist, including the lack of infrastructure in rural communities and under-enrollment for girls. Literacy rates, however, saw sharp increases with only 48.3 percent of women illiterate in 1989 compared to 96 percent of women illiterate in 1956 (Charrad 1997).

The Rise of State Feminism and *Le Pacte National*

In 1987, Habib Bourguiba's three decades of presidency ended after a medical *coup d'état* led by Ben Ali. Although the transition to a new authoritarian bargaining agreement was peaceful, the new changes outlined in Ben Ali's authoritarian agreement led to renewed debates regarding women's rights, which "highlighted the fragility of this process and the urgent need to construct, via an anthropology of culture, a human feminism, as both a legal and a political subject" (Labidi 2007: 25). Bourguiba's quest to both modernize and establish a distinct Tunisian identity resulted in the persecution and suppression of the Islamic faction of society. Ben Ali was tasked with appealing to the different societal groups and bridging differences. Trying to make up for a long history of the marginalization of the Islamist population, while simultaneously attempting to maintain support from the secular communities, created a paradoxical environment for the new president (Bennoune 2012)—a paradox that never fully resolved.

Like Bourguiba's authoritarian bargaining agreement of building the nation through modernization combined with social benefits, the Ben Ali authoritarian bargaining agreements came in the form of *le Changement* and *le Pacte National* and sought to re-build the state through gender politics as a way to accommodate both the Islamists and the secular communities within Tunisia (El Masry 2014). At the onset of Ben Ali's presidency, he aimed for reconciliation and pardoned a large percentage of jailed Islamic activists imprisoned under Bourguiba. Beginning his public speeches with the traditional Islamic phrase, "in the name of God," Ben Ali set himself apart from Bourguiba, especially with the reinstatement of *Madrasat al-Zitouna* in the late 1980s (Jomier 2011). While garnering support from the Islamic faction, Ben Ali also partook in state-sponsored gender policies to cement his rise to power. In 1988, the president showcased his support for gender equality by drafting *le Pacte National* (the National Pact), which would lay out his authoritarian bargaining agreement between him and Tunisians as well as support his drive for modernizing and retaining "a rational orientation toward achieving the full emancipation of women" (Murphy 2003: 177). Through the promotion of a pluralistic outlook, Ben Ali began his reign with strong public support.

Under Ben Ali's authoritarian agreement, which had state support as a central component, an increasing intellectual female populace created a new elite group of activists and autonomous women's organizations (Labidi 2007). Ben Ali's controversial wife, Leila Trabelsi, was viewed as the symbol of modern women (Khalil 2014). Her non-traditional past along with her choice not to wear a hijab again highlighted favoritism toward secular women. Breaking from the former president, conversely, Ben Ali allowed these independent women's organizations, which proliferated through the 1980s and 1990s. In 1989 both the Association of Tunisian Women for Research and Development (*l'Association des Femmes Tunisiennes pour la Recherche* sur le *Développement* [AFTURD]) and the Tunisian Association of Democratic Women (*l'Association Tunisienne des Femmes Démocrates* [ATFD]) gained legal status after operating illegally since the late 1970s (Labidi 2007; Martínez-Fuentes and Ennouri 2014). Prioritizing research activities, AFTURD was composed of professionals, such as journalists, teachers, and healthcare professionals who spread their message through publications and conferences (Labidi 2007). ATFD, focused solely on activism, spearheaded campaigns against domestic violence and other gender-specific causes. While Ben Ali's support for independent feminist organizations was viewed positively, the government began recognizing specific organizations, such as ATFD, which resulted in institutional partnerships with the government instead of activist approaches separate from the government (Murphy 2003). Under the Ben Ali authoritarian agreement, he appeared to embrace grassroots organizations but ultimately aimed to promote feminism through state action and benevolence. As the government made these advances, the advent of "female autonomy constituted a rupture with the existing 'masculine feminism'" (Naciri 2003: 26), which ignited an independent women's movement.

The state continued to advocate for women's rights in the form of state feminism through the creation of the National Commission on Women in Development (*le Commission Nationale Femme et Développement* [CFD]) in 1991 and the State Secretariat for Women and the Family (*le Secrétariat d'État pour les Femmes et la Famille*) in 1992 (Arfaoui 2007). Ben Ali also made concerted efforts to increase the presence of women in higher levels of government. Women were placed in high-level ministry positions, leading to the culmination of various gender-empowered commissions and associations, along with the accession of women into political roles and leadership positions. This ultimately led to the emergence of a feminism housed within the political/public space where women's issues and reactions were not solely just a part of the political structure, but a part of a collective independent female voice that defended women's interests and women's rights (Charrad 1997).

The culmination of this activism led to widespread amendments to the *Code* in 1993, replacing clauses urging women to "respect and obey her husband with a provision making husbands equally responsible for household management" (Murphy 2003: 179). Further, sanctions against domestic violence were established, mothers were given the rights to deny the marriage of their minor daughters, and alimony laws were created. One of the biggest changes to the *Code* granted women the rights to pass citizenship on to their children whether the children were born within Tunisia or outside of the country and granted women the right to pass on citizenship regardless of the nationality of the father (Charrad 2007). Although the state technically made the changes to the *Code*, it was the push from women's associations and women in leadership positions that led to citizenship rights.

By 1995, following Ben Ali's 1991 Law No. 91–65 highlighting the importance of educating girls, enrollment figures for elementary students showed that girls made up 38.6 percent of the student population, which increased to 46 percent by 1997 (Murphy 2003). The Tunisian education systems saw the most enrollment gains for young girls and women in higher education, with 99 percent of six-year-old girls enrolled in first grade and 43.7 percent of women enrolled in higher education in the 1990s (Murphy 2003). Additionally, the university curriculum for women diversified throughout the Ben Ali presidency, with women particularly represented within the fields of science and information technology. Despite significant gains made in access to higher education and vocational education for rural populations, problems persisted, which led to the Eighth Development Plan from 1992 to 1996. The plan highlighted the necessity for programs to reduce illiteracy within rural populations of women (Murphy 2003). In addition to a lack of educational resources, women continued to be overrepresented in traditional female vocations, such as health care and teaching, particularly in rural communities, rather than managerial positions which offered higher pay and leadership opportunities.

The Ben Ali government continued to strategically advocate for women's rights through the rest of his reign. In 2004, Tunisia hosted the 2004 Arab League Summit, which promoted the rights of women. Ben Ali urged fellow member states to "consider the promotion of the rights of Arab women as a fundamental axis of the process of development and modernization of Arab societies" (as cited in Labidi 2007: 7). These actions continued to earn Ben Ali the support of Western countries.

Although Ben Ali remained committed to educational development throughout the rest of his presidency, gaps continued between boys and girls, and urban and rural students. In 2002, the Tunisian Education Act reiterated earlier decrees that stated the necessity of a free education for all Tunisian students regardless of sex, religion, social origin, race, or religion (United Nations 2004). While literacy rates for adult women increased from 55 percent in 1995 to over 64 percent in 2003, gender gaps have persisted within secondary education, albeit there has been improvement (World Bank 2012). According to the *Global Gender Gap Report*, countries in the MENA still struggle to provide adequate education to the entire population. In 2009, Tunisia was placed at one hundred and nine in the Global Gender Gap Index (Megahed and Lack 2011). The most impressive gains in educational attainment for women were made in higher education. In the 2008–2009 school year, "more than half of all university students were women, representing 59.5 percent. However, despite gender parity in Tunisian higher education, school administrations still tend to be male-dominated" (Megahed and Lack 2011: 412). Nonetheless, the biggest education-related issue that plagued the Ben Ali administration, and became one of the main contributing factors to the overthrow of the government, was widespread unemployment throughout the country. In 2005, unemployment for women was at 17.3 percent and 13.1 percent for men (Megahed and Lack 2011).

Picking up where Bourguiba left off, the Ben Ali authoritarian agreement made both education and women's rights a top priority to bolster the development process in the country and to maintain power. Ben Ali utilized gender politics to accomplish his early goals, which focused on establishing relations with Islamists while remaining committed to the secular-oriented polity (El Masry 2014). In the end, Ben Ali never resolved the paradoxical nature of the country. While the country began to protest the president's administration, he promised to create hundreds of thousands of jobs, but his promises came too late (Randeree 2011).

Les Femmes *and* al-Shawa

Women and men from all different backgrounds came together in support of *al-sahwa*, which commenced with the self-immolation of Tunisian street vendor Mohamed Bouazizi on December 17, 2011. As the protests spread from the vendor's hometown to the capital, women and men took to the streets as "equal and active participants within the revolution" (Mulrine 2011: 17). Finally, in January former president Ben Ali fled the country along with his wife, Leila Ben Ali. Women were once again tasked with maintaining their rights, particularly advocating against any threats to the CPS (Arfaoui and Tchaicha 2014). As the regime fell, women for the first time could fully act outside of the confines of the state.

Women's groups and activists were given the "opportunity to create their own political consciousness and be at the forefront of post-revolutionary development" (Joline 2012: 3). Women's associations, such as AFTURD and ATFD along with other activist groups (Equity and Parity, Women's Front for Equality, Women and the Dignity, Tunisian Women's Forum and Citizen Engagement) took on the challenge of spreading awareness of the democratic process and the pressing need to both maintain and push forward greater gender equality (Arfaoui and Tchaicha 2014). Both secular and Islamist women's organizations and activists mobilized after *al-sahwa*. Since Ben Ali continued to persecute Islamists under his reign, Muslim women organizations and activists were sparse. Two of the core issues surrounding the women's movements post-*al-sahwa* were the inclusion of a female Islamist voice and attempts to assess the impact of this new discourse within the political community. Quickly following *al-sahwa*, the Tunisian Women's Association was established as a Muslim women's organization that aimed to educate women about their roles in society and rights as individuals, specifically Muslim women jailed under either the Ben Ali or Bourguiba regimes (Daniele 2014). Feminism became decentralized and a plurality in feminist discourses emerged.

Before post-*al-sahwa* elections were held, the interim government wasted no time before enacting gender-related policies. In 2011, a gender-parity agreement was issued that required every other party candidate listed to be a woman to ensure an equal number of males and females running for office (Joline 2012). Earlier restrictions placed on the creation of non-government organizations were also lifted, which created a space for grassroots organizations to continue to flourish among both the Islamists and secularists. Women were most represented within the *Ennahdha* Party, the modernist Islamist party formally banned under Ben Ali (Joline 2012). Despite tensions due to the rise of the Islamist party, Muslim leaders insisted on a strict adherence to the *Code*. Women within the party fought to keep the *Code* and advocated for a stronger female presence within parliament (Khalil 2014). Tensions still persist between the secular and Muslim communities within Tunisia, despite the same overarching goals between the women's groups. Secular women continued to mistrust the Islamist faction, while Muslim women expressed the need for free religious expression (Kahlil 2014). Women's organizations and female activists collectively spearheaded the call for the interim government to lift previous reservations on

CEDAW. On August 16, 2011, the reservations were lifted under a statement of intent (Arfaoui 2014). They were officially lifted in April 2014.

In addition to gender issues being a point of contestation post-*al-sahwa*, an educated yet highly unemployed young population still struggled to find work. In 2012, unemployment for young Tunisians was at 37.6 percent and overall unemployment at 15.3 percent in 2015 (OECD 2015b). In the post-*al-sahwa* period, young women have the lowest employment figures with 30.3 percent of young women unemployed compared to 13.3 percent of young men unemployed. Further, those with a university degree are at a higher risk of unemployment than those without a degree. Those that are employed often face little job security and poor work quality, with an estimated 50 percent of Tunisian youth working in the informal sector (OECD 2015b). *Al-shawa* finally gave many a voice, but this need for change has yet to materialize institutionally.

Reframing Women's Rights in the Constitution

The new Tunisian Constitution, adopted on January 26, 2014, asserted a continued commitment to women's rights. Article 46 promises "to protect women's established rights and works to strengthen and develop them" and guarantees "equality of opportunities between women and men to have access to all levels of responsibility in all domains" (Government of Tunisia, Tunisian Const., 2014). The article continues to state a commitment to equal representation in elected positions and a promise to eradicate violence against women.

The Constitution also guarantees the right to a free public education at all levels, while stressing the importance of a high-quality education. Article 39 pays heed to the Muslim voice within educational establishments by stressing that the state "shall work to consolidate the Arab–Muslim identity and national belonging in the young generations and to strengthen, promote, and generalize the use of Arab language and to openness to foreign languages, human civilizations and diffusion of the culture of human rights" (Government of Tunisia, Tunisian Const., 2014). Further, Article 40 highlights the rights of Tunisians to work, regardless of gender and guarantees "All citizens, male and female, . . . the right to decent working conditions and to a fair wage" (Government of Tunisia, Tunisian Const., 2014). In contrast to earlier commitments toward education under Bourguiba and Ali, the 2014 Constitution stresses that access is not enough and recognizes the need for plurality in the educational sphere and employment opportunities.

Concluding Thoughts—*Le Code du Statut Personnel* Endures

This chapter problematized the assertion that holds Tunisia as the beacon for feminism within the MENA regions. Under similar authoritarian bargaining agreements, both Bourguiba and Ben Ali championed the rights of women through the *Code* and educational access and they did so to appeal to Western counterparts in a quest to empower the central state and appear modern. Further, Bourguiba and Ben Ali often catered to the more secular-oriented faction of the female population, ignoring the voices of prominent Islamist feminists. That being said, women were able to utilize tenets of state feminism to advance their cause, particularly post-*al-sahwa*, through the advent of women-led civil society organizations. The proliferation of civil society organizations has diversified the feminist voice in Tunisia, resulting in countrywide grassroots efforts for equality, employment, and civil liberties. While the 2014 Constitution has acknowledged issues surrounding women and education within Tunisia, unemployment continues to plague all youth within Tunisia, especially women. In September 2017, President Beji Caid Essebsi's government lifted the 1973 governmental decree that prevented Tunisian Muslim women from marrying non-Muslims. The 1973-ban prohibiting inter-religious marriage was seen as violating the 2014 Constitution. Before the repeal of the marriage decree, a non-Muslim man wishing to marry a Tunisian Muslim woman converted to Islam and submitted proof of his conversion in the form of a certificate; while a Tunisian Muslim man was allowed to marry a non-Muslim woman. Despite the advances that women have made, they still face discrimination across several strata ranging from pay gaps and workplace discrimination to inheritance protocols that stipulate women receive half less than males.

Freedom, Social Media, and Activism

In 2015, four years after *al-sahwa*, the Nobel Peace Prize was awarded to Tunisia's *National Dialogue Quartet*—(UGTT, UTICA, LTDH, and the OTA [Tunisian Order of Lawyers]). This group of civil society organizations, created in 2013 under the banner of Tunisia's *National Dialogue Quartet*, played a pivotal role in securing Tunisia's transition to democracy, particularly serving as mediators between Tunisia's Islamists and secular factions and ensuring both parties engaged in a *National Dialogue* after *al-sahwa*. Due to political assassinations in 2013, the country was in another period of unrest and on the verge of a civil war. Despite setbacks, the organizations vocalized support for the National Constituent Assembly and ultimately aided in getting the Tunisian people behind the constitutional process (BBC 2015). The actions of the quartet and the Tunisian people proved that a pluralistic society with competing ideologies can work toward common goals. In fact, it can be argued that the *National Dialogue Quartet* built its foundation and established its legitimacy after *al-sahwa* from the wreckage of the previous authoritarian agreement left by the Ben Ali regime.

As the dust began to settle in Tunisia after the overthrow of the government in 2011 and the dismantling of Ben Ali's authoritarian agreements—*le Changement* and *le Pacte National*— the struggle for a new form of government, one in which other countries could emulate, began to take form. Questions began to arise as to how such a seemingly polarized nation could ever reach a consensus. As this chapter will showcase, civil societies, labor unions, lawyers, the youth, the employed, and the unemployed all came together to achieve common goals. Striving for a free and stable government, the path toward their current governing structure, a semi-presidential republic, has not been an easy one, as reaching a consensus has proved arduous. However, while many are aware of *al-sahwa*, it is important to note that activism in Tunisia did not begin with the December uprising after the self-immolation of Tarek el-Tayeb Mohamed Bouazizi in 2010 nor did it end with Ben Ali fleeing the country in January 2011. Although the Tunisian voice has been stifled by years of living under an authoritarian government, Tunisians have long been vocal and they continue to fight for change as the country has transitioned into a democracy.

This chapter will contextualize *al-sahwa* and the subsequent unrest through our comparative-historical approach, uncovering the history of activism under different authoritarian agreements and within a country faced with decades of colonial and authoritarian rule. Across this chapter, we argue the activism that led to *al-sahwa* has its heredity in Tunisia's colonial past and was nurtured across the dictatorships of Bourguiba and Ben Ali. Further, we will discuss how these movements have evolved using social media. Finally, this chapter will end by highlighting the newfound freedoms under the constitution, specifically discussing the rights of citizens and the media.

Activism under the French Protectorate

Although the transition from Tunisia's status as a protectorate under France to its independence in 1956 is often considered a smooth transition from the authoritarian agreement between the French and the Bey of Tunis with the citizens of Tunis to a new authoritarian agreement between Habib Bourguiba and the citizenry, it is important to note that Tunisians were active in the fight for their own independence and took to the streets to fight for their autonomy. The first organized attempt toward criticizing the French Protectorate came from French-educated Tunisians, called *The Young Tunisians*, who believed France needed to provide Tunisians with more leadership opportunities (Alexander 2010). Established in 1907, *The Young Tunisians* eventually expanded their efforts and supported protests centered on government corruption, including clashes with police in 1911 due to a construction project encroaching on a cemetery and protests with Tunisian tram-workers demanding an increase in pay. Despite *The Young Tunisians* having little role in organizing these protests, their participation led to the dissolution of the organization. French officials used the unrest as a reason to jail members of the Young Tunisians and shut down its newspaper, *Le Tunisien*. This despotic control quelled any outright attempts toward Tunisian nationalism (Anderson 1999).

The nationalist movement began to take concrete form through the establishment of a well-organized political party. Although the movement was spearheaded through the *Destour* Party, founded in 1920, which later evolved into the *Neo-Destour* Party, led by Habib Bourguiba in 1930, nationalist leaders were not alone in their quest for independence. By 1937, the *Neo-Destour* Party had around 100,000 members with 400 different branches dispersed throughout the country (Okoth 2006). The party succeeded in bringing together not only the top leaders educated within the Franco-Arab education system, but also graduates of *Madrasat al-Zitouna*, who served as "activists at the local level" (Okoth 2006: 233). In 1938, the UGTT, along with *Neo-Destour* supporters, initiated a series of riots aimed at the dismissal of an Algerian worker (Okoth 2006). Riots resulted in one hundred and twelve deaths and the arrest of Bourguiba. Bourguiba spent the next decade as a prisoner and subsequently as an international spokesperson, attempting to bring awareness of Tunisia's movement toward independence. These early events sparked the labor movement in Tunisia.

The advent of the labor movement began in the 1920s, but the official establishment was in 1946 with the birth of the UGTT. The UGTT played a pivotal role in organizing a united anti-colonial front. In 1946, all three organizations and parties, *Destour*, *Neo-Destour*, and the UGTT, took part in a 1946 congress that was held to address Tunisia's independence, and which culminated with leaders vowing to support independence. Despite the police putting a halt to the meeting, activists began to take to the streets. It is during this time we also see the mobilization of women joining men in the public sphere in support of nationalistic causes. As the nationalist movement began to gain momentum, leaders were jailed but unions and Tunisian guerrillas kept the fight for freedom alive, culminating in the independence of Tunisia in 1956 (Okoth 2006). The UGTT was directly responsible for the building of the modern state. Therefore, "the history of Tunisian unions is bound up with the history of Tunisian liberation from colonialism" (Toensing 2011: para. 3). The nationalist movement is also intertwined, specifically the role of unions and organized activism, with *al-sahwa*—an uprising, although seemingly disjointed in the beginning, that used social media and resilience to overthrow the government and demand democracy.

Activism, Militantism, and Bourguibaism: When the Activist becomes the Antagonist

While Bourguiba won the hearts of Tunisians through his leadership during the fight for Tunisian independence, from the beginning of his presidency Bourguiba refused to grant Tunisian civil society groups and activists autonomy. Under the long presidencies of both Bourguiba and Ben Ali and their ensuing authoritarian agreements, autonomous citizen engagement was repressed and a fearful environment was created consisting of executions, trials and torture for those who went against the grain (Aleya-Sghaier 2012). Bourguiba knew firsthand the power of organized action and used his knowledge to systematically control civil society organizations (Foundation for the Future 2013). Independent political organizations and citizen action was stymied through the 1959 Law No. 59, which restricted the creation of associations (Foundation for the Future 2013). The Tunisian Law on Associations stated that, to operate legally, new organizations had to register with the government but the government could refuse their establishment without recourse for the group. Further, organizations were required to publish their names, goals, and descriptive information in a periodical entitled the Official Gazette (Amnesty International 2010).

Bourguiba's main concern after taking office in 1957 was to ensure a "homogeneous, united, modern, Francophile and secular national body" (Marzouki 2011: 17). To achieve this goal, opposition was not tolerated. Although the UGTT worked with the *Neo-Destour* Party to gain independence, Bourguiba attempted to maintain strict control over the UGTT and any other organization. The Tunisian General Labour Union, however, clashed with the regime at times, particularly in the 1970s when the UGTT refused to heed to governmental demands. Setting the tone for the rest of his presidency Bourguiba had union leaders jailed or deported, although UGTT member meetings were still held in secret after the raids. In 1978, the UGTT called for a general strike to protest an increased cost of living due to the adoption of an array of neoliberal policies (Toensing 2011). The strikes again resulted in the persecution of union representatives while the government refused to acknowledge their demands.

Earlier unrest gave way to a more orchestrated attempt at reform with the 1983–1984 "Bread Riots." The violent demonstrations began in the often neglected and impoverished regions of South and Southwest Tunisia (Seddon 1986); regions of the country that continue to plead to this day for economic reform. Protests stemmed from a government measure to remove bread subsidies, (Chossudovsky 2011; Seddon 1986). With the price of bread increasing 100 percent, anger throughout the country was well warranted. Fearing attempts to overthrow the government, the riots turned bloody as security forces opened fire on demonstrators; in the end, reports varied as to the exact death toll, with numbers ranging anywhere from sixty to one hundred and twenty. Even though a state of emergency was declared, a curfew was placed and gatherings were banned, citizens continued to protest (Seddon 1986). Their determination forced Bourguiba to finally relent; appearing on television, he stated his decision to reverse the price hike (Chossudovsky 2011). While Tunisians achieved what they wanted, frustrations with the government began to mount. This was aggravated by "erratic behavior" that Bourguiba began to display in his later years (Schraeder and Redissi 2011). In addition to joining labor unions, Tunisians began joining opposing political groups.

Ennahdha, founded by Rachid al-Ghannouchi and inspired by the Islamic Revolution in Iran, was established in 1981 and quickly started gaining support. Although the movement's goals were overtly religious in nature, aiming for the return of Tunisians to a deeper Islamic lifestyle rather than catering to Western demands, the organization also focused on economic stability and human rights (Esposito and Voll 2001; Reich 1990). The movement was successful in garnering support from all sectors of society, including blue-collar workers, union members, students, the middle class, and even those that held more prestigious positions, such as lawyers, professors, and doctors (Esposito and Voll 2001). Bourguiba, intolerant of any form of opposition, had *Ennahdha's* leaders jailed, including al-Ghannouchi. Although many were released in the mid–1980s, they were accused in 1987 of attempting to overthrow the government and were threatened or imprisoned once again (Reich 1990). In 1987, Ben Ali, the newly appointed Prime Minister, initiated a medical *coup d'état* with the backing of many Tunisians who felt that the transition was well warranted, including the subsequent jailing of the Islamists. Citizens hoped for a new beginning with Ben Ali and he made a staunch commitment to change (Dwyer 1991).

Ben Ali and the Road to *al-Sahwa*

Ben Ali kept his word at the beginning of his presidency and was quick to make some much-needed changes under his authoritarian agreements of *le Changement* and *le Pacte National.* Ben Ali "promised to establish the rule of law, to respect human rights and to implement the kind of democratic political reforms that Bourguiba had steadfastly refused" (Alexander 1997: 2). Ben Ali immediately released an estimated four thousand political prisoners jailed under Bourguiba and reestablished the governmental party from the *Socialist Destourian Party* (PSD) into *Le Rassemblement Constitutionnel Démocratique* (RCD). Further, he organized multiparty elections and abolished lifetime presidential terms, shuttered the state security court, granted more freedoms to the press, and ratified the United Nation's convention against Torture (Alexander 1997; Kingdon 2014). Showcasing his commitment to political plurality, he "invited 16 political organizations and parties, including the banned Islamists, to join him in signing a 'National Pact' to promote national interest, stability and democratic reforms" (Kaboub 2014: 60). Ben Ali also lessened restriction overall on the establishment of associations and political parties. While the initial reforms were well-received and promising, policies throughout the rest of his presidency were reminiscent of the Bourguiba regime. Similar to Bourguiba's early goals after independence, Ben Ali stated his commitment to democracy, but in reality he aimed for social control.

Ben Ali achieved his early goal for a united populace, but not exactly in the way he had imagined. Decades of strict authoritarianism led a large segment of the population to be undivided in their distrust of his regime (Aleya-Sghaier 2012). In the late 1980s, Ben Ali refused to legalize MTI, which renamed itself *Hizb al-Nahda* or *Ennahdha* (the Renaissance Party), albeit the Islamists agreed upon the grounds of competitive democracy (Alexander 1997). In the first presidential and legislative election of the new regime Ben Ali used the old electoral code, which called for a single combined list of candidates. Such election protocols and restrictions on the media allowed for Ben Ali and the RCD to run largely unopposed and the President won his first election with 99.27 percent of the vote (Rand 2013). With some members of *Ennahdha* running as independents, it came as a surprise when party members in the election won between 14 and 25 percent of the vote in some regions, which Ben Ali took as a direct threat to his new regime. This culminated in 1991 when Islamists possibly linked to the *Ennahdha* party set fire to a government office in Tunis, resulting in the death of one employee. Hereafter, Ben Ali launched a vicious attack on *Ennahdha* and by 1991, eight thousand members were arrested, and many tortured. The attack led to the death of 49 members and the exile of Rached al-Ghannouchi (Rand 2013). This was just the beginning of the government's repressive tactics toward Islamists and all those that opposed Ben Ali's leadership.

While Ben Ali became more and more authoritative, Tunisians, particularly those in wealthier regions, put up with restrictive policies as poverty decreased and citizens were given greater access to social welfare (Alexander 1997; Paciello 2011). As the economy continued to grow, Ben Ali could remain in power. However, he used initial reforms and a stable economy to hide his practices of "electoral manipulation, intimidation and favors to co-opt leaders of ruling-party organs and civil society organizations" (Alexander 2011: 3). In the 1990s, Ben Ali also utilized his private police force, *al-mukhabarat*, to ensure the stability of his regime, particularly through surveillance activities (Schraeder and Redissi 2011). Due to the regime's restrictions, few civil society organizations operated outside of state control. ATFD and LTDH, founded in 1977 and 1989 respectively, were two such organizations that attempted to work independently from the state (Deane 2013). In the early 1980s Bourguiba attempted to silence the LTDH but was unsuccessful (Alexander 1997). Nonetheless, lines between independence and state interference were always blurry within the confines of civic action under deep-rooted authoritarianism. This was exacerbated when a united front against the government, calling themselves the Tunisian National Salvation Front, issued a communiqué urging Ben Ali to embrace a true multiparty system. Because the faction had ties to former political leaders, Ben Ali felt especially threatened and viewed any type of civic action as an indicator of resistance to his regime (Alexander 1997).

Ben Ali continued to win election after election (1989, 1994, 1999, 2004, and 2009) but his success and popularity were illusionary. While some legal political parties could participate in elections, they were given a limited number of seats in parliament. Other procedures ensured that elections were uncompetitive. Further, opposing parties and candidates were either barred from running for office or banned from campaigning publicly (Paciello 2011). In 2002, Ben Ali passed a constitutional measure to abolish the three-term presidential limit, attempting to remain President for life. These actions along with deteriorating socio-economic conditions in the 2000s began to make Tunisians weary of the Ben Ali establishment.

Unrest and the Rise of New Media

While poverty rates throughout the coastal regions of Tunisia significantly dropped from 1990 to 2003, the Midwest, the South, and rural regions continued to face widespread poverty and underdevelopment (Aleya-Sghaier 2012; Deane 2013). Rural areas were historically neglected and regions even more prosperous started to struggle as socio-economic conditions began to deteriorate at the turn of the century. Broad disapproval of the regime began "as socio-economic conditions worsened, the tacit social contract between Ben Ali and the Tunisian people, resting upon political repression in exchange for social benefits, was no longer acceptable ..." (Paciello 2011: 5). Socio-economic conditions, in addition to an array of other social and political factors, eventually contributed to the fall of the regime. As noted in Chapter 5, new media technologies became pervasive under Ben Ali, commencing in 2002 under his "Seven-November Internet Bus" project that sought to expand Internet access to the rural areas while cutting traffics. However, such polices did not alleviate unemployment and underemployment.

The large youth population, even those with college degrees, was faced with vast unemployment or underemployment. In 2006–2007, three hundred and thirty-six thousand university graduates were unemployed, compared to one hundred and twenty-one thousand eight hundred in 1996–1997. In 2009 estimates on youth employment ranged from 40 to 60 percent (Aleya-Sghaier 2012). The youth and rural populations were not the only ones experiencing financial hardship. As rising food costs in 2008 reached homes throughout all of Tunisia, the average household was spending around 36 percent of their income on food (Schraeder and Redissi 2011). These economic trends continued up to *al-shawa*.

As Tunisians were faced with little economic security, the rise of social media exposed the lavish lifestyle of dignitaries, particularly Ben Ali's wife, Leila Trabelsi and her entire extended family. In 2007, a YouTube video showed Leila on a European shopping excursion in her family's private jet (Howard et al. 2011). The video was widely viewed and led to increased regulations on streaming sites, such as YouTube and Facebook. Videos of their extravagant lifestyle did not fully detail the breadth of their wealth and control over Tunisia's private sector. Ben Ali and his extended family owned over 200 companies and held 21 percent of net private sector profits. The family owned an array of media enterprises, including Tunis-based radio and television stations, newspapers, and magazines, which in turn led to censorship (Dreisbach and Joyce 2014). As Tunisians became more and more Internet savvy, information about the royal family continued to spread.

Sensing that the regime's strict power over the populace was beginning to wane, Ben Ali attempted to restrict both old and new forms of media. Acknowledging the power of free speech, "the regime exercised tight control over the media; no critical press or independent radio/television was allowed; and Internet censorship became extensive and sophisticated, with Interior Ministry agents routinely monitoring personal email accounts, blocking sensitive websites and supervising Internet cafes to discourage criticism" (Paciello 2011: 2). As early as 2003, reports surfaced of users being jailed (International Crisis Group 2011). Internet activists remained diligent and fought the government's attempt to ban social media platforms—a Facebook ban in 2008 drove Tunisians to remain on the site through proxy servers (Joseph 2011). As the Ben Ali regime became more and more restrictive, Tunisians became increasingly irritated and more fervent and creative in their quest for change.

Wikileaks and the Unraveling of Authoritarian Bargaining

The private jet video, discussed in the previous section, was just the beginning of damaging evidence against the regime, highlighting the power of the digital age in the dissemination of sensitive material. In a series of 2008 US State Department cables, the US ambassador to Tunisia, Robert F. Godec, described in detail the rapacious lifestyle and repressive political tactics utilized by the Ben Ali family (Schraeder and Redissi 2011). While the US State Department tried to withhold the documents from mass release, TuniLeaks, a site associated with an opposition site entitled *Nawaat*, posted the cables for the whole country to see.

The cables detailed the rampant corruption, particularly that more than half of Tunisia's wealthiest corporate leaders were related to Ben Ali, including his three children, seven brothers and sisters, and his wife's ten siblings (Anderson 2011). Godec (2008) went on to describe Ben Ali's family as a "quasi mafia" that had holdings in multiple business sectors, including an airline, hotels, radio stations, assembly plants, real estate, etc. Describing public ridicule of the family and obvious corruption, Godec (2008 para 10) states that the "strong censorship of the press ensures that stories of familial corruption are not published." Further, he described the imprisonment of comedian Hedi Oula Baballa for using the family as the brunt of his stand-up jokes, albeit the government stated it was drug-related. While many Tunisians were aware of such practices, the leaked cables highlighted not only the depth of the corruption, but also showed there was substance to the rumors surrounding the Ben Ali family (Schraeder and Redissi 2011).

As Tunisians became more and more aware of governmental malfeasance, it became more difficult to justify or rationalize their actions. Not only were Tunisians experiencing deteriorating living conditions, but they were also scared to openly discuss government corruption. The Internet worked as an outlet, where one could view information and theoretically post anonymously, but pent-up frustration also made Tunisians less fearful and willing to act regardless of repercussions.

Laying the Foundation: Gafsa's *al-Sahwa*

Frustration with the dire economic situation, particularly in the neglected regions of the South, came to fruition in 2008 in the small town of Redayef, near the mining city of Gafsa. As noted in Chapter 1, workers protested over the hiring practices of a state-owned GPC that initially had promised locals and the labor union that new hires would be given to local families, specifically sons of workers that had died from accidents on the job or had been injured (Marzouki 2011). Instead of keeping their promises and hiring locals, the company offered positions to workers with connections to the government. This was viewed as another blow to both Ben Ali's authoritarian bargaining agreement and to a region experiencing an unemployment rate of 40 percent. Locals took to the streets not only to protest blatant nepotism, but they also accused the local chapter of the UGTT of being in accord with the phosphate company instead of local workers (Chomiak 2011). The protests gained support quickly, spread throughout the Gafsa region and occurred on a regular basis. The unfair hiring practices became a catalyst for a growing restiveness toward the Ben Ali regime.

Despite the unrest, state news channels failed to cover the protests, but "oppositional papers *Al-Maukif, Al-Mouatin and Al-Tariq Al-Jedid* reported on them regularly" (Chomiak 2011: 72). In solidarity, the movement spread and mobilized university students, teachers, spouses of workers, widows, and local union members. As the numbers of protestors grew, the government feared the blatant opposition. Government security forces, including riot squads, were sent to the region and violently arrested, jailed, and tortured protestors, legitimizing their actions by labeling it a coup (Chomiak 2011; Schraeder and Redissi 2011). As protestors refused to back down, the protests culminated when two activists were shot and killed. As the protests became more violent, state-controlled stations remained silent, while international stations were prohibited. In defiance, online activists that were aware of the story took to Facebook and sent emails to spread the word (Chomiak 2011).

In the end, a combination of factors, including the regional containment of the protests, lack of media coverage, and failed support of the UGTT, led to the dissolution of the six-month long movement. In retrospect, frustration over the economic situation in the Southern region of the country would soon lead to national insurrections. The combination of both old and new media, along with the engagement of more organized and committed labor and civil society groups (particularly the UGTT), empowered Tunisian citizens.

In 2010, a Facebook event, entitled *Tunisie en Blanc* (Tunisian in White), was created to bring awareness to Internet censorship. The young group of Tunisians responsible for the page called for sites, such as YouTube and Dailymotion, to be unblocked and for access to international articles critical of the government (Chomiak 2011). Garnering support globally, the event called on members to dress in white and drink coffee in a café on the busy avenue, Habib Bourguiba, in Tunis. In addition, protests were planned near the Ministry of Technology. The group, which reached five thousand members, utilized the space to engage in political debate (Chomiak 2011). Although the protest seemed harmless and stressed the importance of peaceful action, protests of any size were considered serious offenses.

al-Sahwa and Activism

Al-sahwa is often considered to have begun with the self-immolation on December 17, 2010 of Mohamed Bouazizi, a 26-year-old street vendor from Sidi Bouzid. The fruit vendor faced continuous harassment from the local police, who that very day had confiscated his merchandise. A group of teachers from the National Secondary School Teachers Union took Bouazizi to the hospital, where he later died (International Crisis Group 2011). While the tragic death of Bouazizi was certainly a catalyst for *al-shawa*, the impetus for *al-shawa* is much more complicated. Bouazizi, unfortunately, was not the first citizen to immolate himself and previous acts of opposition discussed above contributed to the overthrow of the regime.

In protest of the difficulty of earning a living wage, another struggling street vendor, Abdesslem Trimech, set himself on fire on March 3, 2010. The difference between the two deaths, however, was that Bouazizi's desperate act was recorded and, with support from his mother, quickly posted online by his cousins (Halverson, Ruston and Threthwey 2013; Harrelson-Stephens and Callaway 2014). Quickly, Bouazizi came to symbolize "the plight of millions of Tunisians, especially the unemployed yet educated youth, who were excluded from economic advancement and denied political expression by the repressive and corrupt policies of Ben Ali and his small clan of powerful families" (Chomiak 2011: 70). As the news began to spread, it became clear that Tunisians resonated with the young street vendor and the first protest in Sidi Bouzid took place on the same day that he set himself aflame (Aleya-Sghaier 2012). While in the beginning the protests were spontaneous in nature, various factors, including media attention (both traditional forms and new forms of social media), the support from various civil society groups, and the inaction of the military led to the mass uprising.

Riots began to erupt first on the neglected streets of Sidi Bouzid. The Bouazizi family, along with trade unionists, staked themselves outside of the police headquarters to express their anger (International Crisis Group 2011). The protests were insulated at first, but after a week quickly spread to surrounding areas. The twenty-seven-year-old blogger, Lina Ben Mehnni, reported on her site,

A Tunisian Girl, the unrest early on in Sidi Bouzid and played an important role in disseminating the information that the state media had ignored (Radsch 2012). Working as a "cyberactivist," one who uses digital media and social media to create momentum for political action, Mehnni, and others took to the Internet to spark a movement. Since a large segment of the society had access to the Internet and were active on Facebook, blogging and other social media platforms were highly effective in spreading information (Radsch 2012). A Facebook group entitled, *Mr. President, Tunisians are Setting Themselves on Fire,* was quickly joined by thousands of users, while Twitter messages with hashtags, such as #bouazizi, #tunisia, and #sidibouzid became rallying cries for *al-shawa.* Al-Jazeera's *Mubasher* channel subsequently became the first major media outlet to televise the immolation video, which the station received from Facebook (Halverson, Ruston and Threthwey 2013).

The protests soon moved to neighboring towns and eventually to the southern cities of Gafsa and Kebili. These protests were clearly different from those in 2008, as the police force was unable to contain the protestors and the government failed to block media outlets (Aleya-Sghaier 2012). *Al-sahwa* moved north, finally reaching Sfax and Tunis. Since *al-shawa* did not have a particular leader, truly embodying a grassroots movement, the government was unable to imprison individuals and attempts at blocking media outlets were stifled through both internal and external actors. Young Tunisians, along with the hacking groups Anonymous and Telecomix, used their Internet expertise to ensure that social media sites remained open (Howard et al. 2011). Despite Ben Ali quickly mobilizing his police brigade, videos were rapidly posted online of clashes between protestors and the police, which only fueled the fury of the entire country.

While social media and the Internet provided the momentum for *al-shawa,* especially for young activists, civil society organizations, unions, and students worked to progress the movement. Fighting collectively for bread, freedom, dignity, and social justice (Marzouki 2011; Plaetzer 2014). Tunisians knew that now was the time to act, regardless of social status, religion, or political affiliation. Before *al-shawa,* civil society groups, except for a few, often "acted as mere cogs in the political machine of the national government and therefore were hardly in tune with the reality of societal problems" (Foundation for the Future 2013: 8). Faced with threats of imprisonment or torture, groups had to find ways to work with the government, rather than against it. Conversely, organizations mobilized quickly after the death of Bouazizi on January 4, 2011, with the teacher's union in Sidi Bouzid putting together a "Committee of the Marginalized" to organize protests and the National Secondary Teachers' Union even calling for teachers to stop working for twenty minutes in support of the countrywide unrest. In addition, the UGTT, determined not to repeat their failure during the Gafsa protests, issued a communiqué on January 11, 2011 in support of peaceful protests, which resulted in a turning point in *al-shawa*. The following day, unions in Sfax organized a strike and thirty thousand Tunisians took to the street, the largest demonstration in the country before Ben Ali fled (International Crisis Group 2011). The protests had quickly evolved from at first being spontaneous and focused on socio-economic conditions to becoming political, demanding Ben Ali resign. This shift further cemented the need for civil society organizations to articulate and fight for the country's demands.

One of the most pivotal demonstrations throughout *al-shawa* was on January 14, 2011. Beginning in Mohammad Ali Square near the UGTT headquarters, the protest quickly spread throughout Tunis on Habib Bourguiba Avenue where thousands and thousands of protestors shouted in front of the Ministry of the Interior "Step down! Step down!" (Aleya-Sghaier 2012: 24). Leila Ben Debba, a prominent lawyer in Tunisia, bravely held a Tunisian flag and urged her fellow Tunisians to continue to fight. Meanwhile, civil society groups, such as the LTDH and regional unions expressed their unwavering support for the movement (Schraeder and Redissi 2011). Those most repressed by the government were waiting for this opportunity.

Ben Ali made three televised appearances before he left the country. In his first appearance, December 28, 2014, the President threatened protestors; in the second, January 10, 2011 he described protestors as "terrorists," but promised to create three hundred thousand new jobs. In his last address, January 13, 2011, Ben Ali changed his tone and stated that he would not run for re-election on October 14 (Schraider and Redissi 2011). With the military refusing to heed to his demands and the swarms of protestors too difficult for the police force to contain, Ben Ali was given no choice but to flee. On the same day of the massive protests, the President and his family flew to Saudi Arabia, where they have remained. While Tunisians celebrated the removal of his regime, they knew that *al-sahwa* was far from over—Ben Ali and his extended family were just the leaders of the RCD and the country wanted the regime removed in its entirety.

Activism after Authoritarianism: The Democratic Agreement

A few days after Ben Ali removed himself from office, a temporary president and a "national unity government" took power (Dalacoura 2012: 64). Prime Minister

Mohammad al-Ghannouchi took over as interim president, which was in accordance with the Tunisian Constitution. Tunisians were wary that elements of the government, particularly the police, the Ministry of the Interior, and the RCD would continue to govern the country as though nothing had happened (Aleya-Sghaier 2012). Moreover, al-Ghannouchi's ascension was seen as a continuation of Ben Ali's authoritarian agreement. As a result, Tunisia's second *al-shawa*, the *Kasbah* Coalition, began on January 15, 2011 with demonstrators demanding al-Ghannouchi's resignation.

The *Kasbah*, a plaza in central Tunis, became the epicenter of the second wave, with protestors demonstrating round-the-clock. With the plaza within clear view of the interim president al-Ghannouchi, protestors demanded both his departure and the collapse of the RCD. Demonstrators turned the outside of al-Ghannouchi's office into their canvas and spray-painted caricatures, drew satirical political cartoons, and even created a "blown-up Facebook page that showed how to join the revolution online and handwritten signs in Arabic, French and English" (Coll 2011: para 3). Very articulate in their demands, dissenters expressed that the NCA should focus on rewriting the constitution. The highly-educated populace was a key differentiating factor between the Tunisian *al-shawa* and other countries involved in the Arab Spring—a large proportion of the opposition were able to explain exactly what kind of government would work given the dynamics of the country.

Aleya-Sghaier (2012) states that the second wave was marked by two distinct occurrences: young Tunisians caravanning from rural parts of the country into the capital and a prominent sit-in from February 20, to March 4, 2011 that contained strong representation from the UGTT and *l'Ordre Tunisien des Avocats*. These particular acts disrupted the interim government and forced the al-Ghannouchi government to step down. While the al-Ghannouchi government was perhaps a step in the right direction with newly appointed members more representative of regions throughout the country and more civil society involvement (Paciello 2011), in the end al-Ghannouchi's previous role under the Ben Ali regime could not be ignored. Just ten days after taking office, al-Ghannouchi resigned on February 27, 2011. Tunisians demanded yet another transition in governance and made it clear that the unrest would continue until a fair governance structure was put in place.

A new interim government was established and Beji Caid Essebsi became the country's new leader. Having formerly worked under both Bourguiba and Ben Ali, albeit a critic of both regimes, the eighty-four-year-old supported the abolition of the RCD party. He demanded that high-ranking officials under the former government be arrested and punished and that the special police force be disbanded (Schraeder and Redissi 2011). Heeding to the demands of protestors, the new government was tasked with holding National Assembly Elections and the government also created three transitional management commissions—the Commission on Law Reform, the Commission of Inquiry on Corruption, and the Independent Commission of Inquiry (Aleya-Sghaier 2012). To ensure that truly all voices would be heard on February 11 the National Council for the Protection of the Revolution was formed—members consisted of leftist groups, the Islamist Party, *Ennahdha*, UGTT members, the Association of Lawyers, and the Association of Judges of the Tunisian League of Human Rights. Essebsi then created a High Committee for the Achievement of the Objectives of the Revolution, which represented a wide variety of political parties, civil society organizations, and associations with the main task of providing counsel to the government. There was controversy, however, that with the creation of the High Committee Esbessi was attempting to dissolve the National Council (Aleya-Sghaier 2012).

The civil society structure throughout this interim period largely evolved from the days under authoritarianism. From 2011 to 2013, thousands of additional civil society groups joined the political arena because of the deregulation of the archaic laws on forming associations. Finally opening the doors for political plurality, with a "broad range of activities including civic activism, human rights, social welfare initiatives and direct outreach work with deprived communities across the country" (Fortier 2015: 143), civil societies finally found a space to flourish. Although they were a key component of the *al-shawa*, it was in the post-*al-shawa* period and subsequent unrest that civil society organizations played their largest role, particularly during the multiple rounds of elections that have occurred since *al-shawa*.

On October 23, 2011, Tunisia held its first free elections to elect a Constituent Assembly tasked with rewriting the constitution. Surprising secularists, the Islamist *Ennahdha* party won the most seats in the Constituent Assembly, but failed to win the majority. The leader of the party, Rachid al-Ghannouchi, who was forced into exile under the Ben Ali regime, promised to remain committed to a modernist vision, ensuring women's rights and confirming that Sharia law would not be imposed (Zoubir 2015). Despite the win, *Ennahdha* did not secure the majority, resulting in a coalition between two social democratic parties—highlighting a commitment to plurality. Although the elections were for the most part peaceful and the transition was smooth, after the results were announced violent protests occurred in Sidi Bouzid at the *Ennahdha* headquarters. Demonstrators were angered over the cancellation of seats won from the Popular List party, popular in Sidi Bouzid due to its leader hailing from the region, for alleged financial fraud (BBC 2011). Despite some unrest within Sidi Bouzid, the election process was lauded internationally for a process deemed "free, transparent and fair" (Zoubir 2015: 13)

Although there was deep-seated ideological fragmentation within the newly formed Assembly, parties succeeded in collectively coming together to pass a provisional constitution in December 2011. The twenty-six articles detailed the structure of the newly formed government, including the roles of the executive, legislative, and judiciary sectors. The two hundred and seventeen-member Assembly debated over a five-day period about specific provisions within the constitution. There was wide interest throughout the entire country as they watched the debate aired live on television and discussed over social media platforms. Peaceful demonstrations occurred outside the Assembly as citizens chanted "freedom and dignity." With its passing also came the resignation of Essebsi and a vote from the Assembly elected Moncef Marzouki, a doctor and former head of *La Ligue Tunisienne des Droits de l'Homme*, as the new President (Al Jazeera 2011). Tunisia's path to democracy, albeit arduous, highlighted the power of collective activism.

Tunisia's change of state, although deemed "successful," came with an enormous cost. An estimated three hundred people died during protests and seven hundred were injured, widely the result of the violence used toward protestors by the regime's police force. Human rights groups claimed that imprisonment and torture continued even after Ben Ali fled (Zagger 2011), which encouraged Tunisians to be fully engaged with the transitional process; they wanted to ensure their new leaders were nothing like those in power under the former regimes. An important note is that during this transitory period, no major reforms occurred in education.

Activism under the New "Democratic" Constitution

It would be three years before Tunisia would eventually pass the country's final constitution. While the fall of the Ben Ali regime brought newfound freedom to the country and the opportunity for change, the country still faced high unemployment, terrorist attacks, and polarity between parties. The country almost erupted into chaos with the murders of opposition leaders Chokri Belaid on February 6, 2013 and Mohammed Brahmi on July 25, both of whom belonged to the left-wing nationalist Movement of the People Party. The killing resulted in a "political paralysis" and large-scale demonstrations called for the resignation of the Islamist-led government (Al Jazeera 2013). Jihadists were responsible for the murders, which led to accusations of the ruling *Ennahdha* party's failure to combat terrorism and improve the economy (Zoubir 2015).

Opposition protests organized by the National Salvation Front, a collective of anti-government parties, included tens of thousands of Tunisians who demanded *Ennahdha* resign to bring stability back to the country. The collectivity that embodied the provisional constitution process deteriorated as distrust between secular and moderate Islamists escalated during nationwide discussions. It was at this tense time where the country was at a crossroads that civil society organizations played their biggest role.

Civil society organizations became a key component in the transitional framework and took on the task of pushing the country forward despite continued unrest and ideological divides. Thousands of citizens, three hundred civil society organizations and hundreds of university representatives acted as consultants in the drafting process of the new constitution and pushed the Assembly forward by holding discussions and debates that were often televised. In addition, organizations encouraged and took part in the use of social networks to spread awareness (Jemail 2015). The proactive stance forced politicians to compromise. This was particularly the case in 2013 when a *National Dialogue* was established and a Social Pact agreed upon between UGTT, UTICA, and LTDH and the Tunisian Order of Lawyers in collaboration with the *Ennahdha*-led government. Civil society organizations and opposition leaders were building partnerships and compromising to improve the deteriorating socio-economic condition of the country and also secure a peaceful and nonviolent transformation (Jemail 2015). The pact made politicians accountable and called for a completed constitution, particularly requesting the departure of *Ennahdha* following the continued unrest. *Ennahdha* heeded their demands and stepped down to allow the country to move forward (Zoubir 2015).

After months of deadlock and uncertainty, Tunisia adopted a new constitution in January 2014. Widely heralded internationally as a model to neighboring nations, the progressive constitution "protects civil liberties; separates legislative, executive and judicial powers; guarantees women parity in political bodies; and declares that Islam is the country's official religion, while protecting religious freedom for all" (Zoubir 2015: 14). With two hundred of the two hundred and sixteen members of the NCA voting in favor (and twelve against and four absenting), the constitution marks a new beginning after decades of authoritarian rule. The constitution dedicated an entire chapter to the rights of citizens with 28 articles protecting Tunisians from torture, assuring rights to a fair trial, and freedom of religion (The Guardian 2014). In addition to the constitution, civil society organizations fought for new laws giving Tunisians the rights to form associations and the freedom to acquire and disclose public information. Further, organizations finally could collaborate with international non-profit organizations on an array of development projects, attempting to improve the dire economic conditions throughout impoverished regions (Jemail 2015).

With the drafting of the new constitution, Tunisians are hoping for stability and the power to chart their own course. While the constitution cemented Tunisia's transition to the democracy and freedom Tunisians have yearned for, leaders must remain committed to improving the economic conditions for Tunisians, particularly providing avenues for employment for the younger generation. The constitutional process highlighted the determination of an entire country willing to come together for the chance to have a fresh start. While major education reforms have occurred during the drafting of the new constitution, the 2014 Constitution reaffirmed and enshrined many of the same educational rights that had been guaranteed under the authoritarian agreements of both Bourguiba and Ben Ali.

Concluding Thoughts—A Nobel Peace Prize

The Nobel Peace Prize awarded to *The National Dialogue Quartet* "symbolizes an extraordinary recognition of the achievements of all Tunisians" (Jemail, 2015: para. 8). As this chapter has encapsulated, change did not simply begin with *al-shawa* but instead, decades of activism ultimately effected change. Years of pent-up frustration over authoritative rule along with dire societal conditions made all Tunisians activists, regardless of age, sex, religion, or occupation. The advent of new media, such as social media sites Facebook, YouTube and Twitter, gave all Tunisians both a voice and an outlet. In addition, civil society organizations, fed up with years of repression, worked to not only progress the movement, but also force the government to unite. Economic conditions and security issues continue to plague the nation, creating a need for activists, civil society organizations, and citizens to continue what they have started.

8

The End of Authoritarian Bargaining Agreements and the Rise of Homegrown Militantism

Relying on a comparative-historical approach, across the preceding seven chapters we have reflected on Tunisia's 3,000 years of state-run education under different authoritarian agreements (be it kingdom, Beylic, or dictator) and we argue that Tunisia's youth have historically revolted after being discontented, disillusioned, and disenfranchised with their prospects after studying. We have examined the post-independence educational Masaâdi Plan (under Minister Mohammed Masaâdi) under Bourguiba's dictatorial leadership and showed that in education his authoritarian bargaining agreement focused on expanding mass schooling and access, particularly in the rural areas. The Masaâdi Plan concentrated on ensuring that every Tunisian received six years of basic education while seeking to build a unified system that emphasized technical and vocational education and the training of a corps of Tunisian educators qualified to teach a new uniform school curriculum emphasizing Arabic language and literature, Islam though the history, and geography of the Tunisian and North African region.

The Charfi Plan (under Minister Mohamed Charfi), or the 1991-Education reforms, stemming from Ben Ali's authoritarian agreements of *le Changement* and *le Pacte National* which represented radical reforms, that touched not only the structural aspect of education but they restructured the educational philosophy and theoretical orientations of the system. Ben Ali's education reforms confirmed the principle of the gratuitousness of all education stages, the compulsory character of education to students from ages six to sixteen and the access to nine years of basic education across two cycles. Many of these measures were taken to reduce school failure and truancy. The main objective of the 1991-Educaiton reforms was to ensure that every student developed predefined competencies, which qualifies them for an active social life and integration into Tunisian society. The Rouissi Plan (under Minister Moncer Rouissi), or the 2002-Educaiton reforms, not only continued previous reforms but also stressed the importance of information and communication technologies in the education sector. This emphasis on creating a technological elite society would lay the foundations for *al-sahwa* as educated young people became disgruntled when they could not find jobs.

Regardless of the transition from dictator to dictator and changes in authoritarian agreements, our comparative-historical approach toward understanding Tunisia's educational policies shows that education was used as a social good to achieve the aims of different dictators. In essence, we draw attention to the "transitological monuments" that come to define and dominate the Tunisian educational architecture as new futures are envisioned and as the past gives way to historical revisionism. Such an approach focused on "'transversal' and 'horizontal' comparisons and what links, overlappings and asymmetries we can see as a result ... or what has been called 'situatedness' or 'embeddedness'" (Robertson 2012: 39) to highlight the "politics of knowledge production" (Vavrus and Bartlett 2006). By focusing on different dictatorial regimes and how they used education during and after their transitions, we show how historical shifts in political, economic, and cultural experiences shape pre-modern, modern, and late-modern educational systems. In agreeing with Cowen (2000b: 339), we suggest that education transitologies are not necessarily linear and "educational reform itself helps to construct not sequential equilibrium conditions but more transitologies." Thus, in empirically conceptualizing transitory spaces, we suggest these spaces be viewed as part of a vertical site that encompasses past and present discourses that are "multi-layered and cross cutting proceeds and modes of interaction" (Robertson 2012: 39).

Historically, education has been used and continues to be touted as a way to access middle class-ness in Tunisia. While what constitutes the middle class often remains vague for the regime in power, there is a perception in this homogeneous society that investment in human capital brings economic privilege. Unlike other Arab societies, Tunisia has led the way in girls' schools and gender equity in work. This sense of equity, particularly within the francophone tradition of secularism, has meant that parents ensure both boys and girls attend school. From independence to *al-shawa*, Tunisia's growth model has been summed up by three defining characteristics: (i) a robust neo-corporatist state that promised stability and a corrupt and extensive police state apparatus; (ii) an implied social contract based on active education and social policy, state feminism, and broad-based investment in infrastructure; and (iii) the appearance of sound state-driven economic management under the guise of a liberalized economy.

One year after *al-sahwa,* in the World Economic Forum's 2013–2014 *Global Competitiveness Report,* Tunisia placed eighty-third and in the 2016–2017 Report covering the competitiveness performance of one hundred and thirty-eight economies Tunisia placed ninety-fifth. The overall decline in Tunisia's competitive ratings was attributed to the fallout from the homegrown acts of terrorism of Spring 2015 and their perceived part in the subsequent failure to generate new jobs. In educational areas, Tunisia also ranked the lowest for Levant and North Africa countries. Tunisia ranked 48th (down from 22nd in 2012) for availability of scientists and engineers; 71st (down from 31st in 2012) for quality of math and science education; 89th (down from 71st in 2012) for quality of the education system; 76th (down from 73rd in 2012) for higher education and training; 111th (down from 94th in 2012) for quality of scientific research institutions; and 116th (down from 113th in 2012) for university-industry collaboration in research. These downward trends on key indicators show that Tunisia's transition is turbulent and compounded by numerous internal and external factors.

Yet, the OECD (2015c) cites that Tunisia's educational resources are among the highest-ranked within the global PISA. In 2016, its PISA scores ranked toward the bottom at 69th in math, 66th in reading, and 68th in science out of seventy-two participating countries. The 2014 census revealed that since the previous census of 2004, Tunisia's illiteracy rate had decreased from 23.3 percent to 18.8 percent. However, it was still higher than the global average and Tunisia ranked twelfth out of the twenty-two Arab countries in literacy (Reidy 2015). Illiteracy in rural areas, particularly multi-generational illiteracy, is still high and students still find it difficult to access education due to financial (school fees) and social barriers. According to the World Bank, the turnover of *cours particuliers* (private lessons) in Tunisia amounts to about 700 million dinars. Yet, businesses cannot find the labor needed, universities are packed, and unemployment is rising.

In the preceding chapters, we have used a vertical case study to scrupulously scrutinize the different policy streams that structure educational transitions in Tunisia. We addressed the contemporary problems of the authoritarian bargaining agreement in Chapters 5, 6, and 7 and accounted for the recurrence of internal disruptions and how these shape the different educational transitions. Consistent with our arguments, we have suggested that dictatorial regimes use authoritarian bargaining to shape educational transitologies. In this final chapter, we reflect upon several of the broad themes we have covered in this book. In the first half of this chapter, we discuss the incremental nature of reforms in the post-*al-sahwa* period. We show that after *al-sahwa,* the authoritarian agreements of the past were left intact and few modifications were made to the existing system. In the second part of the chapter, we argue that such incremental policy reforms coupled with high unemployment and underemployment have made the Tunisian education system a ripe breeding ground for the recruitment and training of militant jihadists by *Daesh* (the Islamic State)—where Tunisians make up half of its fighters and leadership. We conclude by discussing the consequences of returning Tunisian *Daesh* fighters, compounded with economic uncertainty, re-entering Tunisia's education system.

Governing through the *Troika* and Educational Politics

On October 23, 2011, *Ennahdha* won a plurality of the first post-*al-sahwa* elections vote for the National Constituent Assembly (NCA). They formed a ruling coalition called the *Troika*—an alliance between *Ennahdha*, *Ettakatol* (the Democratic Forum for Labor and Liberties), and *El Mottamar* (the Congress for the Republic)—through which it ruled the country under Moncef Marzouki as President (from 2011 to 2014) and Hamadi Jebali as Prime Minister (from December 2011 to March 2013). Along with fifty-three independent representatives and four other parties, the *Troika* worked in the NCA to draft the constitution and provisionally govern the country. The NCA was the product of the second Kasbah sit-in[1] in February 2011, which occurred after pressure was placed on the transitional government to convene an assembly to draft a *new* constitution after *al-sahwa* to reflect the sacrifice and aspirations of Tunisians. In fact, the Kasbah sit-in was called because:

> [young people] felt the revolution had been stalled. Why were we not speaking about politics anymore? We are now campaigning for a revolution based on our imaginations and our dreams. We're also rooting out all the hidden names of the RCD, the old dictator's party and its new front parties standing for the elections on 24 July. We're showing the government that we still have our eyes open and we can put them under pressure.
>
> Sebystyen 2011: para 5

Since the NCA had derived its legitimacy out of the ashes of *al-sahwa*, upon taking office the Renaissance Party insisted that the NCA should be maintained until it had drafted and passed a new constitution. The NCA had a year to draft the new constitution, a period during which the Law on the Provisional Organization of Public Powers governed domestic affairs. The NCA consisted of two hundred and seventeen seats, of which the *Troika* occupied one hundred and eighteen and its sole mission was the drafting of the constitution, not governing.

During the time of the NCA, all issues were considered and other fundamental issues, such as Tunisian identity, arose and underwent a laborious process of debate, discussion, and dialogue. During the first days of convening the NCA, every conceivable item, all products of authoritarian bargaining agreements, were deemed problematic. Disagreement engulfed the members at several points and at one particular moment, members protested the use of the French language over Arabic. Certain representatives considered French the language of the colonizers and therefore deemed it should not be used until Tunisians had broken their chains from yet another dictator. For several members, the Arab identity of the country had to be confirmed along with Tunisia's Islamic roots. As the debates inside of the NCA stirred, Tunisians took to the streets and mobilized civil society organizations to advocate for a strong statement of freedom and equity against the predominantly Islamic government.

The NCA actively involved civil society in its process and took almost three years and four successive drafts (August 6, 2012; December 14, 2012; April 22, 2013; and June 1, 2013) to arrive at a final constitution, in January 2014. According to Redissi and Boukhayatia (2015: 5), consensus was hard to garner since "opinions differed more on general principles than on liberties." The Tunisian Constitution has been considered a unique model of women's rights in the Arab world. It contains a preamble and one hundred and forty-nine articles embodied in ten chapters, namely, general principles, rights, liberties, legislative authority, executive authority, independent constitutional bodies, local government, constitutional amendments, final provisions, and transitional provisions.

Concerning education, Article 16 of the 2014 Constitution stipulates, "the state guarantees the impartiality of educational institutions from all partisan instrumentalization" (Government of Tunisia 2014: 6). Like many areas in the Constitution, consensus on matters relating to education was not reached easily, particularly on:

> Article 38 (39, after reordering), which concerns education, was the subject of debate. The right as such was affirmed without difficulty (compulsory free public education and the obligations of the state in this respect). A second paragraph, however, polarised the conflicts because it established a cultural particularism, partially resulting from an amendment: 'Also, the State shall endeavour to root young generations in their Arab Muslim identity, to strengthen, consolidate and generalise the Arabic language.' Only nine deputies from the assorted left voted against this article on 7 January 2014. Rooting in identity was not mentioned at all in the second draft (article 29). The third and fourth drafts restrict themselves to requiring the state to strengthen and consolidate the Arabic language

(respectively article 35 and 38). Once alerted, over 50 associations addressed an open letter to the President of the NCA, requesting that the article be revised. The NCA bowed to the pressure. Article 39 requires that the state both consolidate pupils in their identity and ensure 'openness to foreign languages, human civilisations and the diffusion of a culture of Human Rights.'

Redissi and Boukhayatia 2015: 20

In the end, Article 39, addressing the fundamental issues relating to education, was restructured to balance educational particularism. The final text of Article 39 states that:

> Education shall be mandatory up to the age of sixteen years.
>
> The state guarantees the right to free public education at all levels and ensures provisions of the necessary resources to achieve a high quality of education, teaching and training. It shall also work to consolidate the Arab–Muslim identity and national belonging in the young generations and to strengthen, promote and generalize the use of the Arabic language and to openness to foreign languages, human civilizations and diffusion of the culture of human rights.
>
> Government of Tunisia 2014: 8–9

Further, Article 47 guarantees children the right to an education from their parents and the state. Article 65 denotes education as an "ordinary law," which implies that all matters relating to education can be passed by a "majority of members [of the NCA] who are present, provided that such a majority represents no less than one-third of the members of the Assembly" (Government of Tunisia 2014: 8–9).

The new Constitution that emerged in 2014 was initially crafted with input from a wide cross-section of the educated populace. The public engagement in the constitution drafting, in addition to the tremendous work conducted by the different players of civil society, created one of the most advanced constitutions in the MENA region. Moreover, after *al-sahwa*, Tunisian civil society helped to stabilize the transition by suggesting a road map to evade falling into chaos. The UGTT took the first step in forming a civil society alliance by approaching the UTICA, its historical rival. The Tunisian Human Rights League and the Tunisian Order of Lawyers later joined the coalition. This new alliance, *The National Dialogue Quartet* who later won the 2015 Nobel Peace Prize, served as a mediator and broker between the disputing political parties to end the political instability and deadlock that characterized the transitional period. Civil society has also contributed to building sustainable decision-making partnerships between political stakeholders. However, to execute their missions, Tunisia's civil society actors need to expand their knowledge horizons and attain a level of maturity required to guarantee a smooth transition to democracy.

Early Childhood Care after *al-Sahwa*

After *al-sahwa*, the structure of the education system remained the same and no significant reforms began until late 2016. The early childhood care (EEC) system retained its three-cycle system of nurseries, kindergartens and/or *al-kuttabs*, and the Preparatory year. The most visual, post-*al-sahwa* non-governmental reform that occurred was the proliferation of so-called "Qur'anic kindergartens," which used *Wahhabi* doctrine aimed at enlightening Tunisia's next generation (Zbiss 2013). In the post-*al-sahwa* education system, there was no mixing of genders. In 2013, the Ministry of Education (2012) estimated that 90 percent of the institutions specializing in EEC provisions were private suppliers while the other 10 percent were divided among municipalities, other ministries (such as the Ministry of Defense), and organizations and associations (such as the Tunisian Union of Social Solidarity, the National Union of Tunisian Women, and the Organization of Education and Family).

However, an educational disparity exists between the coastal regions and rural interior of the country. For example, in 2013 education cash transfer programs covered fewer than eighty thousand children. Official estimates published by the Ministry of Education (2015) for 2011 and 2012 demonstrate that the number of *al-kuttabs* (from one thousand two hundred and seventy to one thousand three hundred and seventy-one) and teaching staff (from one thousand one hundred and and thirty-four to one thousand two hundred and thirty-five) continues to increase as the demand for this type of pre-education gains greater momentum. In 2013, the ministry established a committee consisting of heads of *al-kuttabs*, Imams, and school inspectors who provided a recommendation for interventions that would assist in modernizing these institutions. These wide-ranging recommendations called for a review of: (i) the curriculum of *al-kuttabs* to ensure they were using modern methods and providing a pre-primary education in line with the policy positions of the ministry; (ii) staffing qualifications at all levels; (iii) the guarantee of a medical examination for children registered in *al-kuttabs* with help from the Ministry of Health; and (iv) the strength of the role of *al-kuttabs* in providing quality Qur'anic learning. Data shows municipal kindergartens decreased from two thousand and fifteen in 1990 to one hundred and fifty-five in 2000 while private kindergartens increased from two hundred and sixty-two in 1990 to one thousand one hundred and sixty-eight in 2000 (UNESCO 2007). The Ministry of Education (2015) notes that kindergartens reached four thousand and five institutions in 2013 enrolling a total number of one hundred and seventy-nine thousand five hundred and forty-one students, which was a 7.7 percent increase from 2012. Regional disparities of resources still exist between rural and urban kindergartens, while the quality of several private kindergartens has been called into question.

After *al-sahwa*, the number of private *année Préparatoire* (Preparatory year) institutions increased drastically by taking advantage of the unstable political transitions and the absence of a pedagogic and administrative inspection by the Ministry of Education. In 2001–2002, there were three hundred and sixty-two Preparatory schools as compared to two thousand and fifty-five in 2012–2013 (Ministry of Education 2015). In 2013, there were approximately forty-nine thousand six hundred and eighteen children enrolled in *année Préparatoire* across four thousand and five institutions. This increase has occurred mostly in rural areas since the Ministry of Education allowed other suppliers, such as the private and civil society sectors (particularly in the governorate of Monastir), to provide *année Préparatoire*. The Ministry of Education (2015) states it will build approximately three hundred Preparatory classes yearly in primary schools in line with the 2014 Constitution requirements of equity. In 2015, the distribution of Preparatory classes in rural areas reached 58.7 percent while it reached 41.3 percent in urban areas. This reflected the government's policy of emphasizing equity in the countryside and avoiding the competition of the private sector (Ministry of Education 2015). However, there has been a disparity in the quality of pre-primary education offered in Preparatory classes due to a lack of adequately trained teachers, pedagogic assistants, and head teachers. In the immediate *al-sahwa* period, the training program offered by the Ministry of Education, consisting of six courses covering the organization of the spaces, language activities, sports activities, sciences activities, psychological activities, hand activities, and curriculum approaches, has declined significantly.

After *al-sahwa*, statistical data from the Ministry of Education (2015)[2] shows that 97 percent of nurseries are private while the other 3 percent are evenly distributed between organizations and associates, ministries, and municipalities. Data released by the Ministry of Education (2015) indicates that after *al-sahwa*, there was a significant decrease in the number of students registering for nursery education from 17.5 percent between 2009 and 2010 to 10.25 percent between 2012 and 2013. Additionally, the Ministry of Education (2015) notes that in 2013, 56 percent of people who ran and taught in nursery schools were untrained. After *al-sahwa*, access to nursery education remains problematic since there are huge disparities in access and quality across the regions and twenty-four governorates. The World Bank (2015) reports that almost a quarter, or 22 percent, of children aged five are engaged in child labor in Tunisia. The report draws attention to the fact that vast disparities exist in the EEC between the least advantaged children with uneducated parents in the poorest rural homes and the most advantaged children with highly educated parents in wealthy urban areas. In other words, children in the countryside are less likely to survive their first year of life when compared to children born in urban areas. In December 2015, the Ministry of Women, Family and Children began to crack down on unauthorized *al-kuttabs* and elementary schools and eight hundred out of one thousand one hundred schools were closed.

Primary and Secondary Education after *al-Shawa*

Like EEC, little visible reform occurred in primary and secondary education after *al-sahwa*. Under the *Troika*, Minister of Education Taïeb Baccouche (from 2011 to 2014) took a non-interventionist approach to education reforms. In employing a gradualist approach toward education reform, after *al-sahwa*, numerous political reasons were cited for no major reforms. In 2014, the Ministry of Education, under the guidance of a new minister, Fethi Jarray, began releasing annual reports that focused on describing the current education system, the challenges that it faces, and the intended interventions the ministry is proposing. It is interesting in that the ministry, in publishing annual reports on education rather than creating the traditional five-year education policy program, is seeking to: (i) suggest that education programs and processes are open to democratic scrutiny and are a national obligation; and (ii) transparency in the form the reports take will lead to a type of educational revolution. For example, the Ministry of Education (2014: 1) notes that "[its] revolution is not only aiming at fight[ing] corruption, but it is also hoping to fight all areas of poverty, ignorance and illness so that the healthy mind will be in a healthy body" (*author's translation*).

After *al-sahwa*, the primary education cycle remained divided into two schedules. The first schedule lasts six years and the second schedule, junior high school, runs for three years. Under the first timetable, the aim is to teach students about national belonging in addition to learning the tools to acquire basic knowledge for oral and written communication, to develop the abilities to read, and count, and to help the pupil strengthen his mind and his physical qualifications. In the second schedule of primary school, students focus on learning oral skills; attention is given to Arabic, as well as two foreign languages and they are prepared for knowledge in mathematics, sciences, technologies, arts, and social sciences. At the primary level, the Ministry of Education (2015) identified that several new factors are undermining the education system. School violence rose drastically in three areas: (i) from one student toward another; (ii) from a student toward school equipment; and (iii) from a student toward a teacher. Additionally, the Ministry of Education (2015) notes that at the primary level, for example in 2014, teacher absenteeism was prevalent at a yearly rate of 4.9 percent amounting to five hundred and sixteen thousand four hundred and sixty working days equivalent to 23.4 million Tunisian dinars in lost productivity.

An independent study on local governance performance in six governorates[3] by Benstead et al., (2015) found that one in five students had a teacher absent and 70 percent of parents paid for private tutors. While Tunisia has managed to record, according to government figures, enrollment rates for students aged six to eleven, at the primary level in 2013–2014 it had reached 99.4 percent (with 99.2 percent gross enrollment for girls as compared with 98.9 percent for boys). However, numerous challenges still confront the current system. In fact, in the post-*al-sahwa* period, the deficits of systems have become clearer. The system has provided broad access and spent a generous portion of the GDP on education since independence, but the quality, infrastructure, regional disparities, and lack of skills needed to transition from school to work are severely lacking. Additionally, the secondary school cycle runs for four years, where everyone takes the same classes during their first year of secondary education and then moves into specializations in their second through fourth years. In September 2014, *The Social Dialogue on Education* (*al-Hiwar al-Watani Hawla al-Taelim*) was launched and it adopted a participatory approach that included different parties related to the education sector, namely, the Ministry of Education, UGTT, the Tunisian Forum of Social and Economic Rights (FTDES), and the National Observatory of Youth with the aim to reform the education system.

The new Minister of Education, Néji Jalloul, (from 2016 to the present) announced the preparation of a new reform project expected to run until 2021. The proposed reform is expected to increase the class times for primary and secondary school, institute school feeding programs, stop half-day and Saturday schooling, and call for the addition of cultural and sport activities to the program (see Chapter 6). In an interview, Néji Jalloul argues that "schools suffer today from deteriorating infrastructure and equipment, a decline in the intellectual level of pupils and the lack of school, sports, cultural and artistic activities" ("Tunis Afrique" 2015). In 2014–2015, the Ministry of Education budget was 14.9 percent of the total state budget.

In 2015, Minister Jalloul resuscitated *The Societal Dialogue on Education* led by members from the Ministry of Education, UGTT, and the Arab Institute for Human Rights (AIHR) to establish a vision for the country's schools. Consequently, the Beji Caid Essebsi government, elected in 2014, has used the language of "saving" the Tunisian education system and in April 2015, the ministry launched a call to different stakeholders to literally sit at one table to come up with a unified vision of the future national education strategy. These types of "negotiated reforms" or authoritarian bargains have a long history in Tunisia dating back to the social pact of 1977—that focused on wage and inflation—and *The National Dialogue Quartet* of October 2013. This national dialogue relied on various constructive recommendations from the different actors in this process. The series of proposals included the improvement of teachers' social conditions at school, the need for revising school programs, as well as the provision of school handbooks. As for reviewing the school hours, the group estimated that time reduction will make it possible for pupils to practice artistic, cultural, and sporting activities that will shape their cultural personalities.

The Jalloul Plan consisted of organizing four workshops with the participation of the pupils, the teachers, and all the educational body actors. The first workshop focused on access to equal opportunity and questions around reducing recidivism and dropouts. The second workshop focused on the development of competencies. The third workshop dealt with the educational environment and school life, paying attention to the problems of the infrastructural development and rise in school violence. The fourth workshop highlighted the governance issue in the education sector, during which the importance of financial resources as a guarantee of a good education was highlighted. All stakeholders emphasized that the *National Dialogue* and other reforms must conform to general national orientations outlined in the 2014 Constitution of the country and international conventions. Overall, the *National Dialogue* reform discussions have focused on improving teaching quality, teacher training, assessment and evaluation, revision of the school timetable, school dropouts, and assessment of the curricula (see Figure 2). In May 2016, the Ministry of Education published a one hundred and fifty-plus-page "White Paper on Education Reform" as well as a two hundred-page pamphlet entitled "Planned Strategies for the Education Sector 2016–2020" with nine strategic goals, as shown in Figure 2.

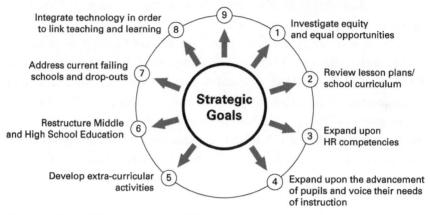

Figure 2 Planned Strategies for the Education Sector 2016–2020

Source: Canavan (2016)

Higher Education after *al-Sahwa*

On June 16, 2015, the Minister of Higher Education and Scientific Research, Chiheb Bouden, announced the launching of the official *Societal Dialogue on the Reform of Higher Education*. The first major post-*al-sahwa* reform project was based on a group of principles ranging from boosting the quality of higher education and the employability of graduates. The reform project in higher education focuses on strengthening university teacher training, promoting research and innovation, reviewing the boards of public universities, and improvising university conditions for students, staff, and faculty members. The reform committee fixed the urgent reforms related to several aspects of good governance, such as the granting of certain prerogatives to the universities and institutions of higher education.

The proposed reform to the higher education and the scientific research system completes the negotiations that lasted four years within the Tunisian university. It represents the starting point of a more extensive *Societal Dialogue* to enrich the reform program and extend the quest for internationalization. Regional workshops and meetings were held from June to September 2015 and the principal reform document outlined several proposed measures for higher education ranging from undertaking a general review of the system; reviewing the orientation, evaluation and training systems; increasing institutional flexibility and interdependence; evaluating teacher accreditation and education;

and redeveloping the research development and technological transfer of capacities and capabilities. During the *Societal Dialogues* on tertiary education, more than four hundred and fifty student representatives, elected from the Scientific Councils, Academic Councils, Unions, and other associations took part in the deliberations. These meetings resulted in various recommendations; some were included in the reform project. During such workshops, many themes were debated, such as the renewed university programs, training, scientific research, food services, psychological support, transportation and accommodation services, and cultural activities. One of the main proposals was that the ministry of higher education committed to create a deputy chamber for university students focused on student life and greater participation (Tap 2016).

Additionally, the Ministry of Higher Education and Scientific Research (MOHESRT) published five priorities for higher education and research—reform of the sector, university autonomy, employability of graduates, improving the education provided by private institutions and increasing efficiency in the use of research facilities—as part of its 2015–2025 strategy. The *Societal Dialogue* on tertiary education is still evolving and it aims at fixing the education and scientific research model to ensure that university training is in line with the skills demanded by the market. The Ministry of Higher Education received a US$70 million support grant in February 2016 from the USA and it has begun decentralizing the administrative structures in public universities, developing labor market information systems, and giving a certain level of autonomy to the research units within public universities while encouraging the expansion of private university suppliers. An exhaustive review of the LMD system is currently underway.

The Rise of the Educated Militant in the Jihad Factory

By the first half of 2017, unemployment in Tunisia stood at 15.5 percent and 32 percent of those without jobs held post-graduate certificates. Today's Tunisian youth, disgruntled by the perceived failure of *al-sahwa*, are caught in the tentacles of three broad strands of Muslim politics that have significant implication for the role of national education. After *al-sahwa*, "political Islamists, salafists, traditional Tunisian religious leaders and jihadi-salafists all competed in an open market of ideas" (Malka 2015: 95). *Ennahdha*, which is the moderate Tunisian offshoot of *Ikhwan* (the Muslim Brotherhood), is transnationally linked and focuses on transforming society through *da'awa* (proselytizing and spiritual outreach), and social and political activism. In the 1980s, *Ennahdha*'s methods were acts of violence against the state and its apparatuses. Their efforts are directed toward making gains in the electoral process through the taking and maintaining of public offices. However, in an era of *Daesh,* political groups, such as *Ennahdha,* are misunderstood by the West and often lumped into the category of an Islamist extremist group. Not all Islamists are extremists or anti-Western. After taking power, the *Ennahdha*-led government granted amnesty to some eight thousand seven hundred people who were imprisoned under the 2003 antiterrorism law and further radicalized (embracing extreme belief systems) while incarcerated (United Nations 2012). Soon after, *Ennahdha* began to centralize mosques and religious spaces resulting in the rise of uncontrolled Qur'anic schools.

In the immediate days after *al-sahwa,* a group of bearded men, calling themselves Salafists, took to the streets. Salafism is a new phenomenon in Tunisia and the root of the word *salafi* means *ancestor* in Arabic; in this sense, the concept refers to following practices of the earliest Muslims (Dreisbach 2013). The post-*al-sahwa* Salafis (*ma baada al-sahwa Salafis*) that filled the streets after *al-sahwa* resulted from an offshoot of "intra-Islamist competition" within *Ennahdha.* Thus, the portrait of the Tunisian Salafist, who is often educated, is of a religious fanatic who has a "phobia toward dissimilarity and a rejection of the other, even to the extent of killing." "The *salafi* school relies on the authority of the literal religious text in its superficial form, steering clear of any interpretation which considers a historical reading of the text" (Lakhdar 2005: para. 4). Following *al-sahwa,* two types of Tunisian *jihadi-salafis* emerged—(i) *al-salafia al-ilmia* (scientific or scripturalist *salafit*) that grew out of *al-shawa* and was politically motivated and (ii) *al-okba ibn Nafaa Brigade* (*al-salafia* or *al-jihadia*) who have posed a security threat by vehemently attacking the Tunisian security forces from their base in the Chaambi Mountains on the Tunisian–Algerian border (Malka 2015; Marks 2012; 2015). Post-*al-sahwa* Salafists began as a monolithic group of highly organized religiously right-wing extremists who seek to emulate the Prophet Muhammad and his earliest followers called *al-salaf al-salih* (the pious ancestors). Initially, the post-*al-sahwa* Salafists were conflated with *Ennahdha* but soon the distinction became clear; the Tunisian press dubbed the post-*al-sahwa* Salafists as the "bearded youths whose rage we don't understand" (Marks 2012: para. 5). Post-*al-sahwa* Salafists are viewed as making an ultra-conservative and violent call for conservative dress and a protest-oriented jihad (viewed as a potentially public violent act of protest). This group viewed the new political freedoms brought by the post-*al-sahwa* Salafists as a way of creating a "land of *da'wa*" and not a "land of *jihad*" where *da'wa* symbolizes the ability to create "more space to practice the rituals of religion and promote ... virtue and prevent ... vice." (Malka 2015: 104 citing Fursan al-Balagh Media 2013). In fact, academics, researchers, and *al-Ulemas* of Islam called for understanding of this phenomenon from an academic perspective to be able to identify the reasons or its emergence and comprehend its effect on Tunisian society.

Immediately after *al-sahwa*, "jihadi-salafists took advantage of the political freedom to organize, preach, and build constituencies. For them, this was an important stage in creating a new social and political order based on Islamic law" (Malka 2015: 95). However, homegrown Tunisian jihadi-Salafists are associated with several acts of violence. Jihadi-Salafists come largely, but not entirely, from economically poorer backgrounds and sought to wage jihad internally. Recently, from January to February 2012, jihadi-Salafists targeted a cultural center in *el-medina* (the old city) of Tunis and attacked brothels in the cities of Tunis, Kairouan, and Sfax. They also levied attacks against alcohol sellers while calling for the creation of a national association aimed at promoting moral rectitude and Sharia rules. Their bid was successful and in February 2012, the Association for the Promotion of Virtue and Prevention of Vice[4] was legalized and described as a centrist association of advocacy and reform since, according to its president in 2012, Adel el Alami, "[Tunisia] has become a haven for obscenity" (Alami 2012). Then on October 9, 2011, a fortnight before the national elections for the Constituent Assembly, some two hundred Salafists tried to burn down the headquarters of *Nessma*, a private television channel in Tunis, which had planned to broadcast *Persepolis*, the Franco-Iranian film by Marjane Satrapi (International Crisis Group 2013).

We label the final political strand as "homegrown jihad militants," consisting of frustrated well-educated Tunisian youths who answered *Daesh's* call to jihad and traveled to the Caliphate, did their service and are returning to Tunisia already radicalized, or willing to radicalize and recruit others. Given the notoriety and international attention Tunisian Salafists have incurred based on their tactics, they are also viewed by *Daesh* as suitable candidates to join its Caliphate. Thus, in the post-*al-sahwa* period, Tunisia has emerged as the principal supply chain for the recruiting and exploration of jihadists for *Daesh*. Tunisia's jihadist output dwarfs the other countries in the region and globally, Tunisia contributed the largest number of foreign fighters to *Daesh's* Islamic Caliphate (a theological empire). As Table 3 shows, official estimates suggest that between six thousand to seven thousand Tunisian Militants have left Tunisia to fight abroad for *Daesh's*

Table 3 Countries with the most/fewest ISIS fighters as a percentage of Muslim population

Country	Muslim Population	ISIS Fighters	Fighters / Population	Country	Muslim Population	ISIS Fighters	Fighters / Population
Finland	42,000	70	0.1667%	Somalia	9,231,000	70	0.0008%
Belgium	638,000	470	0.0737%	Egypt	80,024,000	600	0.0007%
Ireland	43,000	30	0.0698%	Malaysia	17,139,000	100	0.0006%
Sweden	451,000	300	0.0665%	Algeria	34,780,000	170	0.0005%
Maldives	309,000	200	0.0647%	United Arab Emirates	3,577,000	15	0.0004%
Trinidad and Tobago	78,000	50	0.0641%	Indonesia	204,847,000	700	0.0003%
Austria	475,000	300	0.0632%	Sudan	30,855,000	70	0.0002%
Tunisia	10,349,000	6,000	0.0580%	Afghanistan	29,047,000	50	0.0002%
Norway	144,000	81	0.0563%	Pakistan	178,097,000	70	0.0000%
Denmark	226,000	125	0.0553%	India	177,286,000	23	0.0000%

Caliphate while the government has barred approximately fifteen thousand to twenty thousand Tunisians (some estimates are much higher) from traveling to Syria and Iraq (Galka 2016; Trofimov 2016). Today, Tunisians are the backbone of *Daesh* and with *Daesh's* growing presence in neighboring Libya, Tunisian are climbing the ranks of *Daesh's* leadership.

The sending or exportation of educated foreign fighters abroad to fight for terrorist offshoots and splinter groups, such as *al-Qaeda* (the foundation), or the Salafi-jihadist militant group to join *al-Qaeda* in the Islamic Maghreb (AQIM),[5] is nothing new in the Middle East. Unlike *al-Qaeda*, which sees itself as an elite organization, *Daesh* has a much wider appeal and its extremists use Sunniism as their ideological basis. Without reducing religious difference to binary juxtapositions, for the most part, Tunisian educated youth lacks experience with historical sectarian, tribal and religious divides that plague most of North Africa and the Middle East since it is a relatively homogenous country consisting overwhelmingly of Sunni-identifying peoples who have a deep respect for its minorities—Christians and Jews. Scholars have often argued that Tunisian exceptionalism is forged upon its cultural identity (Alexander 2010; Fryer and Jules 2013).

The Perks of Being Educated, Militant, and Amenable to Radicalization

The question beckons: *Why are Tunisians so drawn to Daesh?* The simple answer is that being an educated jihadi has its rewards. The benefits are even better, if one is an educated Tunisian jihadist who is willing to be radicalized. In the past, countries and "international knowledge banks" (such as the World Bank and the IMF, see Jones, 2004) have exploited human capital for economic development. We suggest that *Daesh's* leaders are following the Western economic orthodoxy of efficiently exploiting human capital and human resource development, with an Islamic twist, for its brand of *izdihar al-iktisad al-jihadi* (jihadist development) overseen by the centralized anatomy of its various Councils: (i) Financial Council—manages weapons and oil sales; (ii) Leadership Council—responsible for laws and policies; (iii) Military Council—defends *Daesh*; (iv) Legal Council—runs recruitment and executions; (v) Foreign Fighters Council—provides foreign aid; (vi) Security Council—supervises internal polices of the Caliphate; and (vii) the Intelligence Council—gathers information (Thompson and Shuber 2015). Over its evolution, as Table 4 shows, *Daesh* has developed a complicated

Table 4 *Diwans* and their functions

Government Department	Function
Diwan al-Ta'lim	Education
Diwan al-Khidamat	Public Services (e.g. electricity, water, street cleaning). Management of public facilities (e.g. parks)
Diwan al-Rikaz	Precious resources (two known divisions: fossil fuels and antiquities)
Diwan al-Da'wah wa al-Masajid (wa al-Awqaf)	Da'wah activity and control of the mosques
Diwan al-Sihha	Health
Diwan al-Asha'ir	Tribal outreach
Diwan al-Amn (al-Aam)	Public security
Diwan Bayt al-Mal	Finances and currency system
Diwan al-Hisbah	Enforcement of public morality: Islamic police
Diwan al-Qada wa al-Mazalim	Islamic court, judicial matters, marriages
Diwan al-Alaqat al-Amma	Public relations
Diwan al-Zira'a	Agriculture, environment
Diwan al-Ifta' wa al-Buhuth	Fatwas, textbooks for training camp recruits etc.
Diwan al-Jund	Military and defense

Source: al-Tamimi (2015)

bureaucratic structure with different *Diwans* (departments) reporting to different councils (al-Tamimi 2015).

Tunisians make up the largest contingent of *Daesh fighters* and new recruits; approximately half, as it seeks to promote political, military, and religious governance programs that range from overseeing Sharia type courts, distributing aid, providing law enforcement, and building schools (Gambhir 2014). In fact, the Islamic State's (2014a: 11) recruitment material, the *Dabiq Magazine*, targets well-educated youth by:

> [... making] a special call to the [Muslim] scholars, fuqaha and callers, especially the judges, as well as people with military, administrative and service expertise and medical doctors and engineers of all different specializations and fields. We call them and remind them to fear Allah, for their emigration is wajib 'ayni' (an individual obligation).

Since *Daesh* views itself as neither local nor regional but global, it seeks to fill the vacuum in Tunisia that the Ben Ali regime left and the *Troika*, that ruled from 2011 to 2014 in the post-*al-sahwa* era, was unable to fill. Young Tunisians, who were qualified and could not find good jobs at home, began seeking out alternative paths and the Islamic State has been trying to take advantage of the high pedigree of human resources that Tunisia has to offer. In fact, in their first publication of the *Dabiq Magazine* (Islamic State 2014b: 1), they judiciously recount the ideological tenets of the Islamic State, by arguing that its state-building project commenced with "the spark has been lit here in Iraq and its heat will continue to intensify—by Allah's permission—until it burns the crusader armies in Dabiq". The vacant post-*al-sahwa* space for Tunisian youth became the fit recruitment ground for the Islamic State's call to *hijrah* (migration) by pronouncing that:

> Therefore, rush O Muslims to your state. Yes, it is your state. Rush, because Syria is not for the Syrians and Iraq is not for the Iraqis ... The State is a state for all Muslims. The land is for the Muslims, all the Muslims. O Muslims everywhere, whoever is capable of performing hijrah to the Islamic State, then let him do so, because hijrah to the land of Islam is obligatory.
>
> Islamic State 2014a: 14

For *Daesh,* it envisions *hijrah* to be a place where authority is weak and lawlessness exists, as in Syria, Libya, and Iraq. In its publications, the Islamic State insists that the priority for of all Muslims is to perform the *hijrah.*

When *Daesh* broke ties with *al-Qaeda's* central leadership in February 2014 and its leader Abu Bakr al-Baghdadi declared a Caliphate and himself Caliph, the course of militantism changed. Until then, the perception and picture of the average foreign fighter following jihad had been one viewed as being: (i) a disillusioned Muslim, not necessarily educated, who was infuriated by something the West (either the USA or Europe) had done to Muslims and/or (ii) an individual answering a broad call for *jihad* or *fatwa* put out by some extremist group. In the past, *al-Qaeda's* foot soldiers were described as highly organized and planned jihadists, however, *Daesh* "has encouraged anyone to take up arms in its name and uses a sophisticated campaign of social media to inspire future attacks by unstable individuals with little history of embracing radical Islam" (Mazzetti, Lichtblau and Blinder 2016).

In the Tunisian context, recruits are coming from the hard sciences (doctors, engineers, technicians, and mechanics) who are looking for quick and easy money based on their qualifications. Moreover, Jihadism now relies on satellite television and high-speed Internet, given the advances that have been made in technology, privacy, and security application services and social media platforms. *Daesh* has issued an Operation Security Guide ("Several Cyber" 2015;

Zetter 2015) detailing the best communication platforms recruits should consult. These platforms range from end-to-end encryptions, such as Cryptocat[6], Telegram[7], Signal[8], Sicher[9], WhatsApp[10], and Wickr[11]; email clients, such as, Hushmail[12] and ProtonMail[13]; encrypted phones, such as BlackPhone[14] and Tor Browser, to Tails operating system. Thus, the courtship and recruitment of today's jihadist is not a lengthy process, as in the past with *al-Qaeda*, but one very streamlined and post-bureaucratic, or neo-bureaucratic. Its decisions are based on dialogue and consensus via social media; the organization functions as a horizontal network open at its boundaries, emphasizing meta-decision-making rules, such as a global jihad against everyone, including Muslims.

On the surface, there is no distinction between the purposes of labor under orthodox economic development and jihadist development. However, *Daesh's* self-styled Caliphate, with its bureaucratic trappings and government apparatus of the traditional Westphalia state system, is all but recognized as a country— albeit, a country with an Islamic twist and Islamic laws (Table 4 above). Like any other emerging state, *Daesh's* Caliphate needed educated and stronger professionals to ensure the bureaucratic mechanisms of its Caliphate function efficiently and effectively as it wages *jihad* across the globe. However, what is unique about Tunisians going abroad to fight in *al-Sham* and *al-Iraq* in the *ma baada al-sahwa* is that they are better educated than previous fighters were. While *Daesh* recruits both Tunisian men and women (already radicalized or willing to be radicalized), its recruits come from an assortment of social and economic backgrounds, such as lawyers, traders, small-business owners, university students (across different levels), and government and private service employees. However, the average level of educational attainment for Tunisian recruits is a university degree from one of Tunisia's public universities and the recruit must be someone socially well-connected. As such, Tunisians have come to be the ideal men and women able to keep all the engines of the Caliphate running 24/7.

In fact, a jihadist's level of education is also very important to *Daesh's* leaders and Tunisians are viewed as having the necessary skills worth tapping for jihadist development (World Bank 2016). The allure of militant extremism has both supply and demand attributes. On the demand side, as detailed in a leaked document in March 2016, it shows that *Daesh's* leaders are collecting personal information on militants, as well as paying very close attention to their education level and this is used for retention and promotion (Ramsey 2016). The educated Tunisians arriving in *Daesh*-controlled territory can access essential services, get a wife or "jihadi bride," and find a job. For example, should the new jihadist's wife wish to study, she can attend one of the numerous Sharia Institutes overseen by

Diwans or Islamic service committees (al-Tamimi 2015). However, the new jihadist's children will not have access to certain subjects in school, such as music, social studies, arts, sports, and philosophy since they conflict with the teaching of the Caliphate (Gordts 2014; Harrison 2015). The school curriculum is scrubbed cleaned of anything that defames Islam or is perceived by *al-Diwans* as being too secular, Western, or against the Prophet Mohamad. Teachers are retrained in orthodox or "proper" Islamic studies, students are separated based on their gender and girls must wear the *niqab*.

While education at the beginning of the Caliphate is voluntary, by 2014 school fees in the form of a monthly tax, ranging from "25,000 Iraqi dinars (about $21) for every child attending kindergarten, 50,000 dinars ($42) for high-school students and 75,000 dinars ($62.50) for college undergraduates" (NBC News 2014: para. 1) were introduced in the major cities, such as Mosul. What is troubling is that the children of foreign fighters are now receiving an education that is tailored toward radicalization. Of concern is the amount of educated Tunisian "jihadi brides," close to one thousand by unconfirmed reports, that have been promoted from wifely duties to combat duties and sent from the Islamic State to nearby Libya to fight (The Times 2016).

Revanchism and the Newly Radicalized Tunisian Youth

Al-siraā al-souri (the Syrian conflict) is raging, swaths of territory[15] are swinging back and forth between Iraqi forces and *moukatili Daesh* (Islamic State Fighters), *Ādam al-istikrar al-libi* (Libyan instability) is becoming unsolvable, and the frontiers of Tunisia are being questioned more than before. Radical factions and sleeper cells are incubating and waiting for the perfect time to strike both in and out of Tunisia. A new generation of Tunisians has come of age in an era defined by a new kind of "pan-Arabist identity" that has been shaped in a new Arabic political space defined by social media and *al-Jazeera* (Lynch 2013). The flow of information is no longer controlled by "Orwellian" type bureaucracies and ministries, but by the young themselves. Moreover, modern Tunisian women—educated, underemployed, and Western dressed—have become accustomed to having their social space while at the same time retaining their Arabic and Muslim cultural conceptions of gender roles. In fact, no one foresaw that the space left by Ben Ali's regime would foster extremism and radicalization.

Daesh recruits and radicalizes Tunisians because the vacuum left in the country in the wake of the post-Arab Spring era and the fall of the Ben Ali regime provides a potent mixture of raw, untapped educated talent, dire and more explosive economic and social conditions, linguistic, ethnic and religious homogenization (i.e., strong Sunnification), and an abundance of young workers. As discussed earlier, education was not only used as a means of mobility to the middle class under the Ben Ali regime; it was also employed by the regime to buy time in the hope that their Band-Aid solutions would work. Over time, as policy solutions failed drastically to stimulate the economy or provide jobs while graft and corruption expanded, continued study in Tunisia's fine public universities were encouraged both as a way to keep the youth in check and to fend off unemployment. In the post-*al-sahwa* era, the factors that benefit *Daesh's* "'*jihad* in Syria' phenomenon" (Al-Amin 2014) in recruiting Tunisians are: (i) like other countries across the region real output per person in Tunisia has been affected by economic factors and it is lower today that it was in the 1970s; (ii) stagnant output per person in the 1990s in conjunction with high debt and economic adjustments contributed the current youth bulge that the country is experiencing; and (iii) Tunisians are still fleeing the destruction caused by "total collapse of the economic, social and educational constructs, as well as by the lack of values inherited from the previous regime" (Al-Amin 2014: para. 7).

Furthermore, like Al-Amin (2014), we argue there is an unyielding connection between the rise of militant jihadism in Tunisia and the fall of the Ben Ali regime given that Tunisian jihadists have primarily been emerging from the former strongholds of the Ben Ali regime left in tatters after *al-sahwa*. Added to this complex cocktail is the fact that since the fall of the regime, several of its followers, particularly those comprising the secret police apparatus that played a key role in suppressing the country's opposition, have lost their livelihoods and privileges. Members of the old securocratic state apparatus "did not believe in that regime, but lived, relatively unharmed, in its shadow ... [t]raditionally, they were not children of *Ennahdha* supporters, with some of them coming from families that supported Ben Ali's Democratic Constitutional Rally and others coming from apolitical backgrounds" (Al-Amin 2014: para. 8). Today's contemptuous radicals can be best described as having:

> ... ideological intolerance, which describes a belief system that specifically refuses to tolerate the practices, beliefs and/or tenets of other individuals or groups. It encompasses bigotry and the demonstration of bitterness and/or enmity towards those who dissent or disagree with one's belief systems (presumably the right doctrine), or some aspect of it.
>
> Salaam 2013: para. 5

Once radicalized, educated Tunisians are returning home either disillusioned by the waning fervor for jihad or to inflict harm upon fellow Tunisians. In February 2013, Chokri Belaid, then opposition parliamentarian, was gunned down outside his home and later in July, another opposition politician, Mohammed Brahmi, was assassinated. In early 2014, a group of men were accused of plotting a major terrorist attack leading up to the parliamentary elections. From 2015 to 2016, there were other major terrorist attacks that resulted in the deaths of many people. The Ministry of the Interior is constantly hunting for sleeper cells in Tunisia as Libya plunges deeper into internal ethnic strife, thus cementing it as a failed state in the post-Gaddafi era. Collectively, these events and numerous other political tensions have only plunged the Tunisian economy further into crisis, as jobs are stagnated, real wages unchanged, and unprecedented levels of unemployment persist while students are expected to learn in dilapidated, post-colonial structures with inadequate resources.

Something Old, Something Transitionary, Something Democratic

Tunisia's path to democratization was a minefield dotted with endless challenges and hurdles that accompanied its democratic transition. One of the important lessons transitologies bring to light is whether governments are willing to use a crisis narrative to undertake contested reforms. Tunisia's education system continues to be structured under the Education Act of 2002, constructed under the Ben Ali regime. Nevertheless, the civil society's role in keeping the democratic transition on track has been one of the main reasons why Tunisia could sidestep the scenario of chaotic transition seen in Libya, Syria, and Egypt, which slid back into dictatorship. As one pundit recently stated, "it comes as no surprise, then, that Western countries and international organizations are eager to support what they see as democracy's last outpost in the region" (Cunniffe 2016: para 1). Notwithstanding the fact that Tunisian youth are happy with their freshly triumphant freedom, they show signs of skepticism toward the political parties. In fact, UNESCO and CAAR (2015: 11) note that "these young people who described themselves as the 'guards of the revolution' in 2011 and who complained that politicians have stolen their revolution in 2013, admit in 2014 that contrary to what they expected, the Tunisian revolution simply ended in a rotation of regime elites." The young believe they were excluded and estranged from the political scene, calling to mind the strict monopoly in this territory since none of them could get into pivotal positions. They also feel the existing political parties walk-out on *al-sahwa's* objectives, such as fighting unethical behaviors and adopting transparent and democratic national policies and they are alarmed by the fact that old corruptive methods are still in use. While Ben Ali and his lieutenants have been replaced, the mafia-styled pillage-cum-privatization still operates, but under new leadership. Thus, the sense of mistrust after *al-sahwa* has been a critical factor in shaping the reactions of young activists toward any politician or political party who pretends to defend the youth perspective for a better future.

Economic prosperity is the key toward a stable democracy. Tunisia's political issues, the Libyan conflict the return of hundreds of radicalized Tunisians after the loss of Daesh's Mosul in August 2017 and its *de facto* capital, Raqqa in October 2017, and homegrown militantism have contributed to worsening the country's unstable economy. Increasing unemployment rates, especially among the young, put in jeopardy social peace. Rotten "cartels", left over from the Ben Ali regime, have been grabbing territory and corruption is widespread while the oppressed and the powerless suffer the consequences of another recession. Also, dozens of reforms are desperately needed across sectors, such as taxation, international investment, labor, financial integrity, and banking legal infrastructure. Added to this, one of Tunisia's main economic pillars of its diversified economy—tourism, which employs a large segment of the labor force—is cracking from the bottom upwards because of the rise of homegrown militancy coupled with a lawlessness in the Libyan state and compounded by *Daesh* terrorist attacks that have targeted tourists.

Since the ousting of Moammar Gadhafi in 2011, security has deteriorated and political deadlock between militias remains, in addition, several rival government factions and, the Western-backed unity government are bankrupting the oil-rich country and the Islamic State has a strong contingent of its leadership on the ground. In 2014 and 2015, *Daesh* sent a high-level envoy to Libya to establish its North African Caliphate, the strongest outpost outside of Syria and Iraq. *Deash's* foothold in Libya had drastic implications for Tunisia. As we argued above, the jihadists that Tunisia supplies to the unfettered global terrorist market all have one unique characteristic in that they are well educated and, in many instances, over-educated. Thus, we suggest it was the opening-up of the economy to benefit a selected few that commenced the beginning of the discontent, disillusionment, and disenfranchisement that has led to the post-*al-sahwa* period serving as an incubator for the recruitment of Tunisian youth by *Daesh*. These are youth fleeing in droves to eke out a better standard of living within the Islamic State.

Before the 2014 elections, the country's interim government had to handle different economic prospects due to *al-shawa*-related disruptions and the negative impact of the Libyan conflict, along with higher fuel and food prices. With the economic cost of *al-sahwa* estimated at 5 percent of GDP, growth for 2011 was calculated at between zero and 1 percent. Tourism, which represents 6.5 percent of the GDP and is the largest provider of foreign exchange, declined by more than half in the immediate period of *al-sahwa*. It declined further in 2015 after homegrown militants with allegiance ties to *Daesh* killed twenty-three tourists at the Bardo Museum, thirty-eight people in Port El Kantaoui, twelve presidential guards, and assassinated two Tunisian politicians. Foreign direct investment (FDI) has dwindled by 20 percent and more than eight foreign companies have left the country mainly due to insecurity, especially after the Port El Kantaoui attack. The situation in the labor market has worsened, due to both layoffs and the returning of Tunisian migrant workers fleeing the conflict in Libya. In 2016, estimates suggest the number of unemployed people has increased to around seven hundred thousand, as compared with fewer than five hundred thousand at the end of 2010. As a result, the unemployment rate reached 17 percent in 2016, compared with 14 percent before *al-sahwa*. Both the public deficit and current account deficit have also increased. Moreover, in the post-Brexit era (the United Kingdom's exit from the European Union), Tunisia has access to the European Single Market, of some five hundred million consumers, under the Deep and Comprehensive Free Trade Agreement (DCFTA). Tunisia has had to face the double handicap of a liquidity shortage and the high cost of external finance due to the downgrading of its sovereign debt rating by the three major global credit agencies.

By 2017, six years after the so-called transition to democracy and two successful elections later, nothing significant has taken place in education. Instead, there has been much discourse about what should be done. Central to the arguments of both pundits and skeptics is that the post-Ben Ali system is not broken, it just needs to be tweaked since it is not serving the needs of the labor market. There is widespread agreement that the education system remains disconnected from the realities of the world of work, but no one is quite sure how to remedy this. Instead, attention has been placed on fighting homegrown militants, who are products of the current education system, and on protecting Tunisia's borders. If history serves as a guide, then Tunisia's transition and any comprehensive reforms will not occur before 2026. This would not be an arbitrary year, for as we have demonstrated, it took Bourguiba some sixteen years and a failed socialist experiment to see economic results.

After *al-sahwa*, the direction of the Tunisian education system was one of the most debated issues. However, education reforms were not prioritized until 2016 as it was not deemed important by the *Troika* and then they were put off until the 2014 presidential elections. While the Ministers of Education were continuously changing, it was agreed that all ministries with responsibilities for education should direct their budgets for the improvement of schools and universities to the rural regions. The average job search can last up to eighteen months and many Tunisians grow frustrated and join the informal economy, emigrate (particularly to the glitzy capitals of Qatar, Saudi Arabia, and the United Emirates), go back to school, add on an additional tertiary degree, or join *Daesh*. Economic prosperity is the key to a stable democracy. While politically Tunisians have amassed admiration for earning the Nobel Peace Prize, they have yet to receive a trophy for implementing a growing economy. Tunisia's political issues have worsened the country's unstable economy. Increasing unemployment rates, especially among the young, have jeopardized the country's social peace. The rotten cartels that were a fixture of Bourguiba's and Ben Ali's regimes are still indulging in grafting, rent-seeking activities, oppressing the powerless, and aggravating the protracted recession. Also, dozens of reforms are desperately needed in other vital fields, such as taxation, investment and labor, and banking legal infrastructures. Added to that, one of Tunisia's main economy pillars, tourism, which retains a substantial number of employees, is critically fracturing. This is chiefly because of radicalized Tunisians returning home and attacking fellow Tunisians and tourists.

As we have demonstrated, Tunisia has a rich history of social activism linked to authoritarian bargaining, struck between the people and a despot when that despot comes to power. Tunisia has survived 3,000 years of tyrants, despots, and benevolent dictators because soon after one falls from grace or is deposed, another takes their place. The new charismatic leader then renegotiates the authoritarian bargain and holds it together with post-truths—where *dezinformatsiya* becomes the orthodoxy when the goals of reforms are not materialized. However, *al-sahwa* is different in that it was a leaderless uprising; but it was also an unfinished *al-shawa*. Both a power vacuum and a leadership crisis of legitimacy exist in the post-*al-sahwa* period, something that moderate Islamists could not resolve while ruling through the *Troika* and it leaves a space that *Daesh* is reconfiguring for its long-term endgame.

Notes

Chapter 3

1   Yousra Chatti and Devin Moss contributed research and support to the writing of this chapter.
2   The Fatimids were considered the descendants of Ali ibn Abi Talib and his wife, Fatima, daughter of the Prophet Muhammed.
3   Kheireddine Pacha (or sometimes spelt Khayr al-Din) came from Constantinople as a child and was sold into slavery to Bey Ahmed in 1840. He was educated in the palace and then received military instruction at the Bardo Military Academy. As a military man, he became a cavalry commander and, in 1853, he was sent to Paris and returned in 1857. With the ascension of Bey Muhammad (from 1855 to 1859) to the Beylic, he served as *Wazir al-Bahr* (Minister of Marine) from 1857 to 1859, presided over *al-Majlis al-Akbar* (the Great Council), a parliamentary body established from 1860 to 1862. He then returned to Europe for seven years. In 1869, he returned to Tunisia and was appointed head of the Internal Finance Commission and then Prime Minister from 1873 to 1877 (Islahi 2012).

Chapter 4

1   Arabization "is the process of promoting Modern Standard Arabic (MSA) to the level of a fully functional language in educational, administrative and mass-media domains, to replace the language of the former European colonial powers" (Daoud 1991: 7).
2   The resulting policies' prescriptions are best articulated in the "New Conception of Education in Tunisia 1958–59" (Allman 1979).
3   This position combined the Ministry of Finance, the Ministry of Commerce, and the Industry and the Planning Service.
4   Tunisian Syndicalism has its roots in the work of Mohamed Ali El Hammi (founder of CGTT in 1925) and Farhan Hached (founder of UGTT in 1946).
5   Ministry of National Education Report of Education Development in Tunisia (1981–1984).
6   Rachid Sfar later replaced Mzali as Prime Minister in 1986 and was responsible for the implementation of the first generation of Structural Adjustment Program (SAP)

reforms. To Sfar's credit, *la loi de Finances Complémentaire* (the Supplemental Finances Law) would be passed and the Dinar (the official currency) was devalued by 10 percent, creating a path for the rebuilding of currency reserves and the re-establishment of foreign credit.

7 The Constitution of Tunisia was amended on July 12, 1988; June 29, 1999; June 1, 2002; May 13, 2003; and July 28, 2008. In March 1975, the Constitution was amended to make Bourguiba president for life.

8 SESP (now in Phase II since 2005) aims at increasing the capacity, relevance, and quality of basic and secondary education to ensure that it is harmonized along the trajectories of the national education plan ("AfDB Supports" 2005).

9 Up until 1962, physical education was optional at *le Bac* and only points above the average were considered in calculating the general average grade. In 1963, the physical education test became mandatory for Baccalaureate students and the calculation of the grades were amended in 1981. *Le Bac Sport* has its foundations in Article 72 of Law No. 109 of December 31, 1985, that also created Pierre de Coubertin Sports High School. The sports stream in secondary education and a bachelor of sports was created by Decree No. 1032 of April 26, 2004 and amended on May 10, 2004 and April 20, 2011 to streamline the consistency of the examinations for the high school diploma in sports.

10 Decree No. 2010–2205 of September 6, 2010.

Chapter 5

1 Small sections of this chapter have appeared in Fryer and Jules (2013).

2 *Écoles* are chiefly associated with engineering studies.

3 The Law of January 31, 1996 established *le Système National d'Orientation Universitaire* and it provides the legal framework for the orientation law of scientific research and technology (MOHESRT 2008). However, the system took four years to pick up steam.

4 Created under Decree No. 2007–1713 dated 5 July, 2007, it has only three articles: (i) fixing the hourly remuneration scheme of the different responsibilities of graders for the competitive university reorientation examinations; (ii) the legislative dates of the order; and (iii) the responsibilities and organization of the reorientation examinations falls under the purview of the MOHESRT and the Ministry of Finance (JORT 2007).

5 This data is based on 2007 enrollment rates of three hundred and sixty-four thousand two hundred and eighty-three students in thirteen public universities, twenty-four institutes of technological studies, and twenty private universities (compared to sixty-six in 2016) (Gyimah-Brempong and Ondiege 2011).

6 670 translates to the year 50 in the Islamic calendar.

7 He was a general serving the Umayyad Caliphate that reigned from Damascus from 661 to 750.

8 *Masjid al-Zitouna* Mosque was built in the year 698 and it became a "grand" mosque in 732. The name *Zitouna* translates into "olive tree" in English. The story goes that an olive tree existed on the spot where the mosque was built and with time, the link between Tunisia and the olive tree became synonymous.

9 This includes Al-Azhar University that began its life as an *halqah* (study circle) of *Jami' al-Qahira* (the Mosque of Cairo) in 972. Al-Azhar is thought to be the first university in the East.

10 In 1848, the selling of slaves and the slave market were abolished.

11 Ibn Khaldun (from May 27, 1332 to March 19, 1406) was North Africa's Arab Muslim historiographer and historian. Ibn Khaldun is often viewed as the forerunner and father of modern economics. The Western world credits him as the father of sociology but not a great economist who created its foundations. "[He] was the first to systematically analyze the functioning of an economy, the importance of technology, specialization and foreign trade in economic surplus and the role of government and its stabilization policies to increase output and employment ... [M]oreover, he dealt with the problem of optimum taxation, minimum government services, incentives, institutional framework, law and order, expectations, production and the theory of value" (Cosma 2009: 52–53).

12 The first National Constituent Assembly (*L'Assemblée Nationale Constituante*) had ninety-eight members, it was convened on March 25, 1956 and the future President, Habib Ben Ali Bourguiba, was elected as President of it on April 9, 1956. From 1956 to 1959, the Tunisian legislature was named the National Constituent Assembly, from 1959 to 1981 the National Assembly, from 1981 to 2011 the Chamber of Deputies, and from 2011 to 2014 the National Constituent Assembly. Since 2014, it is called the Assembly of the Representatives of the People.

13 Issued on March 29, 1956, Beylic Decree No. 96 was entitled *le Décret Relatif à la Modernisation de l'Enseignement de la Grande Mosquée et de ses Annexes* (the Modernization of the Teaching of the Great Mosque and its Annexes).

14 Issued on April 26, 1956 the Beylic Decree No. 116 was entitled *le Décret Portant Réorganisation de l'Enseignement al-Zitouna* (the Reorganization of the *Madrasat al-Zitouna* Education System).

15 Issued on March 31, 1961 the Beylic Decree No. 98 is entitled *le Décret Portant Organisation de l'Université de Tunis* (the Organization of the University of Tunis).

16 Issued on March 1, 1961 the Beylic Decree No. 110 entitled *le Décret Complétant le décret No. 60–98 du 31 Mar 1960, Portant Organisation de l'Université de Tunis* (the Decree Supplementing Decree No. 60–98 of March 31, 1960 on the Organization of the University of Tunis).

17 This occurred under Article 1 of Decree No. 110, dated March 1, 1961. Decree-law
   No. 357 dated October 27, 1961 allowed the Faculty of Sharia and the Origins of
   Religion to grant degrees in religion and a certificate in preaching and religious
   guidance. Decree-law No. 164 dated February 15, 1980 codified the mission
   and the organizational structure of the Faculty of Sharia and the Origins of
   Religion.

18 Given that a significant part of higher education is taught in French, with the
   exception of *Ez Zitouna* University the names of universities are listed in French first
   rather than Arabic.

19 It was created August 9, 1986 by Law No. 86–80 (finalized when it was published
   on August 8–12, 1986 in the Official Journal of the Tunisian Republic, No. 44).
   Today, the University of Sfax has five faculties, eleven institutes, and four *écoles
   supérieures.*

20 *Ez Zitouna* University was created in accordance with Law No. 86–80. On
   December 31, 1987, Law No. 83/1987 created *Ez Zitouna* University and endowed
   it with a legal status and an administrative and financial structure. Its curriculum,
   education and scientific research establishments are regulated by Decree
   No. 1939/1989 of December 14, 1989 and the amendments of Decree No. 23/2002
   dated January 8, 2002. Decree No. 865/1995 of May 8, 1995 defines the duties
   of the *Ez Zitouna* University while Decree No. 1708/1995 of September 18, 1995
   defines the general framework of studies and the terms of graduation. Decree-law
   No. 1708, dated September 18, 1995 provides the general educational framework
   for *Ez Zitouna* University and the conditions for obtaining undergraduate and
   master's degrees in Islamic studies. An order dated November 3, 1995, established
   the system of studies and examinations applicable to the Higher Institute of
   Islamic Civilization in order to obtain national undergraduate degrees and master's
   degrees in Islamic Sciences. Ministry of Higher Education departmental orders of
   November 3, 1995 and February 6, 1996 regulate curricula and examinations for the
   first and second academic cycles and the third cycle respectively. The Center for
   Islamic Studies of Kairouan (founded in 2001) is regulated by Decree No. 578 of
   March 30, 1990.

21 Article 19 of Law No. 86–80 regulates the three institutions of the *Ez Zitouna.*

22 On December 31, 1987 Article 97 of Act No. 87–83 created the University of
   Sciences, Technologies and Medicine of Tunis which was later changed on
   November 27, 2000 to University of Tunis El Manar by Decree No. 200–2826.
   Today the University of Tunis El Manar has four faculties, nine institutes, and
   two *écoles supérieures.*

23 The University of Carthage was founded in 1988, today the University of Carthage
   has three faculties, twenty-two institutes, and ten *écoles supérieures.*

24 On July 31, 2000, Decree No. 1801 created the University of Manouba that has one
   faculty, eight institutes, and five *écoles supérieures.*

25 On August 4, 2003, Decree No. 1662 established the University of Gabès. Today it has one faculty, thirteen *instituts supérieurs* (these usually require *Le Bac*), and one *école supérieure*.

26 On August 4, 2003, Decree No. 1662–2003 created the University of Jendouba that has one faculty, ten institutes, and two *écoles supérieures*.

27 On September 2, 2004, Decree No. 2102 established the University of Monastir that has five faculties, nine institutes, and two *écoles supérieures*.

28 On September 2, 2004, Decree No. 2008–2716 called for the creation of the University of Kairouan, but the university was formalized on August 4, 2008 under Decree No. 2008–2716. The University of Kairouan has two faculties and ten institutes.

29 The University of Sousse was created on August 9, 1986 by Law No. 86–80 under the name "the University of Monastir." On December 31, 1991, Law No. 86–80 was changed to Decree No. 91–1999 that created "the University of the Centre" aimed at providing scientific and educational access to the governorates of Sousse, Monastir, Kairouan, and Mahdia. Its current name, University of Sousse, was established on September 2, 2004 by Decree No. 2115–2004. Today University of Sousse has four faculties, ten institutes, and three *ecole supérieures*.

30 On September 2, 2004, Decree No. 2102 created the University of Gafsa that has one faculty, eight institutes (with one institute being regulated by the university and the Higher Institute of Sport and Physical Education of Gafsa), and one *ecole supérieure*.

31 Today, ULT is organized around six faculties: (i) Faculty of Law and Economics; (ii) Faculty of Literature, Arts and Humanities Science; (iii) Polytechnic Institute; (iv) School of Architecture and Design; (v) School of Business; and (vi) International Language School (I.L.S.).

32 Decree No. 112–02 of January 28, 2000 established UVT and Decree No. 1936–1906 of July 10, 2006 laid down the mission of the UVT, its training regime and its relationship with other universities. A Ministerial Order by the Minister of Higher Education, Scientific Research and Technology on July 13, 2007 laid down the conditions for obtaining a Computer and Internet Certificates (amended on April 22, 2013 to Informatics and Internet Certificate) issued by the UVT.

33 On November 6, 2000, Ben Ali launched a new Presidential initiative called the "Seven-November Internet Bus" project with the aim of providing youth in rural areas with access to the Internet and computers. A bus was converted into a classroom featuring thirteen laptops, (including one for the facilitator), a proxy server to optimize the Internet connection, a printer, a monitor and a video projector connected to the facilitator's computer. A wireless network of eleven megabits interconnected the computers and web access was provided by VSAT (satellite) which was installed in another vehicle accompanying the bus. The first leg of the bus's tour covered Tunis to Nabeul, making stops in towns and cities (Sousse, Monastir, Oueslatia, Sebikha, Chrarda, Kef, and Jendouba) that did not have access to the Internet at that time. The last stop was the *Nianou Childhood Festival* in Grombalia, Nabeul.

34 UVT's objectives outlined at the World Summit on Information Technology held in Tunis 2005 calls for it to: "(i) spread distance-education and make it accessible to all qualified people; merge all initiatives in the area of education based on digital multimedia technologies; (ii) foster a continuing learning environment with the vision of building a learning society; upgrade the skills of young professionals through continuing education and training; (iii) address the challenge of the steady growth of students in higher education by progressively spreading distance education in priority disciplines to cover 20 percent of the university curriculum online by 2006–2007; (iv) promote equal opportunities in higher education to all qualified people including non-traditional students; Participate in widening access to higher education and at the same time improve the quality of education; (v) spread continuing open education by making use of advanced digital multimedia technologies and covering the education part of incoming [sic] future students enrolled in higher education institutions" (Government of Tunisia 2005: 2). The Higher Institute of Education and Lifelong Learning (ISEFC) is the only *établissement* (institution) under UVT. ISEFC was created by Law 82–91 of December 31, 1983 and regulated by Decree No. 84–308 of March 21, 1984 (amended by Decree No. 92–629 of March 23, 1992).

35 DEV states that its current focus is on: modernizing tools and learning methods; optimizing the use of online educational resources; the organization of training and mobilization of teachers and other stakeholders; supporting cross-cutting teaching units online; incentives for teachers to produce new online content; monitoring and optimization of online education infrastructure (UVT access centers, video conferencing facilities, and online learning platform); and developing communication tools for students and teachers (UVT 2016).

36 Pedagogical coordinators are university faculty who are responsible for coordinating students and teaching activities and monitoring the progress of students. Course designers are also university faculty members, but they are charged with generating course content. Evaluators are the next university faculty involved. Their role is to evaluate the scientific merit of the online courses. Additionally, tutors help to mentor the students and assist them with their education.

Chapter 6

1 August 13 is celebrated as a national holiday in Tunisia.
2 Under Decree No. 108 of 1985.
3 Historically, women on the island of Djerba have worn *al-hijabs* as a way to cover their heads from the sun but not as a religious garment.

Chapter 8

1 During the first Kasbah sit-in, in the heart of Tunisia's seat of government located in the Kasbah, the first interim government along with its ministers, who were largely from Ben Ali's regime, was ousted. The second Kasbah sit-in, from February 19, 2011 until March 4, 2011, was organized by a nine-member committee and it attracted thousands of Tunisians who camped out in the square, under the guidance of structured committees for safety, the media, food, health, and meals, discussing politics, and listening to radical music.

2 National report on "education for everyone" in the 2015 horizon.

3 Bizerte, Mahdia, Monastir, Sfax, Siliana, and Tunis.

4 Later called *l'Association Modérée pour la Sensibilisation et la Déforme* (the Moderate Association for Awareness and Reform).

5 AQIM (a.k.a. The Organization of Al Qaeda in the Lands of the Islamic Maghreb) has its heredity in *Groupe Islamique Armé, or al-Jama'ah al-Islamiyah al-Musallaha* (a.k.a. GIA, Armed Islamic Group). GIA was one of two Algerian Islamists insurgency groups that arose in the 1990s during Algeria's Civil War or the Dirty War (*la Sale Guerre*) (lasting from 1991 to 1999). In the 2000s, GIA was splintered into *Le Groupe Salafiste pour la Prédication et le Combat* (a.k.a. GSPC, the Salafist Group for Preaching and Combat) and this new cell aligned itself with *al-Qaeda* and changed its name to AQIM.

6 Cryptocat is a free open source chat application that uses Double Ratchet-based encryption protocol.

7 Telegram, is a two-layer encryption cloud-based messenger, founded in 2013 by Russian brothers Pavel and Nikola Durov.

8 Formerly RedPhone and containing all of its features, this application runs on open source, and documents encryption processes. When it was called RedPhone, the application was a password-free, SMS capable phone that allows users to swap out SIM cards when calling over Wi-Fi or a cellular network. For added security, both the caller and receiver can use a randomly generated two-word passphrase.

9 Offers point-to-point 2048-bit encryption and offers self-destructing messages.

10 In 2014, the social networking service Facebook Inc. acquired WhatsApp. On April 5, 2016, WhatsApp's members began using "The Signal Protocol" to encrypt user's communications, including file transfers and voice calls.

11 This application allows for content-expiring messages, such as photos, videos, and file attachments.

12 For a fee, this application offers secure email where messages between Hushmail users are automatically encrypted and users can add a two-step verification method to their accounts.

13 ProtonMail, a free secure email client with end-to-end encryption. The company is incorporated in Switzerland and subject to Swiss laws and privacy practices.

14 Is made by the Swedish company Silent Circle and uses a heavily modified version of the Android platform to encrypt voice, text, and video chat.

15 In May 2016, the US-led coalition estimated that *Daesh* had lost 45 percent of the territory it once controlled in Iraq and 20 percent of areas it held in Syria. In the beginning, *Daesh's* self-proclaimed Caliphate spanned nearly half of Syria and a third of Iraq. By May 2016, *Daesh* had lost big cities, such as Tikrit, Ramadi, and Palmyra. Since the end of the Libyan Civil War in 2011, after the overthrowing and killing of former president Muammar Muhammad Abu Minyar al-Gaddafi (from 1942 to 2011), fighting between numerous factions (including guerrillas, Islamists, and other militias) and the new state security forces has thrown the country into chaos. This has allowed *Daesh* to make territorial advances in Libya, particularly the 120-kilometer stretch of land extending across the East along the coast from the town of Sirte. Territory held by *Daesh* (particularly in its *de facto* capital Mosul and its second city Raqqa) is a major source of revenue since it collects taxes and imposes fines on the people who occupy these lands. By July 2017, *Daesh* had been forced from fifty-six places (villages, cities, dams, gas fields, oil fields, military bases, and mines), it once controlled, including five major cities with a combined population of at least three million seven hundred thousand people. The lost of land by July 2017 amounted to 45 percent of its territory in Syria and 20 percent in Iraq when compared with 2014 estimates. However, in August 2017 after a nine-months of fighting, the Iraqi city of Mosul (the largest city *Daesh* controlled) fell. Other Iraqi cities, such as Tal Afar, Hawija, Ramadi, Fallujah, and the Syrian cities Dabiq and Raqqa have also fallen. By November 2017, *Daesh* had been banished to the desolate landscape of *Badiyat al-Sham*, (the Syrian Desert), which encompasses some 500,000 square kilometers spanning Southeastern Syria, Northeastern Jordan, Northern Saudi Arabia, and Western Iraq, and famous for its caves and rugged mountains.

References

AALAWA (Almarkaz Alwatani Liltajdid Albidaghouji Walbouhouth Altarbawia). (2011), Moujaz Terikh Al Madrasa Al Tounisya Mina Al Madrasa Al Carthegina Bi Ifriqya Ila Al Yaoum (9th, before JC- 2007), Tunis: Almarkaz Alwatani Liltajdid Albidaghouji Walbouhouth Altarbawia [AALAWA].

Abadi, J. (2013). *Tunisia since the Arab conquest: The saga of a Westernized Muslim state.* Berkshire, UK: Ithaca Press.

Abdeljaouad, M. (2014). Mathematics education in Islamic countries in the modern time: Case study of Tunisia. In A. Kaep and G. Schubring (Eds.), *Handbook on the History of Mathematics Education* (405–428). New York, NY: Springer. doi 10.1007/978-1-4614-9155-2_20

Abdessalem, T. (2010). Financing higher education in Tunisia (Working Paper No. 551), Egypt: The Economic Research Forum. Retrieved from http://erf.org.eg/wp-content/uploads/2014/08/551.pdf

Abun-Nasr, J. M. (Ed.). (1987). *A history of the Maghrib in the Islamic period.* Cambridge, UK: Cambridge University Press.

Adjibolosoo, S. B. K. (1995). *The significance of the human factor in African economic development.* Santa Barbara, CA: Greenwood Publishing Group.

AfDB supports Tunisia's Education Policy (2005, Sept. 28), *African Development Bank Group.* Retrieved from https://www.afdb.org/en/news-and-events/afdb-supports-tunisias-education-policy-3598/

African Union (2004). *Ouagadougou declaration and plan of action on employment and poverty alleviation.* Addis Ababa: African Union.

Akkari, A. (2004). Education in the Middle East and North Africa: The current situation and future challenges. *International Education Journal, 5*(2), 144–153.

Al-Amin, H. (2014, November 3). Who is the 'typical' Tunisian jihadist? *Al Monitor.* Retrieved from http://www.al-monitor.com/pulse/security/2014/11/tunisian-jihadis-profile-fighting-syria.html#

Al Jazeera (2011, February 25). Tensions flare in Iraq rallies. *Al Jazeera.* Retrieved from http://english.aljazeera.net/news/middleeast/2011/02/2011224192028229471.html

Al Jazeera (2013, December 18). Arab uprisings: Progress or paralysis? *Al Jazeera.* Retrieved from http://www.aljazeera.com/programmes/insidestory/2013/12/arab-uprisings-progress-paralysis-2013121881411614136.html

al-Tamimi, A. (2015a). The evolution in Islamic State administration: The documentary evidence. *Perspectives on terrorism, 9*(4).

Alam, A. (2011). Islam, bread riots and democratic reforms in North Africa. *Islam and Muslim Societies: A Social Science Journal, 4*(1).

Alami, A. E. (2012, September 18). Our country has become a haven for obscenity! *Correspondent.org*. Retrieved from http://www.correspondents.org/node/780.

Alexander, C. (1997). Back from the democratic brink: Authoritarianism and civil society in Tunisia. *Middle East report, 205*. Retrieved from http://www.jstor.org/stable/3013093?seq=1page_scan_tab_contents

Alexander C. (2010). *Tunisia: Stability and reform in the modern Maghreb*. New York, NY: Routledge.

Alexander, C. (2011, January 2). Tunisia's protest wave: Where it comes from and what it means. *Middle East Foreign Policy*. Retrieved from http://mideast.foreignpolicy.com/posts/2011/01/02/tunisia_s_protest_wave_where_it_comes_fr om_and_what_it_means_for_ben_ali

Aleya-Sghaier, A. (2012). The Tunisian revolution: The revolution of dignity. *Journal of the Middle East and Africa, 3*, 18–45. doi: 10.1080/21520844.2012.675545

Allman, J. (1979). Social mobility, education and development in Tunisia, Vol. 28. *Social, economic and political studies of the Middle East*. Leiden, Netherlands: E.J. Brill.

Altbach, P. G. (2004). Globalization and the university: Myths and realities in an unequal world. *Tertiary Education and Management, 10*(1), 3–25.

Amnesty International (2010, July). *Independent voices stifled in Tunisia*. Retrieved from http://www.amnistia-internacional.pt/files/Relatoriosvarios/Vozes_silenciadas_na_Tunisia.pdf

Anderson, L. (1986). The state and social transformation in Tunisia and Libya, 1830–1980. Princeton, N.J: Princeton University Press.

Anderson, L. (1990). Democracy frustrated: The Mzali Years in Tunisia. In R. S. Simon (Ed.), *The Middle East and North Africa: Essays in honor of JC Hurewitz* (180–195). New York, NY: Columbia University Press.

Anderson, L. (1999). Politics in the Middle East: Opportunities and limits in the quest for theory. In M. Tessler, J. Nachtwey and A. Banda (Eds.), *Area studies and social science: Strategies for understanding Middle East politics* (1–10). Bloomington and Indianapolis, IN: Indiana University Press.

Anderson, L. (2011). Demystifying the Arab Spring. *Foreign Affairs*. Retrieved from https://www.foreignaffairs.com/articles/libya/2011-04-03/demystifying-arab-spring

Appiah, A. and Gates, H. L. (2010). *Encyclopedia of Africa* (Vol. 1). Oxford, UK: Oxford University Press on Demand.

Arfaoui, K. (2007). The development of the feminist movement in Tunisia 1920s–2000s. *The International Journal of the Humanities, 4*(8). Retrieved from http://ijh.cgpublisher.com/product/pub.26/prod.908

Arfaoui, K. (2014). Women's empowerment: The case of Tunisia in the Arab Spring. In M. Ennaji (Ed.), *Multiculturalism and democracy in North Africa* (59–175). Routledge Studies in Middle Eastern Studies. New York, NY: Routledge.

Arfaoui, K. and Tchaicha, J. (2014). Governance, women, and the new Tunisia. *Politics and Religion*, *1*(8). Retrieved from http://www.politicsandreligionjournal.com/images/pdf_files/engleski/volume8_no1/arfaoui.pdf

Aristotle, R. (1991). *Rhetoric: Book 1*. (W. Rhys Roberts, trans.). (Original work published 350 B.C.) Retrieved from http://philosophy.eserver.org/aristotle/rhetoric.txt

Ayadi, M. and Mattoussi, W. (2014) *Scoping of the Tunisian economy*. WIDER Working Paper 2014/074. Helsinki, Finland: UNU-WIDER. Retrieved from https://www.wider.unu.edu/publication/scoping-tunisian-economy

Baliamoune, M. (2011). *The making of gender equality in Tunisia and implications for development*. Retrieved from http://siteresources.worldbank.org/INTWDR2012/Resources/7778105–1299699968583/7786210–1322671773271/baliamoune.pdf

Ball, S. J. (1990). *Politics and policy making in education*. London, UK: Routledge.

Ball S. J. (2016). Following policy: networks, network ethnography and education policy mobilities. *Journal of Education Policy*, *31*(5), 549–566.

Barakat, H. (Ed.) (2015). *Contemporary North Africa: Issues of Development and Integration*. Routledge Library Editions: North Africa. New York, NY: Routledge.

Bartlett, L. and Vavrus, F. (2014). Transversing the vertical case study: A methodological approach to studies of educational policy as practice. *Anthropology & Education*, *45*(2), 131–147.

Baumann, S. (2007). A general theory of artistic legitimation: How art worlds are like social movements. *Poetics*, *35*(1), 47–65. doi:10.1016/j.poetic.2006.06.001.

Bayat, A. (2010). *Life as politics: How ordinary people change the Middle East*. Amsterdam: Amsterdam University Press.

BBC (2011, October 28). Protests hit Sidi Bouzid after historic Tunisia poll. BBC. Retrieved from http://www.bbc.com/news/world-africa-15488077

BBC (2015, October 9). Nobel Peace Prize for Tunisian National Dialogue Quartet. *BBC*. Retrieved from http://www.bbc.com/news/world-europe–34485865

Beinin, J. (2015). *Workers and thieves: Labor movements and popular uprisings in Tunisia and Egypt*. Stanford, CA: Stanford University Press.

Belkhodja, T. (1998). *Les trois décennies bourguiba*. Paris, FR: Aracanteres/ Publisud.

Ben Ali (2004).

Ben Othman, H. (2010). Investigating transparency and disclosure determinants at firm-level in MENA emerging markets. *International Journal of Accounting, Auditing and Performance Evaluation*, *6*(4), 368–396.

Benner, C. (2003). Learning communities in a learning region: The soft infrastructure of cross-firm learning networks in Silicon Valley. *Environment and Planning A 35*, 1809–1830.

Bennoune, K. (2012, March 28). Système dégagé? Women and transitional justice in the wake of the Arab Spring. Paper presented at *American Society of International Law Annual Meeting*. doi: 10.5305/procannmeetasil.106.0502.

Benstead, L, Kao, K, Harris, A, Landry, P, Lust, E. and Stepanova, N. (2015). The Tunisian local governance performance index: Selected findings on education. University of Gothenburg. Retrieved from https://www.academia.edu/19303161/The_Tunisian_Local_Governance_Performance_Index_Selected_Findings_on_Education

Berry, L. and Rinehart, R. (1988). The society and its environment. In H. D. Nelson (Ed.), *Tunisia: A country study* (71–144) Washington, DC: United State Government.

Birzea, C. (1994) *Educational policies of the countries in transition*. Strasbourg, FR: Council of Europe Press.

Borowiec, A. (1998). *Modern Tunisia: A democratic apprenticeship*. Westport, CT: Praeger.

Boulby, M. (1988). The Islamic challenge: Tunisia since independence. *Third World Quarterly*, *10*(2), 590–614.

Bouraoui, A. (1990). Trente années d'éducation en Tunisie. *Le développement en question: dimension, bilan, perspectives: Actes du colloque de Tunis* (423–440). Tunis: CERES.

Breuer, A., Landman, T. and Farquhar, D. (2015). Social media and protest mobilization: Evidence from the Tunisian revolution. *Democratization*, *22*(4), 764–792.

Brisson, Z. and Kronfris, K. (2012). *Tunisia: From revolutions to institutions*. Paris, FR: The World Bank.

Brown, L. C. (2015). *The Tunisia of Ahmad Bey, 1837–1855*. Princeton, NJ: Princeton University Press.

Brown, N. J. (2012). *Constitutions in a nonconstitutional world: Arab basic laws and the prospects for accountable government*. New York: SUNY Press.

Brown, S. (1976). *Modernism, association and panislamism*. Leiden, Netherlands: Brill Archive.

Bsaies, A. (1989). Educational change and the Ulama in 19th and Early 20th Centuries. In M. K. Nabli and J.B. Nugent, (Eds.). *The new institutional economics and development: Theory and applications to Tunisia* (236–265). Paris, FR: Elsevier.

Burnell, P. (2006). Autocratic opening to democracy: why legitimacy matters. *Third World Quarterly*, *27*(4), 545–562. doi:10.1080/01436590600720710.

Burrows, M. (1986). Mission civilisatrice: French cultural policy in the Middle East, 1860–1914. *The Historical Journal*, *29*(1), 109–35.

Carney, S. (2009). Negotiating policy in an age of globalization: Exploring educational "policyscapes" in Denmark, Nepal, and China. *Comparative Education Review*, *53*(1), 63–88.

Cavatorta, F. and Haugbølle, R. H. (2012). The end of authoritarian rule and the mythology of Tunisia under Ben Ali. *Mediterranean politics*, *17*(2), 179–195.

Champagne, J. (2007). "Job seekers" and "enterprise incubator": Educational reform in Tunisia. *Changing English*, *14*(2), 201–215.

Charrad, M. M. (1997). Policy shifts: State, Islam, and gender in Tunisia, 1930s–1990s. Social politics: International studies in gender. *State and Society, 4*(2). doi: 10.1093/sp/4.2.284

Charrad, M. M. (2001). States and women's rights: The making of postcolonial Tunisia, Algeria, and Morocco. Berkeley, CA: University of California Press.

Charrad, M. M. (2007. Tunisia at the forefront of the Arab world: Two waves of gender Legislation. *Washington and Lee Law Review, 64*(4). Retrieved from http://scholarlycommons.law.wlu.edu/wlulr/vol64/iss4/11

Chemingui, M. and Sánchez, M. (2011). *Assessing development strategies to achieve the MDGs in the Republic of Tunisia: Country study.* New York, NY: United Nations Department for Social and Economic Affairs.

Chomiak, L. (2011). The making of a revolution in Tunisia. *Middle East Law and Governance, 3*, 68–83. doi:10.1163/187633711X591431

Chossudovsky, M. (2011, January 20). Tunisia and the IMF's Diktats: How macro economic policy triggers worldwide poverty and unemployment. *Global Research.* Retrieved from http://www.globalresearch.ca/tunisia-and-the-imf-s-diktats-how-macro-economic-policy-triggers-worldwide-poverty-and-unemployment/22867?print=1

Christensen, C. M., Horn, M. B., Caldera, L. and Soares, L. (2011). *Disrupting college: How disruptive innovation can deliver quality and affordability to postsecondary education.* Innosight Institute.

Clancy-Smith, J. (2000). Envisioning knowledge: Educating the Muslim woman in colonial North Africa, c. 1850–1918. In R. Matthee and B. Baron (Eds.), *Iran and beyond: Essays in Middle Eastern history in honor of Nikki R. Keddie* (99–118). Santa Ana, CA: Mazda Publishers.

Clancy-Smith, J. (2013). From Sidi Bou Zid to Sidi Bou Said: A longue durée approach to the Tunisian Revolutions. In M. L. Haas and D. W. Lesch (Eds.), *The Arab Spring: Change and resistance in the Middle East* (13–34). Boulder, CO: Westview Press.

Clark, E. (2005). On not retracting the confessed (222–243). In J. D. Caputo and M J. Scanlon Augustine and Postmodernism: Confessions and Circumfession. Indiana University Press.

Coleman, J. (1965). *Education and political development (SPD-4).* Princeton, NJ: Princeton University Press.

Coll, S. (2011, April 4). The Casbah coalition. *The New Yorker.* Retrieved from http://www.newyorker.com/magazine/2011/04/04/the-casbah-coalition

Conant, J. (2012). *Staying Roman: Conquest and identity in Africa and the Mediterranean, 439–700 (Vol. 82).* New York, NY: Cambridge University Press.

Cory, I. P. and Hodges, E. R. (Eds.). (1876). *Cory's ancient fragments of the Phoenician, Carthaginian, Babylonian, Egyptian and other authors.* London, UK: Reeves and Turner.

Cosma, S. (2009). Ibn Khaldun's economic thinking. *Ovidius University Annals of Economics, XIV*, 52–57.

Covatorta, F. and Haugbølle, R. H. (2012). The end of authoritarian rule and the mythology of Tunisia under Ben Ali. *Mediterranean Politics, 17*(2), 179–195.

Cowen, R. (1982). *International Yearbook of Education 1982, Vol. XXXIV: Educational Structures.* Paris, FR: IBE/UNESCO.

Cowen, R. (1994). Schooling and selected aspects of culture from the perspective of comparative education: Neither a borrower nor a lender be. In E. Thomas (Ed.), *International perspectives on culture and schooling: A symposium proceedings.* London, UK: Institute of Education.

Cowen, R. (1996). *The evaluation of higher education systems.* London, UK: Kogan Page.

Cowen, R. (2000a). Fine-tuning educational earthquakes. *Education in times of transition: World yearbook of education 2000.* London, UK: Kogan Page.

Cowen, R. (2000b). Comparing futures or comparing past? *Comparative Education, 36* (3), 333–42. Retrieved from http://www.tandfonline.com/doi/abs/10.1080/713656619

Cunniffe, E. (2016, March 11). Hypocrisy and resistance: Interactions with the political in Tunisia. *Brown Political Review.* Retrieved from http://www.brownpoliticalreview.org/2016/03/hypocrisy-and-resistance-interactions-with-the-political-in-tunisia/

Dalacoura, K. (2012). The 2011 uprisings in the Arab Middle East: Political change and Geopolitical implications. *International Affairs, 88*(1), 63–79. doi: 10.1111/j.1468-2346.2012.01057.x

Dale, R. (1994). Applied education politics or political sociology of education? In D. Halpin and B. Troyna (Eds.), *Researching education policy: Ethical and methodological issues* (31–41). London, UK: Falmer Press.

Dale, R. (2005). Globalization, knowledge economy and comparative education. *Comparative Education, 41*(2), 117–49. doi: 10.1080 /03050060500150906.

Dale, R. (2006). From comparison to translation: Extending the research imagination? *Globalisation, Societies and Education, 4*(2), 179–192. http://dx.doi.org/10.1080/14767720600750803

Daniele, G. (2014). Tunisian women's activism after the January 14 revolution: Looking within and towards the other side of the Mediterranean. *Journal of International Women's Studies, 15*(2). Retrieved from http://vc.bridgew.edu/jiws/vol15/iss2/2.

Daoud, M. (1991). Arabization in Tunisia: The tug of war. *Issues in Applied Linguistics, 2*(1). Retrieved from http://escholarship.org/uc/item/3v1089k4

Darvas, P. and Tibbitts, F. (1992). Educational change in central and eastern Europe: Tradition, context and new actors, The case of Hungary. In A. Tjeldvoll (Ed.), *Education in East/Central Europe 1991*, Special studies in Comparative Education, number thirty. Buffalo, NY: Graduate School of Education Publications.

Deane, S. (2013, February). Transforming Tunisia: The role of civil society in Tunisia's transition. *International Alert.* Retrieved from http://www.international-alert.org/sites/default/files/publications/Tunisia2013EN.pdf

DeGorge, B. (2002). The modernization of education: A case study of Tunisia and Morocco. *The European Legacy, 7*(5), 579–596.

Desai, R. M., Yousef, T. and Olofsgård, A. (2007). The logic of authoritarian bargains: A test of a structural model. Washington, DC: Brookings Institution. Retrieved from https://www.brookings.edu/wp-content/uploads/2016/06/01globaleconomics_desai.pdf

Di Tommaso, M. R., Lanzoni, E. and Rubini, L. (2001). *Support to SMEs in the Arab region: the case of Tunisia. UNIDO/UNDP, UNIDO* Italia. Retrieved from http://www.unido.org/fileadmin/user_media/MEDEX/med_publications_documents/Support_to_SMEs_in_Arab_Region._The_case_of_Tunisia.pdf

Diamond, L. (2010). Why are there no Arab democracies? *Journal of Democracy, 21*(1). Retrieved from https://cddrl.fsi.stanford.edu/sites/default/files/Larry_Diamond_Arab_Democracy_article.pdf

Dreisbach, T. (2013, March 28). Presidency defends delayed creation of media regulatory authority. *Tunisialive*. Retrieved from www.tunisialive.net

Dreisbach, T. and Joyce, R. (2014, March 27). Revealing Tunisia's corruption under Ben Ali. *Aljazeera*. Retrieved from http://www.aljazeera.com/indepth/features/2014/03/revealing-tunisia-corruption-under-ben-ali–201432785825560542.html

Dridi, F. (2006). *National employment fund: Tunisia inter-regional inequality facility sharing ideas and policies across Africa, Asia and Latin America*. London, UK: Overseas Development Institute (ODI). Retrieved from http://www.odi.org/sites/odi.org.uk/files/odi-assets/publications-opinion-files/4066.pdf

Dwyer, K. (1991). *Arab voices: The human rights debate in the Middle East (Vol. 13)*. Berkeley, CA: University of California Press.

Economist (2016). Black gold, White gold. *The Economist*. Retrieved from http://www.economist.com/news/special-report/21698438-rentier-system-trouble-big-oil-producing-states-and-beyond-black-gold

Eisinger, P. (1973). The conditions of protest behavior in American cities. *American Political Science Review, 67* (1), 11–28.

El-Araby, A. (2011). A comparative assessment of higher education financing in six Arab countries. *Prospects, 41*, 9–21.

El-Ayechi, M. (2012, April). The Civil State and The Zaytouna issue after the independence. Lecture presented on Education Day. Taalimouna, Tunis Tunisia.

El Jorshi, S. (2003). Democratic deficits in the midst of liberalization. In *Social watch report 2003: The poor and the market* (180–181). Uruguay: Instituto Del Tercer Mundo. Retrieved from http://www.iiav.nl/epublications/2003/social_watch_2003.pdf#page=177

El Masry, I. (2014). *Women's movements and countermovements: The quest for gender equality in Southeast Asia and the Middle East*. Newcastle: Cambridge Scholars Publishing.

El-Mesawi, M. T. (2008). Muslim reformist action in nineteenth-century Tunisia. *The American Journal of Islamic Social Sciences, 25*(2), 49–82.

Ennaceur, M. (2000). Les syndicats et la mondialisation: Le cas de la Tunisie [Trade unions and globalization: The case of Tunisia], *Working Papers,* No. DP/120/2000, ILO, Geneva.

Esposito, J. L. and Voll, J. (2001). *Makers of contemporary Islam.* Oxford, UK: Oxford University Press.

European Commission (TEMPUS). (2010). *Higher education in Tunisia, European Commission.* Retrieved from http://eacea.ec.europa.eu/tempus/participating_countries/reviews/tunisia_review_of_higher_education.pdf

Ez Zitouna (2005). Presentation: History. *Ez Zitouna University.* Retrieved from http://www.uz.rnu.tn/en/feature.asp?cid=65

Facci, P. D. (2011). *On human potential: Peace and conflict transformation fostered through dance* (Vol. 3). Münster, Germany: LIT Verlag Münster.

Faour, M. (2012). *Religious education and pluralism in Egypt and Tunisia.* Washington, DC: Carnegie Endowment for International Peace. Retrieved from http://carnegie mec.org/2012/08/13/religious-education-and-pluralism-in-egypt-and-tunisia

Fortier, E. A. (2015). Transition and marginalization: Locating spaces for discursive contestation in post-revolution Tunisia. *Mediterranean Politics, 20*(2), 142–160. doi:10.1080/13629395.2015.1033904

Foundation for the Future. (2013). Study on civil society organizations in Tunisia. Retrieved from http://foundationforfuture.org/en/Portals/0/Publications/Etude %20SC%20english%20Version%20Finale.pdf

Foweraker, J. (1989). *Making democracy in Spain: Grassroots struggle in the South, 1955–1975.* Cambridge, UK: Cambridge University Press.

Foweraker, J. (1995). *Theorizing social movements.* London, UK: Pluto.

Foweraker, J. and Craig A. (1990). *Popular movements and political change in Mexico.* Boulder, CO: Lynne Reiner.

Foweraker, J. and Landman T. (1997). *Citizenship rights and social movements: A comparative and statistical analysis.* Oxford, UK: Oxford University Press.

Freire, P. (2000). *Pedagogy of the oppressed.* London, UK: Bloomsbury Publishing.

Fryer, L. G. and Jules, T. D. (2013). Transitory policy spaces and educational development in the Maghreb region: Higher education in post-revolutionary Tunisia. In A. W. Wiseman and C. C. Wolhuter (Eds.), *The development of higher education in Africa: prospects and challenges (401-426).* Bingley, UK: Emerald Publishing

Fursan al-Balagh Media, (2013, March). An Appeal to the Youth of Islam Who Are Eager to Hijrah for the Sake of Allah in the Islamic Maghreb and Tunisia. Retrieved from https://azelin.files.wordpress.com/2013/03/al-qc481_idah-in-the-islamic-maghrib-22call-to-theyouth-of-islam-to-those-who-aspire-to-hijrah-in-the-way-of-god-in-the-islamic-maghrib-in-general-and-tunisia-in-particular22-en.pdf

Galka, M. (2016, April 27). New research shows ISIS recruitment driven by cultural isolation. *Huffington Post.* Retrieved from http://images.huffingtonpost.com/ 2016-04-26-1461710833-5242966-mostfewestisisfighters.png

Gambhir, H. K. (2014, August 15). Dabiq: The strategic messaging of the Islamic State. *Backgrounder.* Washington DC: Institute for the Study of War. Retrieved from:

http://www.understandingwar.org/sites/default/files/Dabiq%20Backgrounder_Harleen%20Final.pdf

Garton Ash, T. (2009, December 3). Velvet revolutions: The prospects. *New York Review of Books*.

Gelvin, J. (2013, March). The Arab uprisings: Lessons to be learned (and unlearned), Forum: "Arab Springs," *Il Mestiere di Storico*, 5:1.

Geyer, R. (2003). European integration, the problem of complexity and the revision of theory. *Journal of Common Market Studies, 41*, 15–35. doi: 10.1111/1468–5965.t01–1–00409.

Gobe, E. (2010). The Gafsa mining basin between riots and a social movement: Meaning and significance of a protest movement in Ben Ali's Tunisia. *Working Paper, HAL*. Retrieved from https://halshs.archives-ouvertes.fr/halshs-00557826

Godec, R. F. (2008, June 23). Corruption in Tunisia: What's yours is mine. *WikiLeaks* cable: 08TUNIS679_a. Retrieved from https://wikileaks.org/plusd/cables/08TUNIS679_a.html

Gordon, I, Lewis, J and Young, L. J. (1977). Perspectives on policy analysis. *Public Administration Journal, 25*.

Gordts, E. (2014, September 9). This is what education under ISIS in Raqqa will look like. *Huffington Post*. Retrieved from http://www.huffingtonpost.com/2014/09/26/isis-education-raqqa_n_5889884.html

Götz, I. L. (2010). *Conceptions of happiness*. London, UK: Rowman and Littlefield.

Government of Tunisia (1958). Law of November 4, 1958: Concerning the educational reform and the creation of a Tunisian educational system. Government of Tunisia.

Government of Tunisia (1959). Constitution of the Republic of Tunisia. Publication of the Official Printing Office of the Republic of Tunisia, Tunis.

Government of Tunisia (2005). Tunis Virtual University. Government of Tunisia. Retrieved from http://unpan1.un.org/intradoc/groups/public/documents/un-other/unpan022050.pdf

Government of Tunisia (2014). Constitution. Retrieved from https://www.constituteproject.org/constitution/Tunisia_2014.pdf

Granovetter, M. (1978). Threshold models of collective behavior. *American Journal of Sociology*, 1420–1443.

Gray, D. H. (2012). Tunisia after the uprising: Islamist and secular quests for women's rights. *Mediterranean Politics, 17*(3), 285–302. doi: 10.1080/13629395.2012.725298

Green, A. H. (1978). *The Tunisian Ulama 1873–1915: Social structure and response to ideological currents*. Leiden, Netherlands: E. J. Brill.

Griffiths, T. and Millei, Z. (2013), *Logics of socialist education engaging with crisis, insecurity and uncertainty*. New York, NY: Springer.

Gyimah-Brempong, K. and Ondiege, P. (2011). Reforming higher education: Access, equity, and financing in Botswana, Ethiopia, Kenya, South Africa, and Tunisia. *World, 3*, 0–20.

Halverson, J. R., Ruston, S. W. and Trethwey, A. (2013). Mediating martyrs of the Arab Spring: new media, civil religion, and narrative in Tunisia and Egypt. *Journal of Communication, 63*(2), 312–322.

Hanberger, A. (2003). Public policy and legitimacy: A historical policy analysis of the interplay of public policy and legitimacy. *Policy Sciences, 36*(3), 257–278.

Harrelson-Stephens, J. and Callaway, R. L. (2014). You say you want a revolution: The Arab Spring, north diffusion, and the human rights regime. *Human Rights Review, 15,* 413–431. doi:10.1007/s12142–014–0315–5.

Harrison, C. (2015). *Education under ISIS: A generation in darkness.* The Borgen Project. Retrieved from http://borgenproject.org/education-isis-generation-darkness/

Hatem, M. F. (2005). In the shadow of the state: Changing definitions of Arab women's "developmental" citizenship rights. *Journal of Middle East Women's Studies, 1*(3). Retrieved from http://www.jstor.org/stable/40326870

Hawkins, D. (2002). *International human rights and authoritarian rule in Chile.* Lincoln, NE: University of Nebraska Press.

Hawkins, S. (2011). Who wears hijab with the president: Constructing a modern Islam in Tunisia. *Journal of Religion of Africa, 41*(1), 35–58.

Hay, C. (2002). *Political analysis: A critical introduction.* Basingstoke, UK: Palgrave Macmillan.

Henry, F. G. (2008). *Language, culture, and hegemony in modern France: 1539 to the millennium.* Birmingham, AL: Summa Publishing.

Howard, P. N., Duffy, A., Freelon, D., Hussain, M, Mari, W., and Mazaid, M. (2011). *Opening closed regimes: What was the role of social media during the ArabSpring.* (Working Paper No. 2011.1). Retrieved from http://papers.ssrn.com/sol3/papers. cfm?abstract_id=2595096

Hudson, M. (2014). Transition to what? Reflections on the Arab Uprisings. In F. Al-Sumait, N. Lenze and M. C. Hudson (Eds.), *The Arab uprisings: catalysts, dynamics, and trajectories,* 31–45. London, UK: Rowman and Littlefield.

Hudson, M. C. (2015). *The Crisis of the Arab State.* Report for Middle East Initiative, Belfer Center for Science and International Affairs. Retrieved from http://www. belfercenter.org/publication/crisis-arab-state

Iban Abi al-Diyaf, A. (1989). Ithaf Ahi al-zaman bi Akhbar muluk Tunis wa 'Ahd el-Aman. Tunis: Maison Tunisienne de l'édition.

International Crisis Group. (2011). *Popular protest in North Africa and the Middle East (IV): Tunisia's way.* Brussels, Belgium: International Crisis Group. Retrieved from http://www.crisisgroup.org/~/media/Files/Middle%20East%20North%20Africa/ North%20Africa/106%20Popular%20Protests%20in%20North%20Africa%20 and%20the%20Middle%20East%20-IV-%20Tunisias%20Way.pdf

International Crisis Group. (2013, February 13). Tunisia: Violence and the Salafi challenge. *Report Middle East and North Africa,* 137. Retrieved from https://www. crisis group.org/middle-east-north-africa/north-africa/tunisia/tunisia-violence-and-salafi-challenge

International Development Association (IDA). (1962). IDA Press Release No. 62/18. Retrieved from http://siteresources.worldbank.org/IDA/Resources/timeline–1962-September.pdf

ISIS imposes education tax on all students in Iraq's Mosul. (2014, November 19). *NBC News*. Retrieved from http://www.nbcnews.com/storyline/isis-terror/isis-imposes-education-tax-all-students-iraqs-mosul-n251686

Islahi, A. A. (2012). *Economic ideas of a nineteenth century Tunisian statesman: Khayr al-Din al-Tunisi (43519)*. Munich, Germany: University Library of Munich. Retrieved from https://mpra.ub.uni-muenchen.de/43519/

Islamic State (2014a). Dabiq: The return of Khilafah (Issue 1). Retrieved from http://media.clarionproject.org/files/09-2014/isis-isil-islamic-state-magazine-Issue-1-thereturn-of-khilafah.pdf

Islamic State (2014b). Dabiq: The flood. (Issue 2). Retrieved from http://media.clarionproject.org/files/09-2014/isis-isil-islamic-state-magazine-Issue-2-theflood.pdf

Jelassi, T, Bouzguenda, A. and Malzy, T. (2015a). *Fundamentally changing the way we educate students in the Middle East and North Africa (MENA) region*. Addis Ababa, Ethiopia: African Development Bank Group. Retrieved from http://www.afdb.org/fileadmin/uploads/afdb/Documents/Publications/North_Africa

Jelassi, T. Bouzguenda, A. and Malzy, T. (2015b). Report of the National Commission on Employability, Tunis, 2011.

Jemail, D. (2015, October 15). Tunisian civil society: From revolutionaries to peace keepers (Blog). Retrieved from http://blogs.worldbank.org/arabvoices/tunisian-civil-society-revolutionaries-peace-keepers

Jemni, M. (2010). A case study of Tunisia. In M. Masri, N. Jemni, A.M. Al Ghassani and A. A. Badawin (Eds), *Entrepreneurship education in the Arab States*. Beirut, Lebanon: UNESCO.

Joline, C. (2012). *Women in post-revolutionary Tunisia: Political inclusion and prospects for the future*. Retrieved from http://digitalcollections.sit.edu/isp_collection/1272

Jomier, A. (2011). *Secularism and state feminism: Tunisia's smoke and mirrors*. Retrieved from http://www.booksandideas.net/Secularism-and-State-Feminism.html

Jones, M. T. (1980). Education of girls in Tunisia: Policy implications of the drive for universal enrollment. *Comparative Education Review, 24*(2). Retrieved from http://www.jstor.org/stable/1187557

Jones, P. W. (2004). Taking the credit: Financing and policy linkages in the education portfolio of the World Bank. In G. Steiner-Khamsi and T. S. Popkewitz (Eds.), *The global politics of educational borrowing and lending* (188–200). New York, NY: Teachers College Press.

JORT (1987). *Journal Officiel de la République Tunisienne 1987*. Government of Tunisia. Tunis: Tunisia.

JORT (1996). *Journal Officiel de la République Tunisienne 1996*. Government of Tunisia. Tunis: Tunisia.

JORT (2007). *Journal Officiel de la République Tunisienne 2007*. Government of Tunisia. Tunis: Tunisia.

Judy, R. A. (2012). Introduction: For dignity; Tunisia and the poetry of emergent democratic humanism. *Boundary 2, 39*(1), 1–16.

Jules, T. D. (2013a). Going trilingual: Post-revolutionary socialist education reform in Grenada. *Round Table: The Commonwealth Journal of International Relations, 102*(5), 459–470. doi:10.1080/00358533.2013.83373

Jules, T. D. (2013b). Ideological pluralism and revisionism in small (and micro) states: The erection of the Caribbean education policy space. *Globalization, Societies and Education, (April)*, 37–41. http://dx.doi.org/10.1080/14767724.2013.782194

Jules, T. D. (2016). *The new global educational policy environment in the fourth industrial revolution: Gated, regulated and governed.* Bingley, UK: Emerald Publishing.

Jules, T. D. and Barton, T. (2014). Educational governance activities and the rise of educational contagion in the Islamic Maghreb: The case of Tunisia. *Journal of History and Sociology, 2*, 1–29. doi:10.2390/indi-v5- i2–121.

Kaboub, F. (2014). The making of the Tunisian revolution. *Understanding the political economy of the Arab uprisings*, 57–78, Singapore: World Scientific Publishing.

Kallander, A. A. (2013). *Women, gender, and the palace households in Ottoman Tunisia.* Austin, TX: University of Texas Press.

Khalil, A. (2014). *Crowds and politics in North Africa: Tunisia, Algeria and Libya.* Abingdon, Oxon, UK: Routledge.

Khondker, H. H. (2011). Role of the new media in the Arab Spring. *Globalizations, 8*(5), 675–679. http://dx.doi.org/10.1080/14747731.2011.621287

Kingdon, J. (1984). *Agendas, alternatives and public policies.* Boston, MA: Little, Brown.

Koopmans, R. and Olzak S. (2004). Discursive opportunities and the evolution of right-wing violence in Germany. *American Journal of Sociology, 110,* 198–230.

Koopmans, R. and Muis, J. (2009). The rise of right-wing populist Pim Fortuyn in the Netherlands: A discursive opportunity approach. *European Journal of Political Research, 48*(5), 642–664. http://doi.org/10.1111/j.1475–6765.2009.00846.x

Kriesi, H., Koopman, R. Duyvenda, J. W and Giugni, M.G., (1995). *New social movements in Western Europe: A comparative analysis.* Minneapolis, MN: University of Minnesota Press.

Labidi, L. (2007). The nature of transnational alliances in women's associations in the Maghreb: The case of AFTURD and ATFD in Tunisia. *Journal of Middle East Women's Studies, 3*(1). Retrieved from http://www.jstor.org/stable/10.2979/mew.2007.3.1.6

Lakdhar, L. (2005). Moving from Salafi to rationalist education. *The Middle East Review of International Affairs, 9*(1). Retrieved from http://www.mafhoum.com/press7/231C35.htm

Landman, T. (2008). *Issues and methods in comparative politics.* London: Routledge.

Lange, M (2013). Comparative-historical methods: An introduction. In M. Lange (Ed.) *Comparative-historical methods* (1–21). New York NY: Sage Publications.

Larsen, M. (Ed.) (2010). New thinking in comparative education: Honoring Robert Cowen. *Comparative and international education: A diversity of voices, 8*. Rotterdam, Netherlands: Sense Publishers.

Latrech, (2007, March 26). La pensée réformiste de l'intelligentsia tunisienne. *La Presse de Tunisie*.

Le Saout, D. (1988). Les emeutes entre exclusion et sentiment d'injustice, in D. Le Saout and M. Rollinde (Eds.) *Emeutes et mouvements sociaux au Maghreb* (47–65). Paris, Karthala-Institut Maghreb-Europe.

"Le système" (1962, November). Le système d'enseignement de La Tunisie est orienté vers la formation rapide des cadres intellectuels et techniques. Le Monde Diplomatique. Retrieved from https://www.monde-diplomatique.fr/1962/11/A/25034

Lindberg, D. C. (1992). *The beginnings of Western science: The European scientific tradition in philosophical, religious, and institutional context, 600 BC to AD 1450*. Chicago, IL: University of Chicago Press.

Ling, D. L. (1979). *Morocco and Tunisia: A comparative history*. Washington, DC: University Press of America.

Logan, T. P. (2012). When authoritarianism failed in Tunisia: An investigation of the Ben Ali regime and the factors that led to its downfall (Unpublished masters dissertation). Georgetown University, Washington DC. Retrieved from https://repository.library.georgetown.edu/bitstream/handle/10822/557507/Logan_georgetown_0076M_11838.pdf?sequence=1

Lotan, G., Graeff, E., Ananny, M., Gaffney, D. and Pearce, I. (2011). The Arab Spring the revolutions were tweeted: Information flows during the 2011 Tunisian and Egyptian revolutions. *International Journal of Communication, 5*.

Lulat, Y. (2005). *A history of African higher education from antiquity to the present: A critical synthesis*. Westport, CT: Praeger (Greenwood Publishing Group).

Lynch, M. (2013). *The Arab uprising: The unfinished revolutions of the new Middle East*. New York, NY: Public Affairs.

Maalej, Z. A. (2012). The 'Jasmine Revolt' has made the 'Arab Spring': A critical discourse analysis of the last three political speeches of the ousted president of Tunisia. *Discourse & Society, 23*(6), 679–700.

Maas, M. and Kihn, H. (2003). *Exegesis and empire in the Early Byzantine Mediterranean: Junillus Africanus and the Instituta regularia divinae legis (Vol. 17)*. Tübingen: Mohr Siebeck.

Mabrouk, M. (2013). A revolution for dignity and freedom: preliminary observations on the social and cultural background to the Tunisian revolution. In George Joffé (Ed.), *North Africa's Arab Spring* (121–132). New York, NY: Routledge.

Madi, O. (2013, March). Women and the Arab Spring: A missed opportunity? *Turkish Review*. Retrieved from http://www.turkishreview.org/reports/women-and-the-arab-spring-a-missed-opportunity_540509

Mahoney, J. and Rueschemeyer, D. (2003). Comparative historical analysis: Achievements and agendas. In J. Mahoney and D. Rueschemeyer (Eds.), *Comparative historical analysis in the social sciences* (3–38). Cambridge, UK: Cambridge University Press.

Malka, H. (2015). Tunisia: confronting extremism. In M. Barber, H. Malka, H., W. McCants, J. Russakis and T. M. Sanderson, T. M. (Eds.), *Religious radicalism after the Arab uprisings* (92–121). London: Rowman and Littlefield.

Marcus, G. (1995). Ethnography in/of the world system: The emergence of multi-sited ethnography. *Annual Review of Anthropology, 24*, 95–117.

Marginson, S. and Mollis, M. (2001). The door opens and the tiger leaps: Theories and reflexivities of comparative education for a global millennium. *Comparative Education Review, 45*, 581–615. http://dx.doi.org/10.1086/447693

Marks, M. (2012, September 28). Who are Tunisia's Salafis? *Foreign Policy*. Retrieved from foreignpolicy.com/2012/09/28/who-are-tunisias-salafis/

Marks, M. (2015). *Tunisia's Ennahda: Rethinking Islamism in the context of ISIS and the Egyptian coup*. Washington, DC: Brookings Institution. Retrieved from http://www.brookings.edu/~/media/Research/Files/Reports/2015/07/rethinking-political-islam/Tunisia_Marks-FINALE.pdf?la=en

Marrou, H. I. (1956). A *history of education in antiquity*. Madison, WI: University of Wisconsin Press.

Martínez-Fuentes, G. and Ennouri, B. (2014). Change and persistence in the Tunisia organisational network for the promotion of women. In E. Stetter and C. Reuter (Eds.), *Promoting women's rights & gender equality in the Middle East and North Africa*. FEPS. Retrieved from http://www.feps-europe.eu/assets/bd3344d3-a0fc-4582-9842-e3b8ea4724a4/2014%2009%2003%20women%27s%20rights%20mena_final.pdf

Marzouki, N. (2011). *People to citizens in Tunisia*. Middle East Research and Information Project. Retrieved from http://www.jstor.org/stable/41407961

Mason, P. (2013). *Why it's still kicking off everywhere: The new global revolutions, (2nd ed.)*. London, UK: Verso.

Mazzetti, M., Lichtblau, E. and Blinder, A. (2016, June 13). Omar Mateen, twice scrutinized by F. B. I., shows threat of lone terrorists. *New York Times*. Retrieved from https://www.nytimes.com/2016/06/14/us/politics/orlando-shooting-omar-mateen.html?_r=0

Mbougueng, V. (1999). Ben Ali et le modèle Tunisien, Paris: Les Editions de l'Orient.

McAdam, D. (1982). *Political process and the development of Black insurgency, 1930–1970*. Chicago, IL: University of Chicago Press.

McAdam, D., McCarthy, J. and Zald, M. (1996). *Comparative perspectives on social movements, political opportunities, mobilizing structures, and cultural framings*. Cambridge, UK: Cambridge University Press.

McCann, E. and K. Ward. (2012). Assembling urbanism: Following policies and "studying through" the sites and situations of policy making. *Environment and Planning A, 44* (1), 42–51.

McCarthy, J. and Zald, M. (1973). *The trend of social movements*. Morristown, PA: General Learning.

McCarthy, J. and Zald, M. (1977). Resource mobilization and social movements: A partial theory. *The American Journal of Sociology, 82* (6).

McLeish, E. (1998). Processes of educational transition in countries moving from authoritarian rule to democratic government. *Oxford Studies in Comparative Education, 8* (2). United Kingdom: Symposium Books.

Megahed, N. and Lack, S. (2011). Colonial legacy, women's rights and gender-educational inequality in the Arab world with particular reference to Egypt and Tunisia. *International Review of Education, 57*(3), 397–418.

Mekonnen, A. (2015). *The West and China in Africa: Civilization without justice.* Eugene, OR: WIPF and Stock Publishers.

Mettler, S. (2016). The policyscape and the challenges of contemporary politics to policy maintenance. *Perspectives on Politics, 14*(02), 369–390.

Micaud, C. A. (1964). *Tunisia: The politics of modernization.* New York, NY: F.A. Praeger.

MOE (1958). *Law of November 4, 1958.* Tunis, Tunisia: Government of Tunisia.

MOE (2001). *Tunisie.* Tunis, Tunisia: Government of Tunisia.

MOE (2014). Al Taqrir Al Wtanihawla AlTarbya Lil Jamii3 Fi Ofok 2015, MA diss., Ministry of Education.

MOE (2015). *Données globales par gouvernorat.* Retrieved from http://www.edunet.tn/article_education/statistiques/stat2014_2015/tableau187.pdf

MOET (Ministry of Education and Training) (2002). *Education act, 23 July.* Tunis: MOET.

MOET (2003). *The new education reform in Tunisia: An education strategy for the future 2002–2007.* Tunis, Tunisia: MOET.

MOET (2008). *The Development of Education in Tunisia, 2004–2008. National report.* Tunis, Tunisia: MOET.

MOHESRT (2008). *The fiftieth anniversary of the Tunisian university, 1958–2008.* Tunis, Tunisia: Government of Tunisia.

MONE (1981). *Ministry of national education report of education development in Tunisia.* Tunis, Tunisia: Government of Tunisia.

Moore, C. H. (1965). *Tunisia since independence: the dynamics of one-party government.* Berkeley, California: University of California Press.

Mulrine, C. (2011). *Women's organizations in Tunisia: Transforming feminist discourse in a transitioning state.* Retrieved from http://digitalcollections.sit.edu/isp_collection/1136

Murphy E. C. (1999). *Economic and political change in Tunisia: From Bouguiba to Ben Ali.* Houndmills, London, UK: Macmillan Press.

Murphy, E. C. (2003). *Women in Tunisia: Between state feminism and economic reform.* Boulder, Colorado: Lynne Rienner.

Naciri, R. (2003). The women's movement in the Maghreb: With emphasis on Tunisia, Morocco and Algeria. *Al-Raida, 20*(100). Retrieved from http://inhouse.lau.edu.lb/iwsaw/raida100/EN/p020–025.pdf

National Association of Broadcasters (1968). Educational television and educational development in Tunisia. Retrieved from https://archive.org/stream/ERIC_ ED119718/ERIC_ED119718_djvu.txt

Nóvoa, A. and Yariv-Mashal, T. (2003). Comparative research in education: A mode of governance or a historical journey. *Comparative Education, 39*(4), 432–438.

OECD (2015a). *Investing in youth: Tunisia. Strengthening the employability of youth during the transition to a green economy.* Paris, FR: OECD Publishing.

OECD (2015b, March). *Tunisia: A reform agenda to support competitiveness and inclusive growth.* "Better Policies" Series. Paris, FR: OECD Publishing. Retrieved from http://www.oecd.org/countries/tunisia/Tunisia-a-reform-agenda-to-support-competitiveness-and-inclusive-growth.pdf

OECD (2015c). Tunisia student performance (PISA 2015). Retrieved from http:// gpseducation.oecd.org/CountryProfile?primaryCountry=TUN&treshold=10&topic=PI

Okoth, A. (2006). *A history of Africa: African nationalism and the de-colonisation process.* Nairobi, Kenya: East African Educational Publishers, Ltd.

Omri, M. S. (2006). *Nationalism, Islam and world literature: Sites of confluence in the writings of Mahmud Al-Masʾadi.* Oxfordshire, UK: Routledge.

Omri, M. S. (2014, 12 February). The Tunisian constitution: The process and the outcomes. *Jadaliyya.* Retrieved from http://www.economist.com/blogs/ pomegranate/2014/01/tunisias-rural-poor?fsrc=scn/tw_ec/rebel_country

Opeku, F. (1993). Popular and higher education in Africa proconsularis. *SCHOLIA Studies in Classical Antiquity,* 31–44. Retrieved from http://www.casakvsa.org.za/ ScholiaUpdate/Volumes/Scholia2(1993).pdf

Paciello, M. C. (2011, May). Tunisia: Changes and challenges of political transition. *Mediterranean Prospects, 3.* Retrieved from https://www.ceps.eu/system/files/ book/2011/05/MEDPRO%20TR%20No%203%20Paciello%20on%20Tunisia.pdf

Pastuovic, N. (1993). Problems of reforming educational systems in post-communist countries. *International Review of Education, 39,* 405–418.

Peck, J. and Theodore, N. (2012). Follow the policy: A distended case approach. *Environment and Planning A, 44*(1), p. 21–30.

Pekkarinen, T. and Pellicer, M. (2013). Education and allocation of skills in Tunisia: evidence from an education reform. *IZA Journal of Labor & Development, 2*(1), 1–21.

Pena, A. M., Davies, T. and Ryan, H. (2016). Protest, social movements and global democracy since 2011: New perspectives. In P. G. Coy (Ed), *Research in social movements, conflicts and change* (1–39). Bingley, UK: Emerald Publishing.

Perkins, K. J. (1986). *Tunisia: Crossroads of the Islamic and European worlds.* Boulder, CO: Westview Press.

Perrin, B. (1914). *Plutarch's lives.* (Bernadotte Perrin, trans.). Cambridge, MA: Harvard University Press.

Peterson, W. (2008). Tacitus, dialogus (William Peterson, trans.). In T. W Benson and M. H. Prosser (Eds.), *Readings in classical rhetoric* (112–115). New York, NY: Routledge.

Petsinis, V. (2010). Twenty years after 1989: moving on from transitology. *Contemporary Politics, 16*(3), 301–319. doi.org/10.1080/13569775.2010.501652.

Plaetzer, N. (2014). Civil society as domestication: Egyptian and Tunisian uprisings beyond liberal transitology. *Journal of International Affairs, 68*(1). Retrieved from http://jia.sipa.columbia.edu/civil-society-domestication-egyptian-tunisian-uprisings-beyond-liberal-transitology/

Radsch, C. C. (2012). Unveiling the revolutionaries: Cyberactivism and the role of women in the Arab uprisings. Retrieved from http://bakerinstitute.org/files/635/

Ramsay, S. (2016). IS Documents identify thousands of Jihadis. *Sky News* Retrieved from http://news.sky.com/story/is-documents-identify-thousands-of-jihadis-1019855

Rand, D. H. (2013). *Roots of the Arab Spring*. Philadelphia, PA: University of Pennsylvania Press.

Randeree, B. (2011, January 10). Tunisian leader promises new jobs. *Al Jazeera*. Retrieved from http://www.aljazeera.com/news/africa/2011/01/20111110162392 14548.html

Rappleye, J. (2010). Compasses, maps, and mirrors: Relocating episteme(s) of transfer, reorienting the comparative kosmos. In M. Larsen (Ed), *New thinking in comparative education: Honouring the work of Robert Cowen,* (57–79). Rotterdam: Sense Publishers.

Rappleye, J. (2012). *Educational policy transfer in an era of globalization: Theory—history—comparison*. Frankfurt, Germany: Peter Lang.

Redissi, H. and Boukhayatia, R. (2015). EUSpring: The National Constituent Assembly of Tunisia and civil society dynamics. Brussels, Belgium: European Policy Center. Retrieved from http://www.epc.eu/pub_details.php?cat_id=1&pub_id=5815&year= 2015

Reich, B. (1990). *Political leaders of the contemporary Middle East and North Africa: A biographical dictionary*. New York, NY: Greenwood Publishing Group.

Reidy, E. (2015, February 20). Tunisia unity government stirs crisis in leading party. *Al Jazeera*. Retrieved from http://www.aljazeera.com/news/2015/02/tunisia-unity-government-stirs-crisis-leading-party–150215125404882.html

Risse, T., Ropp, S.C. and Sikkink, K. (Eds). (1999). *The power of human rights: International norms and domestic change*. Cambridge, UK: Cambridge University Press.

Rizvi, F. (2006). Imagination and the globalization of educational policy research. *Globalization, Societies, and Education, 4*(2), 193–205.

Robertson, S. and Dale, R. (2008). The World Bank, the IMF and the possibilities of critical education. In M. Apple and L. Gandin (Eds.), *International Handbook of Critical Education* (23–35). New York, NY: Routledge.

Robertson, S. L. (2011). The new spatial politics of (re)bordering and (re)ordering the state-education-citizen relation. *International Review of Education, 57*(3–4), 277–297.

Robertson, S. L. (2012). Researching global education policy: Angles in/on/out... In A. Verger, M. Novelli and H. Altinyelken (Eds). *Global education policy and international development: New agendas, issues and practices*. New York: Continuum Books.

Robertson, S. L., Bonal, X. and Dale, R. (2002). GATS and the Education Service Industry. *Comparative Education Review, 46* (4), 472–497.

Rodney, W. (1982). *How Europe underdeveloped Africa*. Washington, DC: Howard University Press.

Rosenkranz, K. (1894). *The philosophy of education* (Vol. 1, second edition). New York, NY: D. Appleton and Company.

Rossi, P. (1967). *Bourguiba's Tunisia*. Tunis: Editions Kahia.

Sadiki, L. (2002). Ben Ali's Tunisia: Democracy by non-democratic means. *British Journal of Middle Eastern Studies, 29*(1), 57–78.

Sadiqi, F. (2014). *Moroccan feminist discourses*. Basingstoke, UK: Palgrave Macmillan.

Salaam, A. O. (2013). The psychological make-up of Mohammed Yusuf. *E-International Relations*. Retrieved from http://www.e-ir.info/2013/11/04/the-psychological-make-up-of-mohammed-yusuf/

Santos, B. S. (1995). *Toward a new common sense: Law, science and politics in the paradigmatic transition*. New York, NY: Routledge.

Santos, B. S. (2004). Interview with Boaventura de Sousa Santos. *Globalization, Societies & Education, 2*(2), 147–160.

Sayigh, Y. A. (2014). *The economies of the Arab world (RLE Economy of Middle East): Development Since 1945*. New York, NY: Routledge.

Schraeder, P. and Redissi, H. (2011). Ben Ali's fall. *Journal of Democracy, 22* (3), 5–19.

Schram, S.F. (1993). Postmodern policy analysis: Discourse and identity in welfare policy. *Policy Sciences, 26*, 249–270.

Schofield, H. (2008, July 26). Yacht theft makes diplomatic waves: Tunisian–French relations suffer due to inquiry. *Herald Scotland*. Retrieved from http://www.heraldscotland.com/yacht-theftmakes-diplomatic-waves–1.829762

Schriewer, J. (2002). *Educación comparada: Un gran programa ante nue vos desafíos*. Surrey, UK: Surrey Association for Early Childhood Education. Retrieved from http://www.saece.org.ar/relec/revistas/2/art8.pdf

Sebag, P. (2007). Tunis. In C.E. (ed) Bosworth, C. E. *Historic cities of the Islamic world* (535–49). Koninklijke Brill NV, Leiden: The Netherlands.

Sebystyen, A. (2011, May 23). Voices from the Tunisian revolution. *Red Pepper*. Retrieved from http://www.redpepper.org.uk/voices-from-the-tunisian-revolution/

Seddon, D. (1986). Bread riots in North Africa: Economic policy and social unrest in Tunisia and Morocco. In P. Lawrence (Ed.), *World recession and the food crisis in Africa* (177–192). London, UK: James Curry.

"Several Cyber" (2015). Several cyber security to protect your account in the social – networking Twitter. *Wired*. Retrived from https://www.wired.com/wp-content/uploads/2015/11/ISIS-OPSEC-Guide.pdf

Shaw, M. (2000). *Theory of the global state: Globality as an unfinished revolution.* Cambridge, UK: Cambridge University Press.

Shillington, K. (Ed.). (2013). *Encyclopedia of African distory 3-Volume Set.* New York, NY: Routledge.

Siino, F. (2004). *Science et pouvoir dans la Tunisie contemporaine.* Paris/Aix-en- Provence: KARTHALA Editions.

Silova, I. (2009). Varieties of educational transformation: The post-socialist states of Central/Southeastern Europe and the former Soviet Union. In R. Cowen and A. Kazamias (Eds.), *International handbook of Comparative Education* (295–320). Netherlands: Springer Publishers.

Simons, M., Olssen M. and Peters, M. A. (2009). Introduction (1-98). In M. Simons, M. Olssen M. and M. A. Peters (Eds.) *Re-reading education policies: A handbook studying the policy agenda of the 21st century.* Boston, MA: Sense Publishers.

Sizer, C. T. (1971). The development of education in Tunisia. (unpublished masters dissertation). The American University, Washington, DC

Sobe, N. W. and Ortegón, N. D. (2009). Scopic systems, pipes, models and transfers in the global circulation of educational knowledge and practices. In T. Popkewitz and F. Rizvi (Eds.) *Globalization and the Study of Education* (49–66). New York: NSSE/ Teachers College Press.

Stetter, E. and Reuter, C. (2014). *Promoting women's rights & gender equality: In the Middle East and North Africa.* Bruxelles, Belgium: FEPS. Retrieved from http://www. feps-europe.eu/assets/bd3344d3-a0fc–4582–9842- e3b8ea4724a4/2014%2009%20 03%20women's%20rights%20-mena_final.pdf

Suleiman, M. W. (1993). Political orientation of young Tunisians: The impact of gender. *Arab Studies Quarterly, 15*(1). Retrieved from http://www.jstor.org/stable/41858041

Tap (2016). *Tunisie: Lancement du dialogue sociétal sur la réforme du système de l'enseignement supérieur.* Retrieved from http://directinfo.webmanagercenter. com/2015/11/16/neji-jalloul-le-dialogue-national-sur-la-reforme-du-systeme-educatif-na-exclu-aucune-partie

Tarrow, S. (1994). *Power in movement: Social movements, collective action and politics.* Cambridge, UK: Cambridge University Press

TECA (Tunisian External Communications Agency). (1992). *The national pact.* Tunis: TECA.

Tessler, M. and Keppel, E. (1976). Political generations. In R. A. Stone and J. Simmons (Eds.), *Change in Tunisia: Studies in the social sciences* (73–106). Albany, NY: SUNY Press.

Thompson, N. and Shubert, A. (2015, January 1). The anatomy of ISIS: How the 'Islamic State' is run, from oil to beheadings. *CNN.* Retrieved from http://edition.cnn. com/2014/09/18/world/meast/isis-syriairaq-hierarchy/, access: 18.03.2016

Thuy, P., Hansen, E., Price, D., and Perret-Nguyên, H. T. (2001). *The public employment service in a changing labour market.* Geneva: International Labour Office.

Tibi, C. (1974). *Développement économique et aspects financiers de la politique d'éducation en Tunisie, 2,* Paris, FR: UNESCO.

Tilly, C. (1978). *From mobilization to revolution*. New York, NY: Random House.

Time Magazine (1984, January 16). Bourguiba lets them eat bread. *Time Magazine*. Retrieved from http://content.time.com/time/magazine/article/0,9171,921495,00. html

The Times (2016, April 19). Hundreds of jihadi brides sent for combat training. *The Times*. Retrieved from http://www.thetimes.co.uk/article/hundreds-of-jihadi-brides-sent-for-combat-training-cg8pn55nh

Toensing, C. (2011). *Tunisian labor leaders reflect upon revolt*. Middle East Research and Information Project, Inc. (MERIP), 41. Retrieved from http://www.merip.org/mer/mer258/tunisian-labor-leaders-reflect-upon-revolt-0

Torgerson, D. (1996). Power and insight in policy discourse: Post-positivism and problem definition. In H. M. Dobuzinskis and D. Laycock (Eds.), *Policy studies in Canada: The state of the art* (266–298). Toronto, CA: University Press.

Trofimov, Y. (2016). How Tunisia became a top source of ISIS recruits. *Wall Street Journal*. Retrieved from http://www.wsj.com/articles/how-tunisia-became-a-top-source-of-isis-recruits-1456396203

Tullock, G. (1987). *Autocracy*. Dordrecht, the Netherlands: Kluwer Academic.

"Tunis Afrique" (2015). *Tunisia: Education reform is a shared concern – Habib Essid*. Retrieved from http://allafrica.com/stories/201504240368.html

Tunisia signs new constitution. (2014, January 27). *The Guardian*. Retrieved from https://www.theguardian.com/world/2014/jan/27/tunisia-signs-new-constitution-progressive

"Tunisie: PC Familial" (2001). *Tunisie: PC Familial, 74 millions de dinars de crédits en 5 ans*. Retrieved from http://www.turess.com/fr/Wmc/92921

UN Committee on the Rights of the Child (CRC), (1994, June 1). Consideration of reports submitted by States parties under article 44 of the Convention: Convention on the rights of the child: Initial reports of states parties due in 1999, Addendum Tunisia T CRC/C/11/Add.2.

UNESCO (1966). *La planification de l'éducation dans les pays Arabes et ses Possibilités de Développement*. Retrieved from http://unesdoc.unesco.org/images/0014/001481/14815fb.pdf

UNESCO (1980). *Tunisia education and training: Problems and needs*. Paris, FR: UNESCO.

UNESCO. (1992). *Development of education in Tunisia 1990–1992*. Report presented in the 43rd session of the international conference about education, Tunisian national commission for education, science and culture. Geneva, Switzerland: UNESCO-ALESCO-USESCO.

UNESCO (2006). *Country profile prepared for the Education for All Global Monitoring Report 2007. Strong Foundations: Early childhood care and education Tunisia early childhood care and education (ECCE)*. Geneva, Switzerland: UNESCO. Retrieved from http://unesdoc.unesco.org/images/0014/001480/148046e. pdf#page=1&zoom=auto,- 12,738

UNESCO (2007). *UNESCO National education support strategy*. Paris, FR: UNESCO.

UNESCO and CAAR. (2015). *An Arab exception? The role of civil society in Tunisia's democratic transition*. Retrieved from https://www.deakin.edu.au/__data/assets/pdf_file/0006/395718/AE-Program.pdf

UNICEF. (2011). *Tunisia: MENA gender equality profile: Status of women in the Middle East and North Africa*. Retrieved from https://www.unicef.org/gender/files/Tunisia-Gender-Eqaulity-Profile-2011.pdf

UNICEF. (2013). *Tunisia education statistics*. Retrieved from http://www.unicef.org/infobycountry/Tunisia_statistics.html

United Nations (2004). *Tunisia national report on millennium development goals*. Retrieved from http://www.un.org/en/development/desa/policy/mdg_workshops/mdgreports/tunisia/national_report.pdf

United Nations (2012). *Report of the special rapporteur on the promotion and protection of human rights and fundamental freedoms while countering terrorism, Martin Scheinin: Mission to Tunisia*. UN document A/HRC/20/14. Retrieved from http://www.ohchr.org/Documents/HRBodies/HRCouncil/RegularSession/Session20/A-HRC-20-14-Add1_en.pdf

U.S. Department of Commerce (1988). Joint Publications Research Service. and Foreign Broadcast Information Service. *JPRS report. Near East & South Asia*. Retrieved from handle.dtic.mil/100.2/ADA347212

UVT (2016). *2016–2019 Plan stratégique: En quête de devenir une université innovante de référence à l'échelle nationale et internationale*. UVT. Retrieved from http://www.uvt.rnu.tn/documents/plan-strg-uvt.pdf

Vavrus, F. and Bartlett, L. (2006). Comparatively knowing: Making a case for the vertical case study. *Current Issues in Comparative Education, 8*(2), 95–103.

Verger, A. (2009). The merchants of education: Global politics and the uneven education liberalization process within the WTO. *Comparative Education Review, 53*(3), 379–401.

Vidiani (2011). *Detailed administrative map of Tunisia with cities*. Retrieved from http://www.vidiani.com/detailed-administrative-map-of-tunisia-with-cities

Wallerstein, I. (2011). The contradictions of the Arab Spring. *Al Jazeera, 14*. Retrieved from http://www.aljazeera.com/indepth/opinion/2011/11/20111111101711539134.html

Wintrobe, R. (1990). The tinpot and the totalitarian: An economic theory of dictatorship. *American Political Science Review, 84*(03), 849–872.

Wintrobe, R. (1998). *The political economy of dictatorship*. Cambridge, UK: Cambridge University Press.

Wintrobe, R. (2007). Dictatorship: Analytical approaches, in C. Boix and S. Stokes (Ed.) *Oxford handbook of comparative politics* (363–394). Oxford University Press.

White, B. (1996). Talk about school: Education and the colonial project in French and British Africa (1860–1960). *Comparative Education, 32* (1).

Wooten, C. (1988). Roman education and rhetoric. In, M. Grant and R. Kitzinger (Eds.), *Civilization of the ancient Mediterranean: Greece and Rome* (1109–1120). New York, NY: Scribner's, World History in Context.

World Bank. (2002). *Republic of Tunisia: Information and communications technology: Contributions to growth and employment generation.* Retrieved from http://siteresources. worldbank.org/EXTINFORMATIONANDCOMMUNICATIONAND-TECHNOLOGIES/Resources/ICT_Strategy_Tunisia_Vol_I_March2002.pdf

World Bank (2006, August). *Note de politique sectorielle sur le financement de l'enseignement supérieur.* Washington, DC: The World Bank. Retrieved from https:// www.usp.ac.fj/worldbank2009/frame/Documents/Publications_regional/Tunisia-Notedepolitiquesectoriell2006.pdf

World Bank. (2008). *The road not traveled; education reform in the Middle East and North Africa.* Washington, DC: The International Bank for Reconstruction and Development / The World Bank. Retrieved from http://siteresources.worldbank.org/ INTMENA/Resources/EDU_Flagship_Full_ENG.pdf

World Bank (2012). *World development report 2012: Gender equity and development.* Washington, DC: The World Bank. Retrieved from https://siteresources.worldbank. org/INTWDR2012/Resources/7778105-1299699968583/7786210-1315936222006/ Complete-Report.pdf

World Bank. (2015). *Early childhood development in Tunisia.* Washington, DC: The World Bank. Retrieved from http://www.worldbank.org/en/country/tunisia/ publication/ecd2015

World Bank (2016). *Economic and social inclusion to prevent violent extremism.* Washington, DC: The World Bank. Retrieved from http://documents.worldbank. org/curated/en/409591474983005625/Economic-and-social-inclusion-to-prevent-violent-extremism

Zagger, Z. (2011, May 23). UN rights expert: 300 died during Tunisia uprising. *Jurist.* Retrieved from http://www.jurist.org/paperchase/2011/05/un-rights-expert–300-died-during-tunisia-uprising.php

Zbiss, H. (2013, December 20). Quranic kindergartens in Tunisia: Breeding a Wahhabi elite. *Arab Reporters for Investigative Journalism.* Retrieved from http://arij.net/en/ quranic-kindergartens-tunisia-breeding-wahhabi-elite

Zetter, R. (2015). *Protection in crisis: Forced migration and protection in a global era.* Retrieved from https://www.migrationpolicy.org/research/protection-crisis-forced-migration-and-protection-global-era

Zoubir, Y. H. (2015). The democratic transition in Tunisia: A success story in the making. *Conflict Trends,* 10–17. Retrieved from http://dspace.africaportal.org/jspui/ bitstream/123456789/34946/1/ACCORD-Conflict-Trends–2015–1.pdf?1

Index

In this index proper names beginning with the definite article in lower case (e.g. al-) are sorted under the following letter. Therefore *al-sahwa* is sorted under 's'.